# Learn to Program
# with Python 3

## A Step-by-Step Guide
## to Programming

## Second Edition

Irv Kalb

**Apress®**

*Learn to Program with Python 3*

Irv Kalb
Mountain View, California, USA

ISBN-13 (pbk): 978-1-4842-3878-3          ISBN-13 (electronic): 978-1-4842-3879-0
https://doi.org/10.1007/978-1-4842-3879-0

Library of Congress Control Number: 2018954633

Managing Director, Apress Media LLC: Welmoed Spahr
Acquisitions Editor: Todd Green
Development Editor: James Markham
Coordinating Editor: Jill Balzano

Cover designed by eStudioCalamar

Cover image designed by Freepik (www.freepik.com)

Distributed to the book trade worldwide by Springer Science+Business Media New York, 233 Spring Street, 6th Floor, New York, NY 10013. Phone 1-800-SPRINGER, fax (201) 348-4505, e-mail orders-ny@springer-sbm.com, or visit www.springeronline.com. Apress Media, LLC is a California LLC and the sole member (owner) is Springer Science + Business Media Finance Inc (SSBM Finance Inc). SSBM Finance Inc is a **Delaware** corporation.

For information on translations, please e-mail rights@apress.com, or visit www.apress.com/rights-permissions.

Apress titles may be purchased in bulk for academic, corporate, or promotional use. eBook versions and licenses are also available for most titles. For more information, reference our Print and eBook Bulk Sales web page at www.apress.com/bulk-sales.

Any source code or other supplementary material referenced by the author in this book is available to readers on GitHub via the book's product page, located at www.apress.com/9781484238783. For more detailed information, please visit www.apress.com/source-code.

Printed on acid-free paper

*This book is dedicated to the memory of my mother, Lorraine Kalb.*

*I started learning about programming when I was 16 years old, at Columbia High School in Maplewood, New Jersey. We were extremely fortunate to have a very early computer, an IBM 1130, that students could use.*

*I remember learning the basics of the Fortran programming language and writing a simple program that would add two numbers together and print the result. I was thrilled when I finally got my program to work correctly. It was a rewarding feeling to be able to get this huge, complicated machine to do exactly what I wanted it to do.*

*I clearly remember explaining to my mother that I wrote this program that got the computer to add 9 and 5 and come up with an answer of 14. She said that she didn't need a computer to do that. I tried to explain to her that getting the answer of 14 was not the important part. What was important was that I had written a program that would add any two numbers and print the result. She still didn't get it, but she was happy for me and very supportive.*

*Hopefully, through my explanations in this book, you will get it.*

# Table of Contents

# About the Author

 **Irv Kalb** is an adjunct professor at UCSC (University of California, Santa Cruz) Extension Silicon Valley and Cogswell Polytechnical College. He has been teaching software development classes since 2010.

Irv has worked as a software developer, manager of software developers, and manager of software development projects. He has been an independent consultant for many years with his own company, Furry Pants Productions, where he has concentrated on educational software. Prior to that, he worked as an employee for a number of high-tech companies. He has BS and MS degrees in computer science.

Recently, he has been a mentor to a number of local competitive robotics teams.

His previous publications include numerous technical articles, two children's edutainment CD-ROMs (about Darby the Dalmatian), an online e-book on object-oriented programming in the Lingo programming language, and the first book on Ultimate Frisbee, *Ultimate: Fundamentals of the Sport* (Revolutionary Publications, 1983).

He was highly involved in the early development of the sport of Ultimate Frisbee.

# About the Technical Reviewer

**Mark Furman**, MBA is a systems engineer, author, teacher, and entrepreneur. For the last 16 years he has worked in the information technology field with a focus on Linux-based systems and programming in Python. He's worked for a range of companies including Host Gator, Interland, Suntrust Bank, AT&T, and Winn-Dixie. Currently he has been focusing his career on the maker movement and has launched Tech Forge (techforge.org), which focuses on helping people start a makerspace and help sustain current spaces. He holds an MBA degree from Ohio University. You can follow him on Twitter @mfurman.

# Acknowledgments

I would like to thank the following people, without whom this book would not have been possible:

My wonderful wife, Doreen, who is the glue that keeps our family together.

Our two sons, Jamie and Robbie, who keep us on our toes.

Our two cats, Chester and Cody (whom we think of as people).

Mariah Armstrong, who created all the graphics in this book. I am not an artist (I don't even play one on TV). Mariah was able to take my "chicken scratches" and turn them into very clear and understandable pieces of art.

Chris Sasso and Ravi Chityala for their technical reviews and helpful suggestions.

Luke Kwan, Catherine Chanse, and Christina Ri at the Art Institute of California-Silicon Valley.

Andy Hou at the UCSC-Silicon Valley Extension.

Jerome Solomon at Cogswell Polytechnical College, who first suggested that I consider getting into Python.

Jill Balzano, Jim Markham, Mark Furman, and Todd Green at Apress for all the work they did reviewing, editing, and expertly answering all my questions.

All the students who have been in my classes over many years at the Art Institute California-Silicon Valley, Cogswell Polytechnical College, and the UCSC Silicon Valley Extension. Their feedback, suggestions, smiles, frowns, light-bulb moments, frustrations, and knowing head-nods were extremely helpful in shaping the content of this book.

Finally, Guido van Rossum, without whom Python would not exist.

# CHAPTER 1

# Getting Started

Congratulations! You have made a wise decision. No, not the decision to buy this book, although I think that will turn out to be a wise decision also. I mean you have made a wise decision to learn the basics of computer programming using the Python language.

In this book, I teach you the fundamentals of writing computer software. I assume that you have never written any software before, so I start completely from scratch. The only requirements are that you possess a basic knowledge of algebra and a good sense of logic. As the book progresses, each chapter builds upon the information learned in the previous chapter(s). The overall goal is to give you a solid introduction to the way that computer code and data interact to form well-written programs. I introduce the key elements of software, including variables, functions, if/else statements, loops, lists, and strings. I offer many real-world examples that should help explain the uses of each of these elements. I also give definitions to help you with the new vocabulary that I introduce.

This book is not intended to be comprehensive. Rather, it is an introduction that gives you a solid foundation in programming. The approach is highly interactive, asking you to create small programs along the way as a chance to practice what has been explained in each chapter. By the end of the book, you should be comfortable writing small to medium-sized programs in Python.

This first chapter covers the following topics:

- Introducing Python

- Getting Python installed on your computer

- Using IDLE and the Python Shell

- Writing your first program: Hello World

- Creating, saving, and running Python files

- Working with IDLE on multiple platforms

© Irv Kalb 2018
I. Kalb, *Learn to Program with Python 3*, https://doi.org/10.1007/978-1-4842-3879-0_1

# What Is Python?

Python is a general-purpose programming language. That means it was designed and developed to write software for a wide variety of disciplines. Python has been used to write applications to solve problems in biology, chemistry, financial analysis, numerical analysis, robotics, and many other fields. It is also widely used as a *scripting language* for use by computer administrators, who use it to capture and replay sequences of computer commands. It is different from a language like HTML (HyperText Markup Language), which was designed for the single purpose of allowing people to specify the layout of a web page.

Once you learn the basic concepts of a programming language like Python, you find that you can pick up a new computer languages very quickly. No matter what the language (and there are many) the underlying concepts are very similar. The key things that you learn about—variables, assignment statements, if statements, while loops, function calls—are all concepts that are easily transferable to any other programming language.

# Installing Python

Python was created in the 1990s by Guido van Rossum. He is affectionately known as Python's Benevolent Dictator for Life. The language has two current versions: 2.7 and 3.6. Version 2.7 is still widely used, but its "end of life" has recently been announced. Therefore, this version of the book will use the newer *Python 3*, as it is known. With respect to the contents of this book, there are only a few differences between the versions of the language. Where appropriate, I point out how something presented in Python 3 was handled in Python 2.

Python is maintained as an *open source* project by a group called the Python Software Foundation. Because it is open source, Python is free. There is no single company that owns and/or sells the software. You can get everything you need to write and run all the Python programs in this book by simply downloading Python from the Internet. I'll explain how you can get it and install it.

The center of the Python universe is at www.python.org.

Bring up the browser of your choice and go to that address. The site changes over time, but the essential functionality should remain the same. On the main page, there should be a Downloads button or rollover. Once you're in the Downloads area, you should be able to select Windows, Mac, or Other Platforms (which includes Linux). After choosing your operating system, you should get an opportunity to choose between versions 3.x.y (whatever is the current subversion of Python 3) and version 2.x.y (whatever is the current subversion of Python 2). Choose version 3.x.y.

Clicking the button downloads an installer file. On a Mac, the downloaded file has a name like `python-3.6.4-macosx10.6pkg`. On a Windows computer, the file has a name like `python-3.6.4-msi`. On either platform, find the file that was downloaded and double-click it. That should start the installation process, which should be very simple.

# IDLE and the Python Shell

There are many different *software development environments* (applications) that you can use to write code in Python. It may seem odd that you use a program to write a program, but that's what a software development environment is. Some of these environments are free; others can be costly. They differ in the tools they offer to help programmers be more efficient.

The environment we will use in this book is called IDLE. You might think that IDLE is an acronym, maybe Interactive DeveLopment Environment. When the name was chosen, it didn't mean anything. In fact, the name Python doesn't refer to the snake. Apparently, Guido van Rossum was a big fan of *Monty Python's Flying Circus*, a TV series by a well-known comedy group from Britain, and he named the language after them. One of the founding members of Monty Python was Eric Idle. The name IDLE is a reference to him.

IDLE is free. When you download and run the Python installer, it installs IDLE on your computer. Once installed, you can find IDLE on a Mac by opening the applications folder and locating the folder named Python 3.x. Once you open it, you should see the IDLE application. To open IDLE, double-click the icon. On Windows, IDLE is installed in the standard Program Files folder. If your version of Windows has a Start button, click the Start button and type **IDLE** in the type-in field. Otherwise, you might have to do a Control+R or Control+Q to bring up a dialog box where you can type **IDLE**. However you open IDLE, you should see a window with contents that look something like this:

```
Python 3.6.1 (v3.6.1:69c0db5050, Mar 21 2017, 01:21:04)
[GCC 4.2.1 (Apple Inc. build 5666) (dot 3)] on darwin
Type "copyright", "credits" or "license()" for more information.
>>>
```

This window is called the Python Shell. In fact, the title of the window should be Python 3.x.y Shell.

# Hello World

There is a tradition that when programmers learn a new computer language, they try writing what is called the Hello World program. That is, just to make sure they can get something to work, they write a simple program that writes out "Hello World!"

Let's do that now with Python. The Python Shell (commonly just called the Shell) gives you a prompt that looks like three greater-than signs. This is called the *chevron prompt* or simply the *prompt*. When you see the prompt, it means the Shell is ready for you to type something. Throughout this book, I strongly encourage you to use the IDLE environment by trying out code as I explain it. At the prompt, enter the following:

```
>>> print('Hello World!')
```

Then press the Return key or Enter key. When you do, you should see this:

```
>>> print('Hello World!')
Hello World!
>>>
```

Congratulations! You have just written your first computer program. You told the computer to do something, and it did exactly what you told it to do. My work is done here. You're not quite ready to add *Python programmer* to your résumé and get a job as a professional computer programmer, but you are off to a good start!

---

**Note**    If you don't like the font and/or size of the text used in the Shell, you can choose IDLE ➤ Preferences (Mac) or Configure IDLE (Windows) and easily change either or both.

---

One of the key advantages of the Python language is how readable it is. The program you just wrote is simply the word print, an open parenthesis, whatever you want to be printed (inside quotes), and a closing parenthesis. Anyone can understand the Hello World program written in Python. But to make this point very clear, let's see what you have to do to write the Hello World program in some other popular languages.

You've probably heard of the language called C, perhaps the most widely used programming language in the world. Here is what you have to write in C to get the same results:

```c
#include <stdio.h>

int main(void)
{
  printf("Hello World!\n");
  return 0;
}
```

Notice all the brackets, parentheses, braces, and semicolons you need to have, along with how many lines you have to write?

There is another language called C++, which is a modification of the original C language to give it more power. Here's what the Hello World program looks like in C++:

```cpp
#include "std_lib_facilities.h"

int main()
{
    cout << "Hello World!\n";
    return 0;
}
```

Not surprisingly, it also has many brackets, parentheses, braces, and semicolons.

Finally, here is the same Hello World program written in Java, yet another popular computer language:

```java
public class HelloWorld {
  public static void main(String[] args) {
    System.out.println("Hello World!");
  }
}
```

Again, there are many brackets, parentheses, and semicolons, and many words with meanings that are not immediately obvious.

By comparison, notice how English-like, simple, and readable the Python version is. This readability and simplicity are big reasons why Python is growing in popularity, especially as a language used to teach programming to beginners.

# Creating, Saving, and Running a Python File

So far, you have only seen a single line of Python code:

```
>>> print('Hello World!')
```

You typed it into the Shell and pressed Enter or Return to make it run. Typing one line at a time into the Shell is a great way to learn Python, and it is very handy for trying out things quickly. But soon I'll have you writing programs with tens, hundreds, and maybe thousands of lines of code. The Shell is not an appropriate place for writing large programs. Python, like every other computer language, allows you to put the code you write into a file and save it. Programs saved this way can be opened at any time and run without having to retype them. I'll explain how we do this in Python.

Just like any standard word processor or spreadsheet program, to create a new file in IDLE, you go to the File menu and select New File (denoted from here on as File ➤ New File). You can also use the keyboard shortcuts Control+N (Windows) or Command+N (Mac).

This opens a new, blank editing window, waiting for you to enter Python code. It behaves just like any text editing program you have ever used. You enter your Python code, line by line, similar to the way that you did it in the Shell. However, when you press Return or Enter at the end of a line, the line does not run—it does *not* produce immediate results as it did in the Shell. Instead, the cursor just moves down to allow you to enter another line. You can use all the standard text-editing features that you are used to: Cut, Copy, Paste, Find, Replace, and so on. You can move around the lines of code using the arrow keys or by clicking the mouse. When a program gets long enough, scrolling becomes enabled. You can select multiple lines using the standard click-and-drag or click to create a starting point and Shift-click to mark an ending point.

Let's build a simple program containing three print statements. Open a new file. Notice that when you open the file, it is named Untitled in the window title. Enter the following:

```
print('I am now entering Python code into a Python file.')
print('When I press Return or Enter here, nothing happens.')
print('This is the last line.')
```

When you type the word **print**, IDLE colorizes it (both here in the editing window and when you type it in the Shell). This is IDLE letting you know that this is a word that it recognizes. IDLE also turns all the words enclosed in quotes to green. This also is an acknowledgement from IDLE that it has an understanding of what you are trying to say.

Notice that when you started typing, the window title changed to *Untitled*. The asterisks around the name are there to show that the contents of the file have been changed, but the file has not been saved. That is, IDLE knows about the new content, but the content has not yet been written to the hard disk. To save the file, press the standard Control+S (Windows) or Command+S (Mac). Alternatively, you can click File ➤ Save. Because this is the first time the file is being saved, you see the standard Save dialog box. Feel free to navigate to a folder where you are able to find your Python files(s), or click the New Folder button to create a new folder. In the top of the box, where it says "Save As", enter a name for this file. Because we are just testing things out, you can name the file Test. However, Python filenames should always end with a .py extension. Therefore, you should enter the name **Test.py** in the Save As box.

---

**Note**   If you save your Python file without a .py extension, IDLE will not recognize it as a Python file. If Python does not know that your file is a Python file, it will not colorize your code. This may not seem important now, but it will turn out to be very helpful when you start writing larger programs. So make it a habit right from the start to always ensure that your Python file names end with the .py extension.

---

Now that we have a saved Python file, we want to run, or *execute*, the *statements* in the file. To do that, click Run ➤ Run Module or press the F5 shortcut key. If everything went well, the program should print the following in the Shell:

```
I am now entering Python code into a Python file.
When I press Return or Enter here, nothing happens.
This is the last line.
```

Now let's quit IDLE by pressing Control+Q (Windows) or Command+Q (Mac) keys. Alternatively, you can click IDLE ➤ Exit (Windows) or IDLE ➤ Quit IDLE (Mac).

When you are ready to open IDLE again, you have choices. You can open IDLE by typing **IDLE** into the Start menu (Windows) or by double-clicking the IDLE icon (Mac). If you then want to open a previously saved Python file, you can click File ➤ Open and navigate to the file you want to open.

However, if you want to open IDLE and open a previously saved Python file, you can navigate to the saved Python file (for example, find the Test.py file that you just saved) and open IDLE by opening the file. On Windows, if you double-click the icon, a window typically opens and closes very fast. This runs the Python program, but does not keep the window open. Instead, to open the file and IDLE, right-click the file icon. From the context menu that appears, select the second item, Edit with IDLE.

On a Mac, you can simply double-click the file icon. If double-clicking the Python file opens a program other than IDLE, you can fix that with a one-time change. Quit whatever program opened. Select the Python file. Press Command+I (or click File ➤ Get Info), which opens a long dialog box. In the section labeled "Open with", select the IDLE application (IDLE.app). Finally, click the Change All button. Once you do that, you should be able to double-click any file whose name ends in .py, and it should open with IDLE.

Programming typically involves iterations of edits to one or more Python files. Each time you make changes and you want to test the new code, you must save the file and then run it. If you don't save the file before you try to run it, IDLE will prompt you by asking you to save the file. You'll quickly become familiar with the typical development cycle of edit your code, save the file (Command+S or Control+S), and run the program (F5).

# IDLE on Multiple Platforms

One other very nice feature of Python and IDLE is that the environment is almost completely platform independent. That is, the IDLE environment looks almost identical on a Windows computer, Mac, or Linux system. The only differences are those associated with the particular operating system (such as the look of the window's title bar, the location of the menus, the look of the dialog boxes, and so on). These are very minor details. Overall, the platform you run on does not matter.

Perhaps even more importantly, the code you write is platform independent. If you create a Python file on one platform, you can move that file to another platform and it will open and run just fine. Many programmers use multiple systems to develop Python code. In fact, even though I typically develop most of my Python code on a Mac, I often bring these same files into classrooms, open them, teach with them on Windows systems.

# Summary

In this chapter, you got up and running with Python. You should now have Python installed on your computer and have a good understanding of what the IDLE environment is. You built the standard Hello World program in the Shell, and then used the editor window to build, save, and run a simple multiline Python program (whose name ends in `.py`) made up of `print` statements. Finally, you learned that Python and the IDLE environment are platform independent.

# CHAPTER 2

# Variables and Assignment Statements

This chapter covers the following topics:

- A sample Python program
- Building blocks of programming
- Four types of data
- What a variable is
- Rules for naming variables
- Giving a variable a value with an assignment statement
- A good way to name variables
- Special Python keywords
- Case sensitivity
- More complicated assignment statements
- Print statements
- Basic math operators
- Order of operations and parentheses
- A few small sample programs
- Additional naming conventions
- How to add comments in a program
- Use of "whitespace"
- Errors in programs

© Irv Kalb 2018
I. Kalb, *Learn to Program with Python 3*, https://doi.org/10.1007/978-1-4842-3879-0_2

# A Sample Python Program

Let's jump right in and see an example of what Python code looks like. You are probably familiar with a simple toy called the Magic 8-Ball, made by Mattel, Inc. To play with the toy, you ask it a yes-or-no question, turn the ball over, and the ball gives you one of a number of possible answers. Here is the output of a Python program that simulates the Magic 8-Ball:

```
Ask the Magic 8-Ball a question (Return or Enter to quit): Will this be a
great book?
Absolutely!

Ask the Magic 8-Ball a question (Return or Enter to quit): Will I learn to
program in Python?
Answer is foggy, ask again later.

Ask the Magic 8-Ball a question (Return or Enter to quit): Will I learn to
program in Python?
You may rely on it.

Ask the Magic 8-Ball a question (Return or Enter to quit): Will I be able
to play football in the NFL?
No way, dude!

Ask the Magic 8-Ball a question (Return or Enter to quit): Will I make a
million dollars?
Absolutely!

Ask the Magic 8-Ball a question (Return or Enter to quit): Does the Magic
8-Ball ever make mistakes?
No way, dude!

Ask the Magic 8-Ball a question (Return or Enter to quit):
```

Now, let's jump right in and take a look at the underlying code of this program. I'm showing you this just to give you a feeling for what Python code looks like. I am certainly not expecting you to understand much of this code. At this point, the details are unimportant. Here it is:

```python
import random  # Allow the program to use random numbers

while True:
    print() # prints a blank line
    usersQuestion = input('Ask the Magic 8-Ball a question
(press enter to quit): ')
    if usersQuestion == ":
        break    # we're done

    randomAnswer = random.randrange(0, 8)  # pick a random number

    if randomAnswer == 0:
        print('It is certain.')

    elif randomAnswer == 1:
        print('Absolutely!')

    elif randomAnswer == 2:
        print('You may rely on it.')

    elif randomAnswer == 3:
        print('Answer is foggy, ask again later.')

    elif randomAnswer == 4:
        print('Concentrate and ask again.')

    elif randomAnswer == 5:
        print('Unsure at this point, try again.')

    elif randomAnswer == 6:
        print('No way, dude!')

    elif randomAnswer == 7:
        print('No, no, no, no, no.')
```

Here's a very quick explanation: at the top, there is a line that allows the program to use random numbers. Then there is a line that says `while True`. This line creates something called a *loop*, which is a portion of a program that runs over and over again. In this case, it allows the user to ask a question and get an answer, and then enter another question and get another answer, and on and on.

Moving down, there is a line that causes `Ask the Magic 8-Ball a question` to be printed out and allows the user to type a question for the Magic 8-Ball to answer.

Skipping down a few lines, the program generates a random number between 0 and 7. After generating the random number, the program then checks to see if the value of the random number is 0. If so, it tells the user the answer: `It is certain`. Otherwise, if the value of the randomly chosen number is 1, it tells the user: `You may rely on it`.

The rest of the lines work similarly, checking the random number and giving different outputs.

After the program prints an answer, because the program is inside the loop, the program goes around again and tells the user to ask another question. And the process keeps going.

As I said, don't worry about the details of the program—just get a sense of how the program does what it does. But there are some things to notice. First, see how readable this code is. With only this brief introduction, you can probably get a feeling for the basic logical flow of how the program operates. Second, notice that the program asks the user for input, does some computation, and generates some output. These are the three main steps in almost all computer programs.

Let's get into programming 101. This may be extremely basic, but I want to start right at the beginning, create a solid foundation, and then build on that.

# The Building Blocks of Programming

The two basic building blocks of programming are code and data. *Code* is a set of instructions that tell the computer what to perform and how it should perform. But I want to start our discussion with data.

*Data* refers to the quantities, characters, and/or symbols on which operations are performed with a computer. Anything you need the computer to remember is a piece of data. Simple examples of data include the number of students in class, grade point average, name, whether a switch is in an on or off position, and so on.

There are many different types of data, but this book deals mostly with four basic types, which I describe in the next section.

# Four Types of Data

The four basic types of data are called *integer numbers*, *floating-point numbers*, *strings*, and *Booleans*. This section explains and provides examples of each of these types of data.

## Integers

Integer numbers (or simply, *integers*) are counting numbers, like 1, 2, 3, but also include 0 and negative numbers. The following are examples of data that is expressed as integers:

- Number of people in a room
- Personal or team score in a game
- Course number
- Date in a month
- Temperature (in terms of number of degrees)

## Floats

Floating-point numbers (or simply *floats*) are numbers that have a decimal point in them. The following are examples of data that is expressed as floating-point numbers:

- Grade point average
- Price of something
- Percentages
- Irrational numbers, like pi

# Strings

Strings (also called *text*) are any sequences of characters. Examples of data that is expressed as strings include the following:

- Name
- Address
- Course name
- Title of a book, song, or movie
- Sentence
- Name of a file on a computer

# Booleans

Booleans are a type of data that can only have one of two values: True or False. Booleans are named after the English mathematician George Boole, who created an entire field of logic based on these two-state data items. The following are some examples of data that can be expressed as Booleans:

- *The state of a light switch*: True for on, False for off
- *Inside or outside*: True for inside, False for outside
- *Whether someone is alive or not*: True for alive, False for dead
- *If someone is listening*: True for listening, False for not listening

It might seem that integer and floating-point data have overlaps. For example, there is an integer 0 and there is a floating-point 0.0. There is an integer 1 and a floating-point 1.0. Although these may appear to be the same thing to us humans, integers and floats are handled very differently inside the computer. Without getting too wrapped up in the details, it is easier for the computer to represent and operate with integers. But when we have a value with a decimal point, we need to use a floating-point number instead. Whenever we represent a value, we choose the appropriate numeric data type. As you will see, Python makes a clear distinction between these two types of data.

There are many other types of data in the computer world. For example, you are probably familiar with music being stored in MP3 format or video being stored in MP4. These are other representations of data. However, to make things simple and clear, I'll use just the four basic types of data in most of this book.

# Examples of Data

Now let's take a look at what the actual data looks like for each of the four different data types.

- **Integer** numbers are whole or counting numbers. These are some examples:

  ```
  12, 50, 0, -3, -25
  ```

- **Floating-point** numbers are any numbers that contain a decimal point. These are some examples:

  ```
  1.5, .5, -3.21, 1.0, 0.0
  ```

- **Strings** represent textual data or any sequence of characters. String data is always represented with quote characters before and after the sequence of characters. In Python, you can use either the single (') or the double-quote character ("). The following are examples of strings:

  ```
  'Joe', 'Schmoe', "Joe", "Schmoe", 'This is some string data', "OK"
  ```

  The string 'Joe' and the string "Joe" are exactly the same. The quotes are not actually part of the string. They are there to allow Python to understand that you are talking about a string. You can choose to use either pair of quoting characters. Single quotes are generally easier to use because you don't have to hold down the Shift key to type them.

  However, if you want to include a quote character inside a string, you can enclose the string in the other quote characters. For example, you might write this:

  ```
  "Here's a string with a single quote in it"
  ```

  Or this:

  ```
  'Here is a string that includes two "double quote" symbols inside of it'
  ```

  Think back to the Hello World program you wrote in Chapter 1. The 'Hello World!' you used was an example of a string.

- **Boolean** data can only have one of two values: True or False. The words *True* and *False* must be spelled with this capitalization:

```
True
False
```

# Form with Underlying Data

To make the distinctions among these different data types clearer, let's look at a fake but typical form you might see if you bought something online. Imagine you want to buy some widgets (generic items), and you go to the WidgetsRUs.com web site to buy them. You might be presented with a form like the one shown in Figure 2-1.

```
               Widgets'R'Us
                        Name: [                    ]
                     Address: [                    ]
          Number of Widgets: [                    ]
                Total to Pay: [                    ]
                    Receipt?: [  ]
```

*Figure 2-1.  Sample form where the fields represent different types of data*

As the end user, you would type characters into each of these fields. But as the programmer who is writing this program, you have to think about what types of data you would use to represent the information that the user entered into these fields.

The first two fields, Name and Address, call for string data. The user enters characters, and we would think of what they wrote as strings.

The Number of Widgets field represents a piece of integer data—for example, 10. It wouldn't make sense to order 12 and a half widgets, so this is certainly an integer.

Total to Pay would be a floating-point number, such as 37.25. We think of money written as dollars, a decimal point, and cents. So you would use a floating-point piece of data to represent this.

Receipt is what an end user commonly sees as a check box. But if you were writing the program behind this form, you would represent the answer to the receipt question with a Boolean: True if the box is checked on, False if the box is unchecked. From now on, no matter what device you see a form like this on, you will see check boxes differently. Every time you see a check box, you'll realize that the underlying program is representing your choice with a piece of Boolean data.

# Variables

In programming, we need to remember and manipulate data all the time. This is a fundamental part of computer programming. In order to store and manipulate data, we use a variable.

---

**Definition**    A *variable* is a named memory location that holds a value.

---

The contents of a variable can change or vary over time; this is why it's called a *variable*.

You've probably heard that the term RAM stands for *random-access memory*. It is the active part of storage inside your computer. You can think of this memory as a simple list or array of numbered slots, starting at 0 and going up to as much memory as you have in your computer. The amount doesn't matter, but Figure 2-2 is a diagram showing memory starting a slot 0 and going up to the final slot of 4 gigabytes.

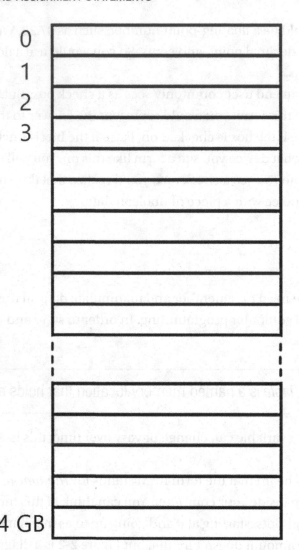

***Figure 2-2.***  *Random-access memory diagram*

Every one of these memory locations can be used as a variable. That is, you can store a piece of data in any free memory slot.

**Note**   Behind the scenes, the way Python stores data and variable names is more complex. For example, different types of data (integer, float, string, and Boolean) take up different amounts of memory, rather than a single "slot." Further, in Python, the name and the data of a variable are actually stored in different places. But thinking of each piece of data as being stored in a single slot in memory provides a good *mental model*—a good way to think about what a variable is.

Let's look at an example of what a variable is and how it might be used. Imagine you are playing a computer game. A game typically has to keep track of your score. To do this, a programmer writes code that creates a variable, gives the variable a name, and puts some starting value into the variable. In a game, a score typically starts with a value of 0, and the value of the variable changes over time. As the game is played, every time something good happens in the game, the programmer's code may add to the value of the variable. If the game calls for it, when something bad happens in the game, the programmer's code could subtract from the value of the variable.

In Figure 2-3, I have arbitrarily chosen slot 3 in memory as the location where the variable score should be saved. Notice that slot 3 is named score and it has a value of 0 in it. In fact, Python makes the choice of where in memory to store data. Because you will always refer to a variable by name, you don't care where in memory the variable is stored. In this example, whenever you use the name score, Python will use the memory location 3.

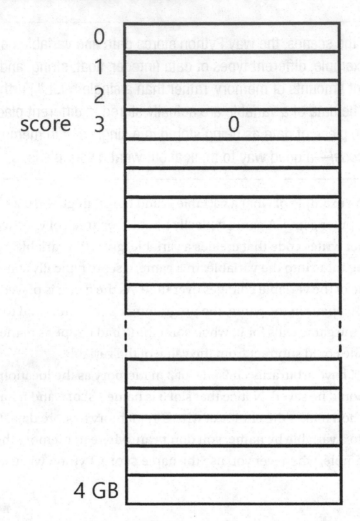

**Figure 2-3.** *Random access memory diagram with one variable defined*

Another way to think of a variable is as an envelope or a box into which you can put a value. In this way of thinking, a variable is a *container*—a storage space—with a name. The contents are the value. The name never changes, but the contents can change over time.

Using the example of a score, imagine that we have an envelope or box with the name *score* on it. Inside, we put the contents—a value. Let's start off with a value of 0, as shown in Figure 2-4.

***Figure 2-4.*** *Visualization of a variable as an envelope*

If the user does something good in the game (kills a bad guy, makes a good shot, finds a hidden item, and so on), the user gains 50 points. We take the current value (contents) of the score, which is 0, and add 50. The value of score becomes 50, as shown in Figure 2-5.

***Figure 2-5.*** *Visualization of a variable with a different value*

Let's say the user does something else good and is awarded another 30 points. We take the current value of 50 and add 30 to it, giving us a total of 80, as shown in Figure 2-6. So we have the variable called score (which is actually a memory location), and its value is changing over time. The program remembers the current value by having it stored in a variable.

**Figure 2-6.** *Visualization of a variable with yet a different value*

# Assignment Statements

I have talked about variables and how they are used to store data, but I haven't shown you yet how to use a variable in Python. Let's do that right now.

So much for the theory. In Python, you create and give a value to a variable with an assignment statement.

---

**Definition**    An *assignment statement* is a line of code in which a variable is given a value.

---

An assignment statement has this general form:

```
<variable> = <expression>
```

When I put things in less-than and greater-than brackets, like this `<variable>`, it means that you should replace that whole thing (including the brackets) with something that you choose. Anything written like `<variable>` is a placeholder.

It works like this: the `<expression>`, or everything on the right side of the equals sign, is evaluated, and a value is computed. The resulting value is *assigned* to (put into) the variable on the left.

This is best explained with some simple examples. Try entering these lines into the Python Shell:

```
>>> age = 29
>>> name = 'Fred'
>>> alive = True
>>> gpa = 3.9
>>>
```

Notice that as soon as you typed an opening quotation mark (such as in typing `Fred` as a value for the variable `name`), IDLE recognizes that you are typing a string and turns all characters green until you type the matching closing quote.

Also notice that when you typed the word `True`, it turned a color (probably purple). This is an indication that Python has recognized a special word.

When Python runs (or *executes*) assignment statements like these, it first looks to see whether the variable to be assigned was previously used. If the variable has never been seen before, Python allocates an empty slot of memory, attaches a name to it, and puts in the given value. Therefore, when you entered the following line and pressed Return or Enter, Python first looked to see if it had ever seen the variable name `age` before:

```
>>> age = 29
>>>
```

Since it had not, it allocated a memory slot somewhere (again, we don't care where) attached the `age` label to it, and then put the value 29 into that memory slot. A similar sequence happened for the other variables.

In pure computer programming terms, the equals sign is not called "equals," it is called the *assignment operator*. In an assignment statement, everything on the right of the equals sign is calculated, and the result is *assigned* to the variable on the left.

Whenever you see an assignment statement, you can read or think of the equals sign as meaning any of the following:

- "is assigned"

- "is given the value of"

- "is set to"

- "becomes"

- "gets"

For example, it might be more helpful and clearer to you to read the line

```
>>> age = 29
```

as "age is assigned 29," or "age is given the value of 29," or "age is set to 29" or "age becomes 29."

After executing that line, enter the following line and press Return or Enter:

```
>>> age = 31
```

Python does the same sequence of steps, but now it finds that there already is a variable named age. Rather than create a new variable, Python overwrites the current value of the variable age with the new value of 31, as shown in Figure 2-7. If you remember the conceptual way of representing a variable as a container (for example, as an envelope), think of this line as replacing the old value inside the envelope with a new value. The variable name age stays the same, but the contents change.

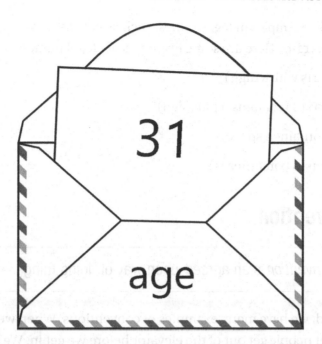

***Figure 2-7.*** *Visualization of a variable as the result of an assignment statement*

# Variable Names

By definition, every variable must have a name. It is best to make variable names as descriptive as possible. For example, let's say I was building a virtual aquarium. I would use a variable to keep track of the number of fish in my aquarium. Python doesn't care what you use for a variable name. You could use a name as simple as x, or you could use some odd sequence of characters, such as xddqfmmp. Or you could create a name like numberOfFishInAquarium. That name is much clearer. Names like that make code much more readable and understandable in the long run.

In Python (and all computer languages), there are some rules about naming a variable, though. Here are Python's rules about the name of a variable:

- Must start with a letter (or an underscore)

- Cannot start with a digit

- Can have up to 256 total characters

- Can include letters, digits, underscores, dollar signs, and other characters

- Cannot contain spaces

- Cannot contain math symbols (+, -, /, *, %, parentheses)

We've seen some examples of legal names, such as `age`, `name`, `score`, `alive`, and `numberOfFishInAquarium`. Here are some examples of illegal names:

- `49ers` (starts with a digit)

- `table+chairs` (contains a plus sign)

- `my age` (contains a space)

- `(coins)` (uses parentheses)

# Naming Convention

---

**Definition**   A *convention* is an agreed-upon way of doing things.

---

In the real world, we have many examples of conventions. When we want to get in an elevator, we let people get out of the elevator before we get in. We always shake hands with our right hand. When we answer a phone, the convention is to say "Hello." In the United States, we drive on the right-hand side of the road. That one is not only a convention, it's the law.

In programming, you can create any variable name you want as long as it follows the rules. However, when creating variable names, I strongly encourage you to use a *naming convention*, by which I mean a consistent approach for creating names for variables. If you create a name like `score`, where the name is just one word, the convention is to use all lowercase letters.

However, we often want to create descriptive names made by putting together two or more words. Take, for example, the variable name `numberOfFishInAquarium`, which is created by putting together five words. In the Python world, there seem to be two common naming conventions.

The first naming convention, and the one that I prefer, is called *camelcase*. The rules of the camelcase convention are very simple:

- The first word is all lowercase.

- For every additional word in the name

  - Make the first letter uppercase.

  - All other letters are lowercase.

Here are some examples of variable names that follow the camelcase naming convention:

```
someVariableName
anotherVariableName
countOfBadGuys
computerScore
humanScore
bonusPointsForCollectingMushrooms
```

The term *camelcase* describes the way variable names look when using this convention. When an uppercase letter starts a new word, it looks like the hump on a camel. Notice how names that follow the camelcase naming convention are easy to read.

There is another convention that many Python programmers use, which is to separate words with underscores:

```
this_is_a_variable_name
number_of_fish_in_aquarium
```

But to me, that's more difficult to both read and write. I am showing this alternative convention here because if you look at other people's code written in Python, you will probably see variable names written with underscores like that.

I have used the camelcase naming convention for years and I will use camelcase throughout this book. If you are coding on your own, obviously you can use whatever names you want, but it really is a good idea to be consistent when naming variables. If you do programming in a class or for a company, the teacher or the company may insist on a particular naming convention so that all programmers can easily understand each other's code.

# Keywords

I'm sure that you have heard that computers only understand ones and zeros. This is true. When you write code in Python, Python cannot run or execute your code directly. Instead, it takes the code that you write and *compiles* it. That is, Python converts your code into a language of ones and zeros that the computer *can* understand. Every language has such a compiler. When the Python compiler reads your code, it looks for special words called *keywords* to understand what your code is trying to say.

**Note**    Python technically has an *interpreter* that turns your code into a machine-independent *byte code*. But to make things simple, I'll refer to this as the Python compiler.

The following is a list of the Python keywords. Don't worry about the details right now. I'm just showing you these now to let you know that you cannot use these words as a variable name:

| | | | | |
|---|---|---|---|---|
| and | as | assert | break | class |
| continue | def | del | elif | else |
| except | finally | for | from | global |
| if | import | in | is | lambda |
| nonlocal | not | or | pass | raise |
| return | try | while | with | yield |
| False | None | True | | |

You have already seen two of these keywords. The words True and False are the only allowable values for a Boolean variable. True, False, and None are the only keywords that begin with an uppercase letter. There are also some words that Python reserves, like the word print that you saw in the Hello World program. Whenever you type a Python keyword or reserved word, IDLE changes the color of the word. Earlier, when you typed the following, the word print turned orange or purple:

```
print('Hello World!')
```

This is IDLE looking over your shoulder and telling you that this is one of Python's reserved words.

**Caution**    The important thing to learn here is that you *cannot* use any of these words as a variable name. If you attempt to do so, the Python compiler will generate an error message when it tries to compile your program.

# Case Sensitivity

The computer language C was developed in the early 1970s. It was one of the first high-level computer languages and has exerted a great deal of influence on many current computer languages. Languages such as C++, JavaScript, ActionScript (the language of Flash), and Java can all trace their roots to C. There are many similarities among these languages, though each one has a different purpose.

As I mentioned, all computer languages have a compiler that changes the code that you write in that language into lower-level instructions (based on ones and zeros) that the computer really understands. This compilation step happens before you run your program. When C was created, computers were very slow. The people who created C wanted the C compiler to be as fast as possible. One way they made it fast was to enforce a rule that said that variable names and keywords would be case sensitive—that is, case matters. As humans, we could certainly recognize if our names were spelled with varying degrees of uppercase or lowercase. If I saw my name written as *irv*, *Irv*, or *IRV*, I would know that someone was talking about or to me.

However, because of the need for speed in the C compiler to read and understand a programmer's variable names, a variable named `myVariable` is *not* the same as one named one named `myvariable` and is *not* the same as one named `MyVariable`. Each of these represents a unique variable.

Python has this same trait. Variable names and keywords in Python are all case sensitive. For example, `print` is not the same as `Print`. This will bite you many times over. You will spend a great deal of time scratching your head about why your program won't compile, only to realize hours later that you used a lowercase letter where you needed an uppercase one.

---

**Tip**   This is another great reason to following a strict naming convention. If you follow a naming convention such as camelcase, you will make fewer uppercase/lowercase naming errors.

---

# More Complicated Assignment Statements

Now that we have an understanding of the rules of naming variables and a naming convention that will help us name variables, let's look at some more details of assignment statements.

Remember, this is the general form of an assignment statement:

```
<variable> = <expression>
```

So far, I've only shown assignment statements that give a variable a simple value. But the `<expression>` part on the right side of the equals sign (actually called the *assignment operator*) can be as simple or as complicated as you need it to be. The right-hand side can also contain variables. Here's an example:

```
>>> myAge = 31
>>> yourAge = myAge
>>>
```

The first line creates and sets a variable named `myAge` to 31. The second line creates a variable named `yourAge` and sets it to the current value of the variable `myAge`. After running these two lines, both variables would be set to the value 31.

An assignment statement computes the value of whatever is on the right-hand side of the equals sign and assigns it to the variable on the left-hand side. Whenever a variable appears in an expression (that is, on the right-hand side of an assignment statement), the expression is evaluated (computed) by using the value of each variable. In other words, as the programmer, you write the name of a variable, but when the statement runs, the computer uses the current value of that variable at that time.

Here's a simple example of doing some addition:

```
>>> numberOfMales = 5
>>> numberOfFemales = 6
>>> numberOfPeople = numberOfMales + numberOfFemales
>>>
```

First, we use two assignment statements to create two variables: `numberOfMales` and `numberOfFemales`. In the third line, we see those two variables on the right side of the equals sign (the assignment operator). To generate a result, Python uses the value of those variables, 5 and 6, does the math, gets an answer of 11, and assigns that result into the variable on the left side of the equals sign: `numberOfPeople`.

I want to make it very clear that the equals sign in an assignment statement is very different from the way an equals sign is used in math. In math, the equals sign implies that the things on the left side and the right side have the same value. In Python, that's not the case.

To drive this point home, consider these two lines of code:

```
>>> myAge = 25
>>> myAge = myAge + 1
>>>
```

If you are a mathematician, the second line will jump out at you as an impossibility— that is, there is no value of myAge for which that statement is true.

However, this is *not* an equation; it is an assignment statement. Here is what the second line says (starting on the right-hand side):

1. Take the current value of the variable myAge

2. Add 1 to it

3. Put the resulting value back in to the variable myAge

This statement effectively changes the value of the variable myAge by adding 1 to it. Using a variable to count something is done all the time in programming, and it is very common to see lines like this in code.

# Print Statements

Now, how do we know if things are working? We would like to have a way to reach into a variable and see the value inside. Remember the print statement from our Hello World program? The print statement is very general purpose. You ask it to print something and it prints whatever you ask it to print into the Shell window. The general print statement looks like this:

```
print(<whatever you want to see>)
```

Here are some examples in the Shell:

```
>>> eggsInOmlette = 3
>>> print(eggsInOmlette)
3
>>> knowsHowToCook = True
>>> print(knowsHowToCook)
True
>>>
```

The print statement can also print multiple things on a single line. You can do this by separating the items you want to print with commas. When the print statement runs, each comma is replaced by a space:

```
>>> print(eggsInOmlette, knowsHowToCook)
3 True
>>>
```

You can use this to nicely format your output. For example, it allows you to print a description of what variable you are printing:

```
>>> eggsInOmlette = 3
>>> print('eggsInOmlette is:', eggsInOmlette)
eggsInOmlette is: 3
>>> knowsHowToCook = True
>>> print('knowsHowToCook is:', knowsHowToCook)
knowsHowToCook is: True
>>> print('eggsInOmlette and knowsHowToCook are', eggsInOmlette, 'and',
knowsHowToCook)
eggsInOmlette and knowsHowToCook are 3 and True
>>>
```

Here are more examples of assignment statements and print statements, using all four types of data:

```
>>> numberInADozen = 12
>>> print('There are', numberInADozen, 'items in a dozen')
There are 12 items in a dozen
>>> learningPython = True
```

```
>>> print('It is', learningPython, 'that I am learning Python')
It is True that I am learning Python
>>> priceOfCandy = 1.99
>>> print('My candy costs', priceOfCandy)
My candy costs 1.99
>>> myFullName = 'Irv Kalb'
>>> print('My full name is', myFullName)
My full name is Irv Kalb
>>>
```

There is one additional note about the print statement. To make things a little clearer in your output, you may want to include one or more blank lines. To create a blank line of output, you can use an empty print statement. Just write the word print with a set of open and close parentheses, like this:

```
>>> print()
```

---

**Note**    In Python 2, the print statement has a different form (syntax). In Python 2, the print statement did not require the parentheses around the item(s) that you want to print. It looked like this: print <item1>, <item2>, ... This is perhaps the most noticeable difference between Python 2 and Python 3. If you see code elsewhere written in Python 2 that is missing parentheses in print statements, you can often modify these statements to work in Python 3 by adding an outermost set of parentheses.

---

# Simple Math

Now let's move on to some simple math for use in assignment statements. Python recognizes the following set of math operators:

- + Add

- - Subtract

- * Multiply

- / Divide

- // Integer Divide

- ** Raise to the power of

- % Modulo (also known as *remainder*)

- ( ) Grouping (we'll come back to this)

Let's try some very simple math. For demonstration purposes, I'll just use variables named x and y. In the Shell, try the following:

```
>>> x = 9
>>> y = 6
>>> print(x + y)
15
>>> print(x - y)
3
>>> print(x * y)
54
>>> print(x / y)
1.5
>>> print(x // y)
1
```

---

**Note**   In Python 2, the divide operator worked differently. If you divided an integer by an integer, you got an integer as a result. For example if you divided 9 by 6, you got 1. The behavior of the divide operator was changed in Python 3 to always give a floating-point answer, and the integer divide operator (with two slashes) was added.

---

| COMPUTERS CAN REPRESENT INTEGERS PERFECTLY |
|---|

As humans, we represent integers using base 10 (digits from 0 to 9). Computers represent integers using base 2 (using only 1 and 0). But there is an exact mapping between the two bases. For every base 10 number, there is an exactly equivalent base 2 number. However, because of the way computers represent floating-point numbers, this is not the case for floating-point numbers. There is no such mapping between base 10 fractions and base

2 fractions. When representing floating-point fractional numbers, there is often some small amount of rounding; that is, floating-point fractional numbers are a close approximation of the intended number. For example, if we attempt to divide 5.0 by 9.0, we see this:

```
>>> print(5.0 / 9.0)
0.555555555556
```

The decimal values goes on forever, but when represented as a float, the value gets rounded off.

Let's try out the last two math operators. "Raise to the power of" is very straightforward. In the following code, we want to raise x to the power of y:

```
>>> x = 2
>>> y = 3
>>> print(x ** y)
8
>>>
```

Finally, there is modulo. The *modulo operator*—the percent sign—gives you the remainder of a division. With an integer division, the result is just the integer result. The modulo operator allows you to get the remainder. Here's an example. Imagine that you have a puppy that is 29 months old. Using an integer divide and the modulo operator, we can do an easy conversion to find out the age of the puppy is in years and months.

```
>>> ageInMonths = 29
>>> years = ageInMonths // 12
>>> months = ageInMonths % 12
>>> print("My puppy's age is", years, "years and", months, "months.")
My puppy's age is 2 years and 5 months.
>>>
```

If we reverse the process, you can see how we can get back to the original number:

```
>>> puppysAge = (years * 12) + months
>>> print("Puppy's age in months is:", puppysAge)
Puppy's age in months is: 29
```

# Order of Operations

Back in elementary school, in a lesson about math, my teacher went through a long description of a topic called the *order of operations*. We were told that some math operators had precedence over other ones. For example, look at this assignment statement:

```
x = 5 + 4 * 9 / 6
```

What operations are done in what order? The teacher explained that the acronym PEMDAS would help us to figure out the order. PEMDAS described the precedence order as follows:

1. Parentheses

2. Exponents

3. Multiplication

4. Division

5. Addition

6. Subtraction

However, I thought that it was a terrible idea to have some implied, seemingly arbitrary ordering of math operators. Let's look at the assignment statement again:

```
x = 5 + 4 * 9 / 6
```

You must understand the PEMDAS ordering to figure it out. First, you would multiply 4 by 9, take the result and divide that by 6, and then add 5, before storing the answer in x.

Because of my conviction for clarity, I feel that writing an assignment statement like this is an extremely poor technique. You are writing in a way that forces future readers to have an understanding of PEMDAS in order to infer what you meant by this statement.

Instead, it would be much clearer to both you and future readers if you were to use parentheses to group operations. Using parentheses allows you to "force" the order of operations so that the steps happen in whatever order you want. If you wanted to write the line in a way that reflects what would happen following PEMDAS, it would look like this:

```
x = 5 + ((4 * 9) / 6)
```

When you have nested sets of parentheses, the only rule you need to know is that sets of parentheses are evaluated from the innermost set to the outmost set. In this example, (4 * 9) is evaluated first, that result is then divided by 6, and then 5 is added tothat result. If you wanted the operations performed in a different order, you could use parentheses to create different groupings. For example:

```
x = (5 + 4) * (9 / 6)
```

These parentheses say that you should add 5 and 4, divide 9 by 6, and then multiply the results.

---

**Tip**  Adding parentheses as in the preceding statements makes your intent much clearer and does not rely on the reader to understand the PEMDAS rules. I strongly encourage you to add parentheses like these to force the order of operations.

---

# First Python Programs

Let's take everything we've learned in this chapter and write some very small but useful Python programs. We'll start by writing a simple program to add up the value of all the one-dollar bills and five-dollar bills that are in a wallet. Start by opening a new Python editor window (Control+N (Windows) or Command+N (Mac), or File ➤ New). This is what that code could look like:

```
numberOfOneDollarBills = 3
numberOFiveDollarBills = 2
total = numberOfOneDollarBills + (numberOFiveDollarBills * 5)
print('Total amount is:', total)
```

Again, none of these lines execute immediately; they have all just been entered into a file. In order to see any results, we have to run (execute) the program we have just written.

First, save the file (press Control+S (Windows) or Command+S (Mac) or click File ➤ Save). The first time you save a new file like this, you must give it a name. All Python file names should end in .py, so name this file something like MoneyInWallet.py.

Now that the file is saved, you are ready to run the program by pressing the F5 shortcut key or clicking Run ➤ Run Module. If there are no errors in your program, you will see the output of your program show up in the Shell. You should see this:

```
Total amount is: 13
```

If you had any errors, read the bottom line of the error message, identify what you typed incorrectly, fix it, save, and run again.

Let's build another simple program. In IDLE, open a new file (Command/Control+N). This time we'll write a program to calculate how much money you should be paid for working at a job. For the first 40 hours, you should be paid at an hourly rate. Any hours over 40 should be paid at time and a half—one and a half times the rate:

```
rate = 10.00
totalHours = 45
regularHours = 40
overTimeHours = totalHours - regularHours
pay = (rate * regularHours) + ((rate * 1.5) * overTimeHours)
print('For working', totalHours, 'hours, I should be paid', pay)
```

When you have that working, you should see the following in the Shell window:

```
For working 45 hours, I should be paid 475.0
```

Here is one more program that involves just a little bit of algebra. Again, open a new file for this program. You are probably familiar with the Pythagorean theorem for finding the hypotenuse of a triangle:

$$hypot^2 = side1^2 + side2^2$$

We cannot use the formula that way directly in a Python assignment statement. We cannot have a squared symbol attached to a variable, but we can simplify by taking the square root of both sides:

$$hypot = square\ root\ of\ (side1^2 + side2^2)$$

Then we can use the Python ** (raise to the power) operator to square both side lengths:

```
hypot = square root of ((side1 ** 2) + (side2 ** 2))
```

Finally, we can use the ** operator again. Raising something to the one-half (0.5) power is the equivalent of taking a square root:

```
hypot = ((side1 ** 2) + (side2 ** 2)) ** 0.5
```

This is a legal Python statement. Now we can build the full program. Let's try side lengths of 3 and 4 and see what our program generates for the hypotenuse:

```
side1 = 3
side2 = 4
hypot = ((side1 ** 2) + (side2 ** 2)) ** 0.5
print('Side 1 is', side1, ' Side 2 is', side2, ' Hypotenuse is:', hypot)
```

In the Shell window, you should see this:

```
Side 1 is 3   Side 2 is 4   Hypotenuse is: 5.0
```

# Shorthand Naming Convention

I want to introduce one more minor convention for naming variables. In addition to the camelcase naming convention, I use shorthand in some of my variable names. It turns out we often use variables to keep track of the number of items we have. In a game, we might use variables to keep track of the number of bad guys or good guys. In a testing program, we might use a variable to keep track of the number of right answers, and so on.

Programmers often start the variables with a numberOf prefix. This happens so often that I use shorthand. Rather than creating this variable name:

```
numberOf<Whatever>
```

I shorten that to where n stands for "number of"—like this:

```
n<Whatever>
```

For example, instead of writing this

```
numberOfJellyBeansInJar
numberOfGoodGuys
numberOfCorretAnswers
```

I write this:

```
nJellyBeansInJar
nGoodGuys
nCorrectAnswers
```

Let's revisit the earlier `MoneyInWallet.py` program and apply this additional naming convention. Here is the original code:

```
numberOfOneDollarBills = 3
numberOfFiveDollarBills = 2
total = numberOfOneDollarBills + (numberOfFiveDollarBills * 5)
print('Total amount is', total)
```

Apply this new naming convention to make it look like this:

```
nOneDollarBills = 3
nFiveDollarBills = 2
total = nOneDollarBills + (nFiveDollarBills * 5)
print('Total amount is', total)
```

If you want, you can do this by making changes on each line. But you could do it faster by doing a Find and Replace. Go to the Edit menu and choose Replace. Fill out the dialog box, as shown in Figure 2-8.

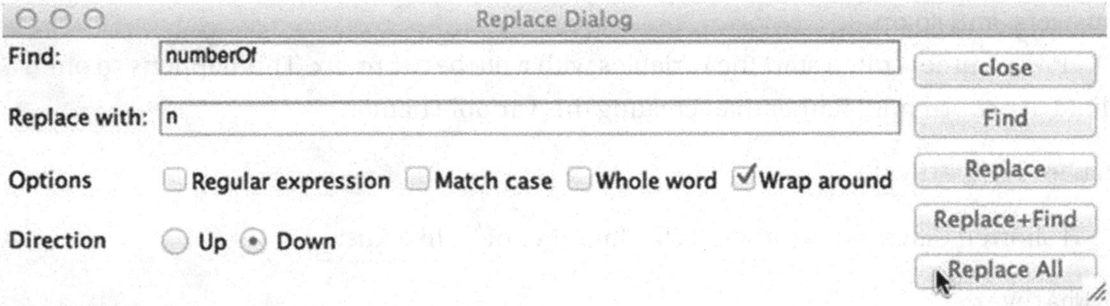

*Figure 2-8.* *Replace dialog box*

Then click Replace All. Save and run the program. You should see these identical results:

```
Total amount is 13
```

Finally, let's modify the program to allow us to count the ten-dollar bills and the twenty-dollar bills in the wallet.

```
nTwentyDollarBills = 5
nTenDollarBills = 4
nFiveDollarBills = 8
nOneDollarBills = 2
total = (nTwentyDollarBills * 20) + (nTenDollarBills * 10) + \
                (nFiveDollarBills * 5) + nOneDollarBills
print('Total amount is', total)
```

Notice that the line got a little long in the assignment statement that does the calculation. If you think a line is getting too long to read, you can add a backslash character (\) at a logical breaking point to indicate that the line should continue to the next line.

# Adding Comments

When you are writing software, you wind up making a lot of decisions about how you approach different problems. Sometimes your solutions are not exactly apparent and could use some documentation. You may want to explain to the reader (who could be a future version of you, or someone else) why you did something the way you wound up doing it, or how some intricate piece of code works.

Documentation like that, written directly in your code, is called a *comment*. Comments are completely ignored by Python; they are only there for humans. There are three ways to write comments in Python: provide a full-line comment, add a comment after a line of code, or use a multiline comment.

## Full-Line Comment

Start a line with the # character, followed by your comment:

```
# This whole line is a comment
# This is another comment line
# All comment lines are ignored by Python
# Even though the next line looks like code, it's just a comment
#  x = 1
#  -------------------------------------
```

Notice that when you type the #, the symbol and all characters after it turn red. This is IDLE recognizing that you are typing a comment.

## Add a Comment After a Line of Code

You can put a comment at the end of a line of code to explain what is going on inside that line. The following lines are very simple and don't really need comments, but they should serve as a good example of how to add this type of comment:

```
score = 0      #  Initializing the score
priceWithTax = price * 1.09  # add in 9% tax
```

## Multiline Comment

You can create a comment that spans any number of lines by making one line with three quote marks (single or double quotes), writing any number of comment lines, and ending with the same three quote characters (single or double quotes) on the last line, as follows:

```
"'
A multiline comment starts with a line of three quote characters (above)
This is a long comment block
It can be any length
You do not need to use the # character here
You end it by entering the same three quotes you used to start (below)
"'
```

There are times, when you are experimenting with code, that you may want to temporarily *comment out* a block of code. For example, you try writing something one way, and it's close to what you want but it's not exactly right. You don't want to delete it because you may want to do a little experiment to see if you can write the code in a better way.

Let's say that you have five lines of code that you want to comment out. You certainly could put the cursor at the beginning of a line and add the # symbol at the beginning of each line. Or you could put a triple quote before and after the block of code. But there is an easier way.

To comment out a block of lines, first select all the lines that you want to comment out. You can click at a beginning point in your code and drag across the lines you want to comment out, or you can click at the beginning point and Shift-click at the ending point. Then go to the Format menu and choose Comment Out Region. (For some reason, IDLE adds two pound-sign characters (##) when doing this, but that works fine.) Later, if you decide that you want to uncomment a block, select the region the same way, go to the Format menu, and choose Uncomment Region.

Finally, comments are often used at the top of a complicated program to build a *revision history*. That is, every time there is a significant change to a program, programmers often add a comment with a date, name, and message about what changed. For example:

```
# 03/27/15  DG  Modified to add ability to ...
# 01/02/14  IK  Modified to handle the ..
# 09/09/13  IK  First version
```

# Whitespace

Python ignores all invisible characters. For now, all of our statements must start in column 1 of each line, but you can add as many space characters as you want in between items on a line. You can also add blank lines anywhere you want in Python. When files get long, added blank lines can aid in readability. (I will talk about readability a lot!) When you press the Return or Enter key when typing in a Python file, IDLE adds an invisible RETURN character at the end of the line.

As with the naming conventions for variables, most programmers put spaces around math operators as another convention. Here is an example of clearly written code with good spacing:

```
myVariable = var1 + var2  #space on either side of equals and plus
(preferred)
```

But it could be written like this:

```
myVariable=var1+var2            #no spaces
```

Or even like this:

```
myVariable        =        \
         var1     +        var2  #lots of spaces
```

45

These lines all do the same thing. The extra spaces are *whitespace*, which is ignored by the Python compiler. Adding a single space before and after all operators makes your code more readable by humans.

Spaces will become important later.

# Errors

When writing and trying to run computer code, everyone makes mistakes. To help you build a correct program, Python tries to catch errors as early as possible. There are three different types of errors you encounter when doing Python programming: syntax errors, exception errors, and logic errors.

## Syntax Error

The first type of error is a *compile error* (the generic name for it in programming), which is known as a *syntax error* in Python.

Consider the following two-line program:

```
learningPython = True
print(learningpython)
```

When this program is run, we see this:

```
Traceback (most recent call last):
  File "<test>", line 2, in <module>
    print(learningpython)
NameError: name 'learningpython' is not defined
```

This is called a *traceback*, a term that won't make a lot of sense at the moment. For now, just recognize that this is a Python error message. Python is trying to help you by telling you that something has gone wrong. To understand what Python is trying to say, look at the last line first. In this case, it says the following:

```
NameError: name 'learningpython' is not defined
```

And this is exactly the problem. The first line created a variable named learningPython, but learningpython (with a lowercase *p*) has never been defined. The wording of the last line of the traceback is very clear in explaining what went wrong. The middle two lines of the traceback tell you the line where the error occurred:

```
File "<test>", line 2, in <module>
    print(learningpython)
```

Errors in variable names will be the cause of many early errors in your programming. This is why I strongly recommend using the camelcase convention. If you follow the convention consistently, you won't have as many of these types of errors.

Here's a second example of a compilation error:

```
a = 5 5
```

A line like this one breaks the rules of Python. Python understands the first part of it as an assignment statement, but when it sees 5 space 5, it doesn't know what you mean. When you try to compile a program with a line like this, you get an error dialog saying that there was a syntax error. IDLE also puts a red highlight box in your source code that indicates where it thinks your error is. When you get a compile error, Python cannot run your program, so it does not even try. You need to study the line with the error, figure out what is wrong, and fix the error.

Here is a third type of syntax error. In the following, the first line has open parentheses, but no closing parentheses:

```
y = (5 +
x = 1
```

In code like this, Python reads what you wrote, finds the opening parenthesis, and looks for the matching close parenthesis. It doesn't find one on the first line, so it continues to the second line. When it finds what it thinks is a second equals sign, it knows that something is wrong because you cannot have two equals signs in an assignment statement. Therefore, you see the red error box on an incorrect line.

---

**Note**  If you run into an error like this, where the line of code looks correct (x = 1 is correct), the actual error might have occurred on the line above.

---

# Exception Error

The second type of error is a *runtime* error (its generic name in programming), which is known as an *exception error* in Python:

```
x = 5 + 'abc'
```

You can't really add a number and a string. If you try to run this line, Python generates the following error:

```
Traceback (most recent call last):
  File "<pyshell#0>", line 1, in <module>
    x = 5 + 'abc'
TypeError: unsupported operand type(s) for +: 'int' and 'str'
```

When you get a traceback, the first thing to do is read the bottom line first. This one may be a little difficult to read, but what it's saying is that for the plus operator, Python does not allow you to try to combine an integer and a string.

Here is another example. Assume you have not used a variable named xyz, and you try to use this variable in a line like this

```
print(xyz)
```

or this:

```
y = xyz + 1
```

These are valid Python statements, but because xyz was not defined before running these lines, Python gives you the following error message:

```
Traceback (most recent call last):
  File "<pyshell#2>", line 1, in <module>
    print(xyz)
NameError: name 'xyz' is not defined
```

The wording of the last line of this error message is very clear. When you see this type of error, you have most likely misspelled or miscapitalized a variable name. Remember, all uppercase/lowercase letters in a variable name must be the same every time the variable is used. Variables ABC and abc are completely different variables.

# Logic Error

The third type of error is a wrong answer, also known as a *logic error*.

Let's say you are attempting to do simple addition. In trying to write the code, you inadvertently write the following:

```
# Attempt to ADD 2 and 5
total = 2 * 5
print(total)
```

These lines of code are valid Python statements, and the program will run without any error messages. But it produces an incorrect answer. This type of error is often difficult to track down.

In this small example, it is obvious what's wrong: the asterisk (multiplication) should have been a plus (addition). But when you start to write larger programs, it gets more and more difficult to find such errors. To track down this type of error, you generally add `print` statements to write out the values of your variables at different points in the program. You run your program and compare the output of your `print` statements against your expected results. Using that approach helps narrow down the location of the error.

# Summary

In this chapter, you learned about data, variables, and assignment statements. We discussed the four main types of data: integers, floats, strings, and Booleans. You got an in-depth understanding of what a variable is and learned a convention for how a variable should be named. And you saw how to give a variable a value with an assignment statement. I introduced the math operators in Python and showed a few sample programs. You saw how to add comments to code, learned about whitespace, and were introduced to the types of errors you will see when writing code.

# CHAPTER 3

# Built-in Functions

Just as Python has a number of built-in operators (such as + for addition, - for subtraction, * for multiplication, and so on), it also comes with a number of what are called *built-in functions*.

This chapter discusses the following topics:

- Built-in functions

- Using a function/function call

- Arguments

- Getting a result back from a function

- The type function

- Getting input from the user using `input`

- Conversion functions: `int`, `float`, and `str`

- Building our first real programs

- Concatenation, or adding strings together

- Another programming exercise

- Using function calls inside assignment statements

## Overview of Built-in Functions

I'll give you an analogy to explain what a built-in function is. My car has a built-in radio. The radio is not really the car itself; it was developed separately, probably by a different company. But when I bought the car, it had a radio in it. When I want the radio to do something, I press its buttons or turn its dials, and the radio responds appropriately. I don't need to know *how* the radio works, I just need to know how to use the radio's

© Irv Kalb 2018
I. Kalb, *Learn to Program with Python 3*, https://doi.org/10.1007/978-1-4842-3879-0_3

controls. Similarly, in a typical kitchen there are number of built-in appliances. The inner workings of a home bread maker are a mystery to most people, but the average person can read the manual and figure out how to use the controls to have it make a delicious loaf of bread.

Python has a number of things like this called *built-in functions*. They are pieces of code that are available for you to use in your programs. (The real power of programming comes when we build our own functions, which we will get to in the next chapter.) When you want to use a built-in function, you specify its name and typically give it some information. The function does some work with that information and gives you back some result.

# Function Call

Using a function is known as *calling* a function, or making a *function call*, or making a *call* to a function. To call a function, you supply the name of the function, followed by a set of open/close parentheses. This is the generic form:

```
<functionName>()
```

However, most built-in functions expect you to supply one or more pieces of information in addition to the function name. This is commonly called *passing* data to a function.

# Arguments

---

**Definition**   An *argument* is a value that is passed when you call a function.

---

Inside the function call's parentheses, you put any data you want, called an *argument*, to send to that function. Here's what a generic call to a function with arguments looks like:

```
<functionName>(<argument1>, <argument2>, ...)
```

# Results

When you call a built-in function, the function does its work and typically hands back a result. When the function is finished, the result replaces the call and its arguments; that is, the line continues to execute using the returned value in place of the call. Very often when you make a call to a function, you assign the returned value to a variable using an assignment statement, as follows:

```
<variable> = <functionName>(<argument1>, <argument2>, ...)
```

# Built-in type Function

Let's start with a simple example to demonstrate this in context. Python has a built-in function that can tell us the data *type* of any variable or value. Not surprisingly, it is called type. Again, the sequence is that you call a function and pass in a value or values (arguments), the function does some work using the value(s) you provided, and then it gives back an answer. Let's find out the data type of the number 10:

```
>>> typeOfTen = type(10)
>>> print(typeOf10)
<class 'int'>
```

In the first line, we call the type function passing in 10. The function does its work, and when the function is done, it gives back a result. We take that returned result and assign it to a variable, typeOfTen. Finally, we print out typeOfTen. As expected, we see that typeOfTen is an integer. (The word class here means type.)

Alternatively, when making a call to a function, you can pass in a variable instead of a number (or string or Boolean). When you do, Python uses the value of the variable at that time. Here we use a variable named age and make a similar call:

```
>>> age = 18
>>> typeOfAge = type(age)
>>> print(typeOfAge)
<class 'int'>
```

The first line executes and sets the variable age to 18. When the second line runs, Python sees the variable name, looks up the variable's value, and passes the value of the variable. Therefore, when that line executes, your code will run exactly as though it said this:

```
>>> typeOfAge = type(18)
```

Further, when making a call to a function, we do not necessarily need to use an assignment statement. We could just use a print statement to see the returned value:

```
>>> age = 18
>>> print(type(age))
<class 'int'>
```

We don't know *how* the type function does what it does, and frankly, we don't care. It's kind of like how most of us think about a microwave oven, or TV, or phone. Most of us don't know how these things work internally, but we are happy using them as long as they continue to do what we need them to do.

Now, let's try using the type function with a different data type:

```
>>> print(type(123.45))
<class 'float'>
```

To show that the type function works with any data type, we'll try it with a string and then a Boolean:

```
>>> print(type('This could be any string'))
<class 'str'>
>>> print(type(True))
<class 'bool'>
```

Now, let's try to confuse you. Let's create a new variable, myVar, and give it a value:

```
myVar = '1234'
```

What do you think the type of myVar is? Let's ask Python to tell us, again using the type function:

```
>>> print(type(myVar))
<class 'str'>
```

Even though the characters are all digits, this is a string because there is an opening and closing quotation mark. Now let's execute this line:

```
>>> myVar = 1234
```

That line changes the contents of the myVar variable to an integer. Therefore, the same variable is now considered an integer variable:

```
>>> print(type(myVar))
<class 'int'>
```

The important thing to notice here is that 1234 and '1234' are very different things. 1234 is an integer number, and '1234' is a string of characters. These are totally different values. We'll see how to switch between these types very soon.

This ability for variables to switch data types at any time is not typical. In most other computer languages, you must declare the data type of each variable before it is used. Then throughout the program, variables can only be given values of that type. Python is called a *dynamically typed* language because the type of a variable can change over time.

# Getting Input from the User

This is the typical flow of a simple computer program:

1. Input data.

2. Work with data. Do some computation(s).

3. Output some answer(s).

In Python, we can get input from the user using a built-in function called input. Here's how it is used, most typically in an assignment statement:

```
<variable> = input(<prompt string>)
```

On the right side of the equals sign is the call to the input built-in function. When you make the call, you must pass in a *prompt string*, which is any string that you want the user to see. The prompt is a question you want the user to answer. The input function returns all the characters that the user types, as a string. Here is an example of how input might be used in a program:

```
favoriteColor = input('What is your favorite color? ')
print('Your favorite color is', favoriteColor)
```

When the assignment statement runs, the following steps happen in order:

1.  The prompt string is printed to the Shell.

2.  The program stops and waits for the user to type a response.

3.  The user enters some sequence of characters into the Shell as an answer.

4.  When the user presses the Enter key (Windows) or the Return key (Mac), input returns the characters that the user typed.

5.  Typically, input is used on the right-hand side of an assignment statement. The user's response is stored into the variable on the left-hand side of the equals sign.

In the preceding example, as a favorite color, let's say that the user entered **purple**. The variable favoriteColor is given the value of the string 'purple'. favoriteColor is a string variable, because anything the user types is a string of characters.

That works great for this example asking for a favorite color. But what if you want the user to enter a number? Consider what happens when you run the following:

```
nDollars = input('How many dollars do you have? ')
print(type(nDollars))
```

You would probably want nDollars to be an integer because you may want to use that variable in some numerical calculation. However, when run, this code would report that nDollars is a string variable. This happens because input always returns the characters that the user types, even if those characters are digits. If the user typed the characters **12**, then nDollars is given the value of the string '12', not the number 12. As you now know, these two values are very different.

Assuming we want to do some math with the variable nDollars, we need a way to take the string that the user typed and turn it into a number. Let's see how Python provides exactly what we need.

# Conversion Functions

Python has three built-in *conversion* functions that can change a value from one data type to another: the int function, the float function, and the str function.

# int Function

To convert from a string (or a float) to an integer, there is the int function. You call the function, pass in a string or a float value, and it returns an integer version of what was passed in; for example:

```
nDollars = input('How many dollars do you have in your wallet? ')
nDollars = int(nDollars)
```

A call to input returns whatever the user types in as a string. The call to int converts the variable nDollars from the string the user typed into an integer. The call to the int function is shown here in an assignment statement, where we take the resulting integer value and put it back into the same variable, nDollars. This is a very typical use case. Knowing that nDollars has been converted to an integer, we can now do some math with it.

# float Function

To convert from a string (or integer) to a float, there is the float function. For example:

```
thePrice = input('Enter the price: ')
thePrice = float(thePrice)
```

The user is asked to enter a price. Whatever characters the user types are assigned into the thePrice variable. The second line converts the thePrice variable from a string to a float and assigns the resulting float value back into the same variable. Similar to using the int function, now we can do some math with thePrice variable, knowing here that it is a floating-point variable.

# str Function

To convert from an integer or float to a string, there is the str built-in function. For example:

```
myAge = 37
myAge = str(myAge)
aPrice = 150.75
aPrice = str(aPrice)
```

These lines convert from an integer or float to a string. We will use the str function later when we want to build long, nicely formatted strings for output.

Python has many built-in functions, but you will find the five we have discussed to be particularly useful. Each requires that you send in a single argument, and then each returns a result:

```
type(<valueOrVariable>)
# returns data type of the argument passed in
```

```
input(<promptStringOrStringVariable>)
# asks the user a question, and returns the user's response as a string
```

```
int(<valueOrVariable>)
# returns an integer version of the argument passed in
```

```
float(<valueOrVariable>)
# returns a float version of the argument passed in
```

```
str(<valueOrVariable>)
# returns a string version of the argument passed in
```

There is another built-in function that we have already seen. Although I referred to the print *statement* earlier, print is actually another built-in function. The print function works a little differently in that you can pass in as many arguments as you want (separated by commas) and it does not return any value:

```
print(<valueOrVariable>, <valueOrVariable>, ...)
# returns nothing
```

# First Real Programs

We now have discussed all the tools needed to write our first simple programs that incorporate the basic steps of input, processing, and output. As an exercise, the following is a specification of a program for you to build:

1.  Prompt the user to enter a number.

2.  Prompt the user to enter a second number.

3.  Using a third variable, add the user's two numbers together.

4.  Print a nicely formatted line that shows the input and the output.
    For example:

```
The sum of 2 and 8 is 10
```

Once you understand what is being asked, close the book, open a new Python file in IDLE, and try to write and run the program.

Here is the solution:

```python
# Simple addition program

value1 = input('Please enter a number: ')
value1 = int(value1)
value2 = input('Please enter another number: ')
value2 = int(value2)
total = value1 + value2
print('The sum of', value1, 'and', value2, 'is', total)
```

Input to the program is handled by two calls to input, each asking the user to input a number. Because the user's response to input is always a string, we need to use the int function to convert both responses to integers. The calculation of the total is a very simple assignment statement. Finally, we output the answer with a nicely formatted print statement.

Notice that in both of the calls to input, the prompt string has been set up to have an extra space at the end. This is purely aesthetic. It is done this way to allow for a blank space between the question that is asked and the user's input.

To make this point about calling a function and the resulting value even clearer, consider this variation of the code:

```python
value1 = input('Please enter a number: ')
value2 = input('Please enter another number: ')
total = int(value1) + int(value2)
print('The sum of', value1, 'and', value2, 'is', total)
```

Notice the line that calculates the total. I'll go over the sequence of operations. First, int is called to change value1 to an integer. Then int is called again to change value2 to an integer. Each of these calls returns a result. Next, the two returned integer values are added together. Finally, the resulting sum is assigned to the total variable.

Here is a second challenge, very similar to the first. Write and run a program that simulates a cash register:

1.   Prompt the user to enter the cost of an item.

2.   Prompt the user to enter the cash paid for the item (for example, 10 for a ten-dollar bill).

3.   Using a third variable, calculate how much change the user should get back.

4.   Print a nicely formatted line that shows the input and the output. For example:

```
Your item costs 6.75 and you gave me 10.0 dollars.
Your change is 3.25
```

Again, once you understand what is being asked, close the book, open a new Python file in IDLE, and try to write and run the program.

Here is the solution:

```
# Simple cash register

cost = input('Please enter the cost of the item: ')
cost = float(cost)
cash = input('Please enter the cash given: ')
cash = float(cash)
change = cash - cost
print('Your item costs', cost, 'and you gave me', cash, 'dollars.
Your change is', change)
```

This program is almost identical to the first simple addition program. There are only two differences. First, because we are dealing with money expressed in dollars and cents, the cost of the item and the cash amount should be expressed as floating-point numbers. Therefore, cost and cash need to be converted to numbers using the float built-in function. Second, to calculate the change, we need to subtract the cost of the item from the cash. There are ways to format floating-point numbers to display a given number of decimal places, but we won't get into that right now.

# Concatenation

We know that there are a number of operations you can do with numbers (+, -, *, /, //,**, %). But if you try to *add* strings, that doesn't really make sense. Or does it?

Well, you can't really add strings in the way you add numbers. It doesn't really make sense to add a string like 'Joe' and a string like 'Schmoe'.

```
      'Joe'
+    'Schmoe'
_____
    ???????
```

But what if we applied a slightly different meaning to the plus sign when dealing with strings? That is, when dealing with strings, we could redefine the plus operator to mean "Take the first string and add the second string onto the end of the first one." That's exactly what happens in Python.

---

**Definition**    *Concatenate* means take a string and add another string.

---

In Python, along with most other languages, when dealing with strings, the + is called the *concatenation operator*. Here is an example:

```
firstString = 'Hot'
secondString = 'Coffee'
concatenatedString = firstString + secondString
print('The result of concatenation is: ', concatenatedString)
```

When run, the preceding code produces this:

```
The result of concatenation is: HotCoffee
```

# Another Programming Exercise

Here is another exercise for you; this one involves concatenation:

1.  Ask the user to enter their first name.

2.  Ask the user to enter their last name.

3.  Using concatenation, create a string of the user's full name, with a space between the first and last names. Store the full name into a third variable.

4.  Print out a nice greeting using the full name (using *Joe* as the first name and *Schmoe* as the last name), like this:

```
Hello Joe Schmoe I hope you are doing well.
```

```
# Greeting creator

firstName = input('Please enter your first name: ')
lastName = input('Please enter your last name: ')
fullName = firstName + ' ' + lastName

print('Hello', fullName, 'I hope you are doing well. ')
```

This program turns out to be simple. The only tricky part is in the concatenation of the first and last name, because there needs to be a space between the names. With simple addition, it would be obvious that you could add three numbers together by doing something like 5 + 2 + 3 to get 10. The concatenation operator works in a similar way. Just as you can concatenate two strings together, you can concatenate three strings (or for that matter, any number of strings) by using the concatenation operator multiple times. To put a space in between the first and last names, we take the first name, concatenate a single space character (' '), and then concatenate the last name.

Earlier, we built a simple cash register program. It used this line at the end to print the answers:

```
print('Your item costs', cost, 'and you gave me', cash, 'dollars. Your
change is', change)
```

It generated an output like this:

```
Your item costs 6.75 and you gave me 10.0 dollars. Your change is 3.25
```

But what if we wanted to write output using the dollar sign, like this:

```
Your item costs $6.75 and you gave me $10.0. Your change is $3.25
```

We could try adding the dollar sign to our text, like this:

```
print('Your item costs $', cost, 'and you gave me $', cash, ' Your change
is $', change)
```

But the output would have an annoying extra space after every dollar sign:

```
Your item costs $ 6.75 and you gave me $ 10.0. Your change is $ 3.25
```

To fix this, we can use concatenation and the str built-in function:

```
print('Your item costs $' + str(cost) + ' and you gave me $' + str(cash) +
'. Your change is $' + str(change))
```

Notice that in the preceding line, we are calling the str built-in function three times. Rather than saving the "stringified" version of cost, cash, and change, we are just calling the str function "in-line." Each call results in a string version of the numeric variable. We use each resulting string to build up a long string answer before printing.

# Using Function Calls Inside Assignment Statements

In the previous chapter, we built a simple program to calculate the number of dollars a person has in his or her wallet. Let's revisit that code, but now using built-in functions. In the following program, we will ask the user to tell us how many of each denomination of bills they have, and the program will calculate the total. In the following code, we are using three different built-in functions:

```
# Calculate the amount of money interactively

# Use input to get info from the user
nOnes = input('How many ones do you have? ')
nFives = input('How many fives do you have? ')
nTens = input('How many tens do you have? ')
nTwenties = input('How many twenties do you have? ')
```

```
# Use int to convert the inputted strings to integer values before multiplying
total = int(nOnes) + (int(nFives) * 5) + (int(nTens) * 10) +
(int(nTwenties) * 20)

# Use str to convert to a string, then concatenate on a decimal point and
zeros
totalAsString = str(total) + '.00'

# Concatentate strings and print
print('You have $' + totalAsString)
```

Let's take a closer look at this line:

```
total = int(nOnes) + (int(nFives) * 5) + (int(nTens) * 10) +
(int(nTwenties) * 20)
```

There, we have four calls to the int built-in function. Let's walk through how this statement works. As an example, let's assume that the user answered the questions saying that she had 2 ones, 3 fives, 4 tens, and 5 twenties. Therefore, when the preceding line runs, Python substitutes the current values for the variables nOnes, nFives, nTens, and nTwenties. So, when running, Python effectively sees this:

```
total = int('2') + (int('3') * 5) + (int('4') * 10) + (int('5') * 20)
```

Each of the calls to the int function runs and converts each string argument into an integer *before* each value is multiplied. In our earlier code, we typically took the result of calling the int function and assigned it to a variable. Instead, we can use a function call directly inside of a longer expression. When this line runs, you can think of an intermediate step where each call to the int function has been replaced by the returned integer version of each string:

```
total = 2 + (3 * 5) + (4 * 10) + (4 * 20)
```

Then—because of the proper use of parentheses—the numbers are multiplied:

```
total = 2 + 15 + 40 + 80
```

Next, the numbers are added:

```
total = 157
```

Finally, the resulting value is assigned into the variable total.

Python has many additional highly useful built-in functions, which are introduced at the appropriate times throughout this book. Most of them work in a similar way to the `type`, `input`, `int`, `float`, and `str` built-in functions discussed in this chapter.

## Summary

This chapter was all about some of Python's built-in functions, which are pieces of code that Python provides for you. You learned how to call a function and pass arguments. When a function is done, it typically returns a value that you often store in a variable. I introduced the `input` function that allows you to get input from the user. Then we saw the conversion functions of `int`, `float`, and `str`, which are used to change data from one type to another. We found that `print` is also a Python built-in function. Using these built-in functions, we worked through building our first useful programs. You learned how to add strings using concatenation. Finally, you got some experience in writing your own small programs.

# CHAPTER 4

# User-Defined Functions

Software is a detailed set of instructions that tell the computer what to do. There are numerous examples where we, as humans, follow a set of such instructions. As a simple example, many pieces of furniture from IKEA come with a set of high-level instructions in the form of pictures. When creating these instructions, the people at IKEA assume a certain level of basic knowledge of how to use tools, such as a wrench, a screwdriver, a hammer, and so on.

But using tools could be broken down into simpler steps. Using a hammer could be broken down into grip the hammer by the handle, hold the nail perpendicular to the surface, tap the nail with the head of the hammer to get it started, then hit the nail harder, and so forth. Once you understand the steps involved in using a hammer, you can apply your hammer skills any time a set of instructions calls for you to use one, without having to worry about the details. Creating detailed low-level descriptions of steps (like how to use a hammer) is very similar to the way that software is built. In this chapter, you learn how to create these types of software groupings.

This chapter covers the following topics:

- A recipe as an analogy for building software
- Definition of a function
- Building our first function
- Calling a user-defined function
- Receiving data in a user-defined function: parameters
- Building user-defined functions with parameters
- Building a simple function that does addition
- Building a function to calculate an average
- Returning a value from a function: the return statement
- Returning no value: None

67

© Irv Kalb 2018
I. Kalb, *Learn to Program with Python 3*, https://doi.org/10.1007/978-1-4842-3879-0_4

- Returning more than one value

- Specific and general variable names in calls and functions

- Temperature conversion functions

- Placement of functions in a Python file

- Never writing multiple copies of the same code

- Constants

- Scope of variables: global and local

- Global and local variables with the same names

- Finding errors inside functions: traceback

# A Recipe as an Analogy for Building Software

Cooking and baking also have detailed lists of instructions. Let's take a look at a recipe to see how we can use it as an analogy for building software. Here is a recipe for baking a (very delicious) chocolate cake:

## Ingredients

1 box of cake mix (chocolate)

1 box of Jell-O Instant Pudding (chocolate)

1/4 pound chocolate chips

4 eggs

3/4 cup of water

1/3 cup of oil

## Directions

Preheat oven to 350 degrees.

Crack eggs into a bowl.

Blend eggs (high, 4 minutes).

Add the water.

Add the oil.

Blend (medium, 1 minute).

Add the cake mix.

Add the Jell-O mix.

Blend (medium, 10 minutes).

Add the chocolate chips.

Blend (low, 1 minute).

Grease the Bundt pan.

Pour mixture into a pan.

Bake at 350 degrees for 45 minutes.

Remove from oven.

All recipes contain two basic parts: ingredients and directions. The analogy to software works like this. The *ingredients* (such as eggs, water, oil) are always nouns. Think of these as data. Then there are the *directions*, which are always actions. The directions always start with a verb (in this recipe: *preheat, crack, blend, add,* and so on). Think of these as the code that acts on the data.

Just as using a hammer is made up of a number of smaller steps, the steps in our recipe can be broken down further and further. This process is called *stepwise refinement*. For example, "Crack eggs into bowl" can be broken down as follows.

For each egg:

Remove egg from carton.

Hit egg gently on surface.

Move egg over a bowl.

Crack open egg.

Dump all egg goop into bowl.

Discard eggshell.

Once you have developed the detailed, lower-level steps you need to take for "Crack eggs into bowl," and you have tested those steps to know that they work correctly, you can think of the higher-level concept of "Crack eggs into bowl" without having to worry about the lower-level details. If our cake recipe had the need for two different steps where you had to crack eggs into a bowl, you would perform the exact same set of instructions at both points.

Now that we have the detailed procedure for cracking eggs into a bowl, if we found another recipe that called for cracking eggs into a bowl, we do not need to describe those steps again. Someday, if someone invents a laser egg splitter that makes it easier and more efficient to get the contents of an egg out of the shell, then we would modify the steps involved in "Crack eggs into bowl" to use the laser egg splitter, and these new steps would be applied in any recipe that called for cracking eggs.

Notice in the chocolate cake recipe that there are many times when we need to blend ingredients in a mixer. In fact, there are four different places. Also notice that every time we blend, we are also specifying different details for each blend.

Preheat oven to 350 degrees.

Crack eggs into bowl.

**Blend (high, 4 minutes).**

Add the water.

Add the oil.

**Blend (medium, 1 minute).**

Add the cake mix.

Add the Jell-O mix

**Blend (medium, 10 minutes).**

Add the chocolate chips.

**Blend (low, 1 minute).**

Grease the Bundt pan.

Pour the mixture into the pan.

Bake at 350 for 45 minutes.

Remove from oven.

Let's take a closer look at the word *blend* in the directions. We could break down—or define—*blend* into something like the following.

**Blend** with a given electric mixer setting and number of minutes:

Turn on the electric mixer to the given setting.

Set a timer for the specified number of minutes.

Until time is up:

> Stir slowly with spatula.
>
> Break up any lumps.
>
> Scrape sides of the bowl.

When you are following a recipe and it tells you to blend something, you perform the steps inside this definition of blend. This is the basic idea behind how we write code. Software is typically built in groups of lines like this. Such a grouping has traditionally been called a *routine* (also known as a *subroutine* or even a *subprogram*). Every routine like this is given a unique name. Once you test the instructions and know that they work the right way, you can use or invoke the routine by stating the name of the routine. When your program runs, any time the program gets to a line that includes the name of a routine, the statements inside that routine run and do what they do to complete that task.

Within our blend example, the word *stir* could be broken down into a more detailed list of operations, such as "Grab spatula, place under mixture, rotate mixture upward toward the beaters," and so forth. Software works analogously in that a routine can invoke another routine to do another predefined job. In a recipe or in software, you can go down any number of levels until some basic operations are understood without further explanation.

# Definition of a Function

In Python, a routine, like any of the ones described in the preceding section, is known as a *user-defined function*, or more simply, a *function*.

---

**Definition**   A *function* is a series of related steps (statements) that make up a larger task, which is often called from multiple places in a program.

---

Here is the generic form of a function in Python:

```
def <functionName>(<optionalParameters>): # notice the parentheses and the
ending colon
    <indented statement(s)> # the 'body' of the function
```

The word def is short for *definition*. You are defining a function. def is one of the special reserved Python keywords. When you type a keyword such as def, IDLE changes its color to show you that it recognizes it. Next, you supply a name for the function. You can choose any name—although it is recommended that you continue to follow the camelcase naming convention. It's worth it to take time to create a name that makes it very clear what the function does. A set of parentheses follows the name. Let's ignore the <optionalParameters> for now; we'll come back to it shortly. The line ends with a colon (:), which is very important.

All the statements that make up the function, called the *body* of the function, are indented from the def statement. Python relies on indenting to show a grouping of lines. The convention is to indent four spaces. (You can change this in the IDLE preferences, but it defaults to 4, and four spaces is a broadly accepted convention.) If you have ever seen code written in the C, Java, or JavaScript languages, you might know that these languages define similar blocks of code with open and close braces { }. However, C, Java, and JavaScript programmers almost universally use indenting in addition to the braces. Python's use of indenting only (with no braces) is unique and helps make Python code much more readable than most other languages.

# Building Our First Function

Let's build our first function. Open a new file in IDLE and type the following. IDLE helps with the indenting. When you type a def statement to start the definition of a function, IDLE automatically indents the next line (and all successive lines) by the default number of spaces. To tell IDLE that you no longer want to indent code, you must press the Delete key (Mac) or the Backspace key (Windows). Moving the cursor back four spaces by pressing Backspace or Delete is known as a *dedent* or *outdent*:

```
def getGroceries():
    print('milk')
    print('flour')
```

```
print('sugar')
print('butter')
print()    #blank line
```

This is the definition of a function. It is the detailed implementation of something that you want the computer to be able to do. It's like the steps of "Crack eggs into bowl" in our earlier recipe. The name of the function is getGroceries. It contains a series of detailed instructions that make up a larger task. Each of these instruction lines is indented. The code of the function is made up of five simple print statements. Enter the code, save the file, and run the program to see it in action.

When you run it, woo-hoo! Absolutely nothing happens! Why? Because we didn't ask our program to do anything. You probably know how to throw a ball, sing a song, open a can, and make a peanut butter sandwich. But if you are reading this book and no one asks you to do any of these things, you will most likely not perform any of those actions.

If you want a function to run, you have to tell the computer to run it. Chapter 3 discussed a number of Python's built-in functions (type, input, int, float, and str). Python knows what code to run for each of these, but none of these built-in functions will do anything until and unless a call to one of these functions executes in the currently running program.

# Calling a User-Defined Function

Just as we did with built-in functions, when you want to use a user-defined function, you call a user-defined function by specifying the name of the function, followed by a set of parentheses, and include any data (arguments) that you want the function to act on, as follows:

```
<functionName>(<argument1>, <argument2>, ...)
```

Because our getGroceries function does not operate on any data, to call the getGroceries function, we only need to specify its name, followed by an empty set of parentheses:

```
getGroceries()  # calling the function, must have parentheses, even if
there are no arguments
```

In our Python file, we'll add a call to the function after the function definition. The area below any functions is typically referred to as the *main* code. Save and run the program:

```python
def getGroceries():
    print('milk')
    print('flour')
    print('sugar')
    print('butter')
    print()   #blank line

# Main code starts here
getGroceries()
```

When you save and run this code, you should see the following output in the Shell:

```
milk
flour
sugar
butter
```

Let's add a second call to the same function in the main code:

```python
def getGroceries():
    print('milk')
    print('flour')
    print('sugar')
    print('butter')
    print()    #blank line

# Main code starts here:
getGroceries()
getGroceries()
```

After this change, you should see the following in the Shell:

```
milk
flour
sugar
butter
```

```
milk
flour
sugar
butter
```

Until now, you have only seen code that runs strictly from the top down. With the ability to create and use functions, we can affect the "order of execution" of a program; that is, we can jump around within the program.

Let's modify the code just slightly to show how a function can call another function. Here is another variation of the program that does just that:

```
# This function just prints a line of asterisks followed by a blank line
def separateRuns():
    print('*****************')
    print()         #blank line

def getGroceries():
    print('milk')
    print('flour')
    print('sugar')
    print('butter')
    separateRuns()      # call another function

# Main code starts here:
getGroceries()
getGroceries()
```

When we run this version, you should see the following in the Shell:

```
milk
flour
sugar
butter
*****************

milk
flour
sugar
butter
*****************
```

Here is what happens when you run this code. Python sees the first `def` statement for `separateRuns` and recognizes that it is the definition of a function. Python remembers where this function is and skips over the body of the function (the indented lines). Next, it sees the `def` statement for the `getGroceries` function. Again, it remembers where this is and skips over the body of this function. Eventually, it finds the first real line of the executable code—the first call to `getGroceries()`.

When this line runs, because it has a call to a function, Python remembers where it was, and execution jumps to the `def` statement for the `getGroceries` function. Each `print` statement inside the function runs and each writes out its appropriate value. At the last statement, Python finds a call to another function: `separateRuns`. Python remembers where it came from and transfers control into that function. The `separateRuns` function first prints a line of asterisks (to show the end of a run) and then a blank line (to separate the output from other runs). Because there is no more work for this function to do, control is transferred back to where it was called from (inside `getGroceries`). And because this is the last line of `getGroceries`, control is transferred back to where that function was called from (in the main code). On the next line, Python finds another call to `getGroceries`. Control is transferred into the function once again, and the entire sequence is repeated. After the second call to `getGroceries` completes, Python finds no more lines of code to run, and the program terminates.

# Receiving Data in a User-Defined Function: Parameters

Our `getGroceries` function is a good example of what a user-defined function looks like, but it's not very useful. Every time you call `getGroceries`, it does the exact same thing: this is an example of what is known as *hard-coding*. It would be more interesting and useful to have a function that would do something different depending on the data that is passed in.

Remember from our earlier discussion of built-in functions that when you call a function, you can pass data. Each piece of data that you pass is called an *argument*. When we pass arguments with a function call, the function can be written to do different work and/or generate different results, depending on the value(s) of data. Now we can look at the other side of the call: how to receive the data that is passed in to a function.

---

**Definition**    A *parameter* is a variable (defined in the def statement of a function) that is given a value when a function starts. (It is also known as a *parameter variable*.)

---

Think back to our chocolate cake recipe example. When discussing that recipe, we said that *blend* is like a function. The definition of blend is a series of steps that made up a larger task; it was used in many places in our recipe. Further, remember that in our chocolate cake recipe, whenever we were directed to blend, two pieces of information were always specified: the mixer's power setting and the number of minutes the mixer needed to operate. If you think of *blend* as a Python function, then the two pieces of data that are passed with every call are received and used inside the function. The Python version of a blend function might look like this:

```
def blend(powerSetting, nMinutes):

    <indented block of code>
```

In this definition of blend, powerSetting and nMinutes are parameters. They are variables whose values are assigned when another piece of code calls the function and the function starts to run. Here are examples of different calls to the blend function.

```
blend('high', 10)
...
blend('medium', 1)
...
blend('low', 1)
...
desiredSetting = 'high'
numberOfMinutes = 8
blend(desiredSetting, numberOfMinutes)
```

In each of these calls to the blend function, we are passing in different values for the power setting and the number of minutes. When each call happens, the value of the first argument is put into the first parameter of the function: powerSetting. Then the value of the second argument is put into the second parameter of the function: nMinutes. When the first call happens, control is transferred to blend, powerSetting is set to the string 'high', and nMinutes is set to the value 10. In the last call we pass in the *values* of the variables desiredSetting and numberOfMinutes (see Figure 4-1).

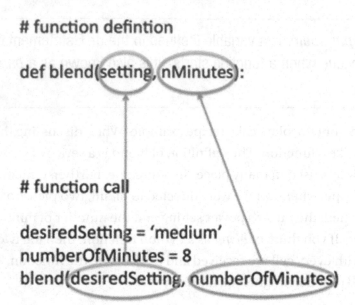

**Figure 4-1.** *The values of arguments are assigned to the parameters in a function*

You can think of it like there is an assignment statement assigning a value from each argument to the associated parameter variable.

# Building User-Defined Functions with Parameters

Let's try this out for real in Python. We'll modify the getGroceries function to use one parameter. That is, instead of always printing *milk* as the first item in our grocery list, we want to allow the caller to call getGroceries and pass in one item to get—but we always want to print the remaining three hard-coded items. Whatever the caller passes in should be printed as the first item. To do this, in the definition of getGroceries, we include one parameter, which we name item1 (just an example name—parameter variables can have any legal variable name):

```
def getGroceries(item1):    # uses one parameter variable
    print(item1)  # prints the contents of the item1 variable
    print('flour')
    print('sugar')
    print('butter')
    separateRuns()
```

And here are some sample calls to getGroceries using different argument values:

```
getGroceries('eggs')
getGroceries('beer')
getGroceries('apples')
```

When each of these calls runs, the first print statement of getGroceries prints the value that was passed in with each call. The output looks like this:

```
eggs
flour
sugar
butter
****************

beer
flour
sugar
butter
****************

apples
flour
sugar
butter
****************
```

Notice that the first item of each grouping is different and matches what was passed in. Now, let's modify getGroceries again, this time so that it accepts four parameters. We'll also change each hard-coded print statement to print an appropriate parameter:

```
def getGroceries(item1, item2, item3, item4):
    print(item1)
    print(item2)
    print(item3)
    print(item4)
    separateRuns()
```

Given this definition, we now have to call our function with four arguments:

```
# Now call the function with four arguments
getGroceries('eggs', 'soap', 'lettuce', 'cat food')
getGroceries('beer', 'milk', 'soda', 'peas')
```

The order of the arguments and the parameters is important. That is, the value of the first argument is given to the first parameter, the value of the second argument is given to the second parameter, and so on for however many arguments and parameters there are. Further, the number of arguments in a call must match the number of parameters in the called function. If these don't match in number, Python will generate an error message. The output of the preceding calls looks like this:

```
eggs
soap
lettuce
cat food
****************

beer
milk
soda
peas
****************
```

We are calling the same function, but because we are passing different arguments, the function does something different; in this case, it prints different results. We can also call a function using variables for any of the arguments:

```
mustGet = 'paper plates'
mustAlsoGet = 'chocolate candy bars'
getGroceries(mustGet, mustAlsoGet, 'lettuce', 'cat food')
```

These lines generate the following output:

```
paper plates
chocolate candy bars
lettuce
cat food
****************
```

In the last call, the `mustGet` and `mustAlsoGet` variables are evaluated, and the values of 'paper plates' and 'chocolate candy bars' are passed as arguments along with 'lettuce' and 'cat food'.

# Building a Simple Function That Does Addition

Let's build a slightly more useful example. In the following, we'll build a function whose purpose is to accept a numeric parameter, add two to it, and print the result:

```
def addTwo(startingValue):
    endingValue = startingValue + 2
    print('The sum of', startingValue, 'and 2 is:', endingValue)
# Call the function twice with different arguments
addTwo(5)
addTwo(10)
```

Each parameter variable takes on the value of the matching argument that was passed in. In this example, from the first call, `startingValue` is assigned 5. In the second call, `startingValue` is given the value 10. This is the output of the two calls to `addTwo`:

```
The sum of 5 and 2 is: 7
The sum of 10 and 2 is: 12
```

# Building a Function to Calculate an Average

Let's build something that is a little more useful and realistic. Here is a function that calculates the average of four numbers. Again, we could use any legal variable name for parameter variables—here we are just showing names like `param1`, `param2`, and so forth, for simplicity:

```
def calculateAverage(param1, param2, param3, param4):
    # Add up numbers, divide by the number of numbers
    total = param1 + param2 + param3 + param4
    average = total / 4.0
    print('Average value is:', average)

calculateAverage(2, 3, 4, 5)
calculateAverage(-3, 5.2, 15, 1000.8)
calculateAverage(1.4, -2.5, 14.3, 200.5)
```

This generates the following output:

```
Average value is: 3.5
Average value is: 254.5
Average value is: 53.425
```

This example demonstrates one of Python's inherent features. In the three calls to calculateAverage, we passed in different mixes of integer and float values. The function calculated and printed the proper result in all cases. Look again at the second call. The first argument is an integer, –3, and the second argument is a float with a value of 5.2. However, as the writer of the function, you don't have to worry about this possibility or do anything special to allow the calculations to work with different types of data. Each parameter in the function (param1, param2, param3, and param4) takes on the value and the type of whatever argument is passed in. This is highly unusual in programming languages and shows off the flexibility of Python's dynamic data typing.

# Returning a Value from a Function: The return Statement

Python recognizes the end of a function by the indenting—or more accurately, by the lack of indenting. As soon as a line is found that has the same indenting as the def statement that started the definition of the function, Python knows that it has reached the end of the definition of a function. After the last indented statement runs, control passes back to a point just past where the function was called.

In the small functions shown so far, each function ends by executing a print statement to print out some result. But in most cases, user-defined functions are typically built to do some calculation(s) to generate an answer and give that answer back to the caller. Remember, this is the way all the built-in functions you have seen operate.

This concept might be best explained through an analogy. Say I am a manager and I have an employee who is a specialist in analyzing the cost of widgets. I am a proud manager because I hired this employee and trained her in the best ways of doing this analysis. The employee can now do the cost analysis all on her own. I have grown to trust that the employee is doing excellent work and always gives correct answers. Because of this, as a manager, I can now think of problems at a higher level and no longer have to worry about the details of analyzing the cost of widgets myself. I know that any time I need to get the best price for a widget, I can ask my employee and I will get a correct cost answer.

This is the way a typical function works. First, you have to write the function's code (train your employee). But once you trust that the function works the right way (the employee is giving you proper results), you come to trust the function (employee). You no longer have to worry about how the lower-level job gets done. You can work at a higher level and assume that the function will respond correctly.

In Python, when a function wants to give a result to a caller, it uses a `return` statement and specifies the value to hand back. The generic form looks like this:

```
return <returnValue>
```

The caller can use the resulting value for whatever it needs. Often, the caller will take the resulting value and store it in a variable. For example, here is a modified version of the previous addTwo function that returns a single number value:

```
def addTwo(startingValue):
    endingValue = startingValue + 2
    return endingValue  # returns a result to the caller

sum1 = addTwo(5)
sum2 = addTwo(10)

print('The results of adding 2 to 5 and 2 to 10 are:', sum1, 'and', sum2)
```

In this example, we first call the addTwo function with an argument of 5. Inside the function, that value is assigned to the startingValue parameter variable. The function runs and calculates an endingValue of 7. Using a return statement, the function hands back a result to the caller. In the assignment statement in the main code, the value of the call addTwo(5) becomes 7, the rest of the assignment statement runs, and the variable sum1 is set to 7. The second call then runs the same way, and the variable sum2 is set to 12. This is the output of the code:

```
The results of adding 2 to 5 and 2 to 10 are: 7 and 12
```

Let's modify the earlier calculateAverage function so that rather than printing a result, it returns its result to the caller. Here's how we can do that:

```
def calculateAverage(param1, param2, param3, param4):
    # Add up numbers, divide by the number of numbers
    total = param1 + param2 + param3 + param4
    average = total / 4.0
    return average    # hand the answer back to the caller
```

83

```
average1 = calculateAverage(2, 3, 4, 5)
average2 = calculateAverage(-3, 5.2, 15,1000.8)
average3 = calculateAverage(1.4, -2.5, 14.3, 200.5)
print('The three averages are:', average1, average2, average3)
```

We call the calculateAverage function three times and pass in four values as arguments with each call. For each call, the function runs and returns a value. The result of each call to calculateAverage is stored into a separate variable. This is the resulting output:

```
The three averages are: 3.5 254.5 53.425
```

# Returning No Value: None

When we first started discussing functions, we saw how a function could simply end without using a return statement at all. When a function does not have an explicit return statement, Python builds an implied return statement that returns no value. In fact, you can write a return statement that does not give back a value:

```
return   # no return value specified
```

But when a return statement is executed without any returned value, Python actually returns a special value of None. None is a Python keyword that means *no value*. The following function multiplies a number times itself (squares the number):

```
def square(number):
    answer = number * number
    return     # Note: this is an error, does not return an answer

userNumber = input('Enter a number: ')
userNumber = float(userNumber)   # convert to a float
numberSquared = square(userNumber)   # call the function and save the
result
print('The square of your number is', numberSquared)
```

When we run this code and enter any number, this is the output:

```
The square of your number is None
```

That's certainly not what you want or expect. But if you understand that None is the value returned by a function when there is a simple return statement, then you can easily track down this type of error and correct it. Here is the corrected version:

```
def square(number):
    answer = number * number
    return answer    # This returns the correct answer
```

# Returning More Than One Value

Python has a further extension of the return statement. In most other programming languages, the return statement can only return either no values or a single value. In Python, just as you can pass as many values as you want into a function, you can also return any number of values:

```
return <value1>, <value2>, <value3>, ...
```

For example, you could create a function that returns three values, like this:

```
def myFunction(parameter1, parameter2):
    #
    # Body of the function, calculates
    # values for answer1, answer2, and answer3

    return answer1, answer2, answer3   # hand back three answers to the caller
```

Then you would call myFunction with code like this:

```
variable1, variable2, variable3 = myFunction(argument1, argument2)
```

That is, you call myFunction, passing in two arguments. The function does whatever it needs to do and returns three values. The call was actually part of an assignment statement. When the function is finished and executes its return statement, the three returned values are stored into the three variables on the left-hand side of the assignment operator (equals sign). The order of the variables in the assignment statement matches the order of the answer variables in the function's return statement.

There is one more clarification about return statements. Whenever a function executes any type of return statement (returning no value, one value, or multiple values), execution of code exits the function immediately and returns control just past the point from where it was called. If you have any code below that return statement, it will not be executed. This is often confusing for new programmers. Here is a simple example:

```
def sayHello(name):
    print('Hello')
    return
    print(name)
```

When called, this function prints the word Hello, and then returns immediately. The second print statement would not execute.

# Specific and General Variable Names in Calls and Functions

New programmers often struggle with creating different names for variables outside of and inside of functions. Here is a general way to think about such variable names. Part of the definition of a function is that functions are often called from different parts of a program. The data being passed in from different calls might have significantly different meanings. Often, though, the code of the function does not know and does not need to know the underlying meaning of the data it is working with.

For example, earlier we saw a function to calculate an average. The function is passed a sequence of numbers, but the function does not need to understand what the numbers represent. Its job is just to do the calculation of the average. Only the code calling the function needs know the meaning of the values it is passing in. The following program has the same calculateAverage function. In the main code, we are calling the function to calculate two different averages of statistics from a football game: the yardage gained on the first four running plays and the first four passing plays:

```
def calculateAverage(param1, param2, param3, param4):
    # Add up the numbers and divide by the number of numbers
    total = param1 + param2 + param3 + param4
    average = total / 4.0
    return average # hand back the answer to the caller

yardsOnRun1 = 4
yardsOnRun2 = 6.5
```

```
yardsOnRun3 = 2.5
yardsOnRun4 = -2

averageYardsPerRun = calculateAverage(yardsOnRun1, yardsOnRun2,
yardsOnRun3, yardsOnRun4)
print('Average yards per run is:', averageYardsPerRun)

yardsOnPass1 = 0
yardsOnPass2 = 25.5
yardsOnPass3 = 0
yardsOnPass4 = 12

averageYardsPerPass = calculateAverage(yardsOnPass1, yardsOnPass2,
yardsOnPass3, yardsOnPass4)
print('Average yards per pass is:', averageYardsPerPass)
```

In the main code, we have four variables that are set to the yardage gained on each of the first four runs. These variables are named to express the data they represent (yardsOnRun1, yardsOnRun2, and so on). Then there is a call to the calculateAverage function, passing in the value of these variables. In the main code, the variable names (which are used as arguments in the function call) are extremely specific. However, inside the calculateAverage function call, the values that are received as parameters are given generic parameter variable names (param1, param2, param3, and param4). The function does the appropriate calculation and stores its answer in a variable with a generic name of average. When the function returns the result, the main code stores the result into the specifically named variable averageYardsPerRun.

The process is repeated, but this time, we are using variable names that imply the yardage gained on each pass play (yardsOnPass1, yardsOnPass2, and so forth). Again, these very specifically named variables are passed in with the call to the function. The function receives the values and puts them into the more generic parameters variables. When the function returns the result, the main code stores this result into the variable with the meaningful name averageYardsPerPass. This is a good pattern to follow.

---

**Tip**   When creating names of parameter variables, try to use generic names that still imply meaning. But when using variables in calls to functions, try to use variable names that are as specific as possible. This way, you typically avoid using the same variable names in calls and in function definitions.

---

# Temperature Conversion Functions

To put all these pieces together, let's walk through the process of creating two very useful functions. In the United States, temperature is measured using the Fahrenheit scale. Most of the rest of the world uses the Centigrade (or Celsius) scale. The scales are very different, but two simple formulas can be used to easily convert between them. These are the formulas:

Fahrenheit to Centigrade:

$$C = (F - 32) \times (5/9)$$

Centigrade to Fahrenheit:

$$F = (1.8 \times C) + 32$$

Here are two Python functions that will do these conversions. For both functions, we pass in a value in one scale, and each returns the value in the other scale:

```
def F2C(nDegreesF):
    nDegreesC = (nDegreesF - 32) * (5.0 / 9.0)
    return nDegreesC

def C2F(nDegreesC):
    nDegreesF = (1.8 * nDegreesC) + 32
    return nDegreesF
```

Given these function definitions, we can now build some main code to use these functions interactively. We can ask the user for a temperature in each scale and then convert and print it in the other scale:

```
# Code to ask the user to input values for conversion:

usersTempF = input('Enter a value of degrees Fahrenheit: ')
usersTempF = float(usersTempF)
convertedTempC = F2C(usersTempF)
print(usersTempF, 'degrees Fahrenheit is:', convertedTempC, 'degrees
Centigrade.')

usersTempC = sinput('Enter a value of degrees Celsius: ')
usersTempC = float(usersTempC)
convertedTempF = C2F(usersTempC)
print(usersTempC, 'degrees Centigrade is:', convertedTempF, 'degrees
Fahrenheit.')
```

Here is what we see if we input the Fahrenheit value of 212 (the boiling point of water) and the Centigrade value of 0 (the freezing point of water):

```
Enter a value of degrees Fahrenheit: 212
212.0 degrees Fahrenheit is: 100.0 degrees Centigrade.
Enter a value of degrees Celsius: 0
0.0 degrees Centigrade is: 32.0 degrees Fahrenheit.
```

These functions yield results that are inverses of each other. The following is an interesting test of the functions using an arbitrary value:

```
>>> print(F2C(C2F(123.45)))
123.45
```

In this code, the innermost function call to C2F runs first, which converts the Centigrade value of 123.45 to its Fahrenheit equivalent. Then that value (whatever it is) is passed into the F2C function, which converts it back to Fahrenheit. The result is the number we started with.

# Placement of Functions in a Python File

Notice that in all the examples of functions and function calls, the code that defines the functions is always at the top of the Python file. The main code of the program, which typically incorporates calls to those functions, is written below the function definitions. This is how a typical story is written. When a character is introduced, some details about his personality are given—maybe there is some description of how the character looks, or maybe a backstory is given—before the character is given any dialog.

If your main code tries to call a function before it is defined, Python gives an error. Remember that when you run a program, Python reads through all of your code before execution starts. Python remembers where functions are defined in your code, but it does not run those functions. Instead, it keeps scanning until it finds the first statement that is not inside any function; this is where execution actually starts. When executing code, if Python were to try a call to a function that it had not seen yet, Python wouldn't know where the function is, and would give an error message saying that the function is undefined.

# Never Write Multiple Copies of the Same Code

A key concept in writing software is that you never want to have multiple copies of the same code. Earlier in this book, we developed the Python code for calculating the hypotenuse (longest side) of a right triangle. Here is an example of what that might look like, where we want to ask the user for two different sets of sides of right triangles:

```
firstTriangleSide1 = input('Enter side 1: ')
firstTriangleSide2 = input('Enter side 2: ')
firstTriangleSide1 = float(firstTriangleSide1)
firstTriangleSide2 = float(firstTriangleSide2)
firstTriangleHypot = ((firstTriangleSide1 ** 2) +
                      (firstTriangleSide2 ** 2)) ** 0.5
print('The hypotenuse of the first triangle is:', firstTriangleHypot)

secondTriangleSide1 = input('Enter the first side: ')
secondTriangleSide2 = input('Enter second side: ')
secondTriangleSide1 = float(secondTriangleSide1)
secondTriangleSide2 = float(secondTriangleSide2)
secondTriangleHypot = ((secondTriangleSide1 ** 2) +
                       (secondTriangleSide2 ** 2)) ** 0.5
print('The hypotenuse of the second triangle is:', secondTriangleHypot)
```

Whenever you find that you have written essentially the same code in multiple places, it should be an immediate trigger for changing such code into a function. The following is a variation of the previous code, but using a function and passing parameters instead:

```
# Assumes that values passed in could be values representing strings
def calculateHypotenuse(side1, side2):
    side1= float(side1)
    side2 = float(side2)
    hypot = ((side1 ** 2) + (side2 ** 2)) ** 0.5
    return hypot

firstTriangleSide1 = input('Enter side 1: ')
firstTriangleSide2 = input('Enter side 2: ')
```

```
hypot1 = calculateHypotenuse(firstTriangleSide1, firstTriangleSide2)
# call function to do calc

secondTriangeSide1 = input('Enter the first side: ')
secondTriangeSide2 = input('Enter second side: ')
hypot2 = calculateHypotenuse(secondTriangeSide1, secondTriangeSide2)
# call function to do calc

print('The hypotenuse of the first triangle is: ', hypot1)
print('The hypotenuse of the second triangle is: ', hypot2)
```

The thinking behind building and using functions this way is twofold.

First, creating a function to do lower-level work allows you to give a name to a sequence of instructions. In this example, using a name like calculateHypotenuse makes it extremely clear what the purpose of the function is. And as I described earlier, when you have written a function like this once, you can think of calling the function by using its name, and you don't have to worry about the details of the internals of the function.

Second, and more importantly, code inside a function is centralized. That is, if you ever need to change the code of a function, you only need to change it in one place. If code like the preceding was not in a function, and you had multiple copies of it, think about what you would have to do to make a change. Imagine that you find a bug in your hypotenuse formula. You would have to look through all your code and make the same change in every place where this calculation is done. That may not seem like a big task in small programs like the ones that we have built so far, but when you start to write large programs, having only one copy of code is critical to building and maintaining reliable software.

---

**Note**   This principle of never writing multiple copies of the same code is known as the DRY principle: Don't Repeat Yourself.

---

# Constants

In a program, there is often the need for a number or string that doesn't change. For example, imagine that you're working on a program that calculates the price of a bill at a restaurant. Let's say the cost of a hamburger is three dollars. While the program is running, that value never changes. So, to calculate the cost of all the hamburgers in an order, you could write a line of code where you calculate the cost of hamburgers by multiplying the number of hamburgers by 3.00. Let's also say that you sell milkshakes at your restaurant and the cost of a milkshake is also three dollars.

As the restaurant owner, you decide that you need to raise the price of your hamburger from three dollars to three dollars and twenty-five cents. To update your program, you could use IDLE and select Edit ➤ Replace to replace all occurrences of 3.00 with 3.25. But if you do that, you have not only raised the price of hamburgers, but also milkshakes and anything else on your menu that had a price of three dollars. That is clearly the wrong approach. Instead, you would have to find every occurrence of 3.00 in your program and decide on a line-by-line basis whether the 3.00 represents a hamburger or a something else, and only change the appropriate one(s). Though that may be very simple in a small restaurant program, this type of change can take a great deal of time and be very error prone in a large program.

In Python, we can create a variable for a number like this so that it can be referred to *by name* throughout the program.

---

**Definition**   A *constant* is a variable whose value does not change throughout a program.

---

A constant is created using a simple assignment statement, typically placed at the top of the program—even before any function definitions. Here is an example:

```
costPerHamburger = 3.00
```

There is nothing special about creating a constant. It really is just another variable. How do we ensure that it that no other piece of code changes this value? Unfortunately, there is no way to prevent a constant from being changed. But there is a widely accepted Python naming convention for constants. When defining a variable to be used as a constant, create a name where all the letters are in uppercase, and separate words are strung together with underscores. Naming a variable this way serves as a signal to yourself and other programmers that this variable is a constant and its value should never be reassigned. Here are some examples that might be used in a program like our restaurant program:

```
COST_PER_HAMBURGER = 3.00
COST_PER_HOT_DOG = 2.00
COST_PER_MILK_SHAKE = 3.00
```

Then we would use COST_PER_HAMBURGER, COST_PER_HOT_DOG, COST_PER_MILK_ SHAKE, and so on in the calculations instead of the numeric prices. That way, if the cost of an item changes, only one line of code needs to be changed: the original assignment statement for that constant. No other changes are needed *and* your code becomes more readable. This is another example of using the DRY principle.

# Scope

We've talked about how variables have a type (integer, float, Boolean, string). But variables also have a lifetime. Let's start with another definition.

---

**Definition**   *Scope* is the amount of code over which a variable is active.

---

In Python, there are three levels of scope for variables. In this book, though, we'll only talk about two levels of scope: global and local.

Global variables are created at the top level of a program, in the main code. They have what is called *global scope*. Global variables maintain their values and are available throughout a program. Here is the code we recently looked at about calling functions:

```
firstTriangleSide1 = input('Enter side 1: ')
firstTriangleSide2 = input('Enter side 2: ')
hypot1 = calculateHypotenuse(firstTriangleSide1, firstTriangleSide2)
# call function to do calc

secondTriangeSide1 = input('Enter the first side: ')
secondTriangeSide2 = input('Enter second side: ')
hypot2 = calculateHypotenuse(secondTriangeSide1, secondTriangeSide2)
# call function to do calc

print('The hypotenuse of the first triangle is:', hypot1)
print('The hypotenuse of the second triangle is:', hypot2)
```

The variables firstTriangleSide1, firstTriangleSide2, hypot1, secondTriangleSide1, secondTriangleSide2, and hypot2 are all global variables. Notice that the code is written in a way that assumes that they maintain their values even where there are calls to functions in between lines where they are used.

*Global variables* (created in the main program code) can legally be used inside functions. However, it is strongly recommended to *never* do this. Using global variables inside functions leads to a poor coding practice called *spaghetti code*, where these variables can be used and modified all over a program. This style of programming makes the code very hard to understand and extremely difficult to maintain and modify, because any call to any function might change one or more global variables.

Instead of using global variables inside functions, whenever a function needs a value that is held in a global variable, that value should be passed as an argument into the function when the function is called. If the function wants to effectively change the value of a global variable, the function should return a value, and the caller can set a new value for the global variable as the result of the call.

The previous section talked about constants. I suggested that constants be created at the top level of a program. When created this way, constants also have global scope. Because constants are global, they are available and can be used inside any function in the program. Global constants are good things. Constants help clarify meaning rather than having "magic numbers" interspersed throughout code.

Consider the following example of a program to calculate the cost of purchasing some number of small and large widgets. In this program, small widgets cost five dollars each, large widgets cost eight dollars each, and there is a tax rate of nine percent:

```
TAX_RATE = .09  # 9 percent tax
COST_PER_SMALL_WIDGET = 5.00
COST_PER_LARGE_WIDGET = 8.00

def calculateCost(nSmallWidgets, nLargeWidgets):
    subTotal = (nSmallWidgets * COST_PER_SMALL_WIDGET) +
    (nLargeWidgets * COST_PER_LARGE_WIDGET)
    taxAmount = subTotal * TAX_RATE
    totalCost = subTotal + taxAmount
    return totalCost

total1 = calculateCost(4, 8)  #  4 small and 8 large widgets
print('Total for the first order is', total1)
total2 = calculateCost(12, 15)
print('Total for the second order is', total2)
```

Notice the TAX_RATE, COST_PER_SMALL_WIDGETS, and COST_PER_LARGE_WIDGET variables at the top of the program, outside of any function. The naming convention implies that these are intended to be constants. Because they have global scope, they can be used (correctly and clearly) inside the calculateCost function.

*Local variables* are created inside a function. The scope of a local variable ranges from the point where it is first used in a function to the end of that function. When the function ends, any local variables used inside the function literally disappear. Here is the same code again, but used to demonstrate the local variables inside the calculateCost function:

```
TAX_RATE = .09  # 9 percent tax
COST_PER_SMALL_WIDGET = 5.00
COST_PER_LARGE_WIDGET = 8.00

def calculateCost(nSmallWidgets, nLargeWidgets):
    subTotal = (nSmallWidgets * COST_PER_SMALL_WIDGET) +
    (nLargeWidgets * COST_PER_LARGE_WIDGET)
    taxAmount = subTotal * TAX_RATE
    totalCost = subTotal + taxAmount
    return totalCost

total1 = calculateCost(4, 8)   # 4 small and 8 large widgets
print('Total for first order is', total1)
total2 = calculateCost(12, 15)
print('Total for second order is', total2)
```

Inside the function, we are creating and using subTotal, taxAmount, and totalCost local variables. They are local variables because they are only used inside of a function. In addition, all parameter variables, the ones listed in the def statement, are also local variables. Parameters (or parameter variables) are given their values when a function is called, and they go away when the function is finished.

You cannot access local variables outside of a function because those variables are out of scope and no longer exist. In the following, there is an additional line in the main code that tries to print the amount of tax that was calculated inside the function. Any attempt to access a local variable in the main code of a program will result in an error message:

```
TAX_RATE = .09  # 9 percent tax
COST_PER_SMALL_WIDGET = 5.00
COST_PER_LARGE_WIDGET = 8.00
```

```
def calculateCost(nSmallWidgets, nLargeWidgets):
    subTotal = (nSmallWidgets * COST_PER_SMALL_WIDGET) +
    (nLargeWidgets * COST_PER_LARGE_WIDGET)
    taxAmount = subTotal * TAX_RATE
    totalCost = subTotal + taxAmount
    return totalCost

total1 = calculateCost(4, 8)  #  4 small and 8 large widgets
print(taxAmount)              # Trying to access local variable from the
above function
print('Total for first order is', total1)
total2 = calculateCost(12, 15)
print('Total for second order is', total2)
```

This generates the following error:

```
Traceback (most recent call last):

File "/Learn to Program with Python/Chapter 4 - User-Defined Functions/
CostsWithTaxError.py",
line 12, in <module>
    print(taxAmount)
NameError: name 'taxAmount' is not defined
```

You can think of it this way: when you call a function from the main code, or from another function, the caller's code has its set of variables that it remembers, and the called function has a set of variables that it uses. With the exception of global constants, these sets of variables should be considered completely independent.

---

**Note**   The third type of scope is called *class scope*, which deals with how variables are used inside objects in object-oriented programming. Unfortunately, that is beyond the scope of this book.

---

# Global Variables and Local Variables with the Same Names

Take a look at the following code:

```
def myFunction():
    someVariable = 5

someVariable = 10
myFunction()
print(someVariable)
```

In this code, we assign 10 to a variable named someVariable. Then we call a function. But inside the function, there is another assignment statement setting someVariable to 5. If we run this code, perhaps surprisingly, we see an output of 10. What's going on here?

In the main code, the first executable line creates a global variable named someVariable. Then there is a function call. As I said earlier, any variable created inside a function is a local variable whose scope is only within the function. Python allows you to create a local variable that has the same name as a global variable. Within this function, the someVariable local variable is given a value of 5. But when that function is finished, the someVariable local variable goes away. When the function returns, the final print statement executes. The someVariable in that final print statement is the global version, and the program outputs its value: 10.

Although using the same variable name for a global and a local variable *is* supported by Python, it is best to never get into this situation in the first place. Using the same name for global and local variables only leads to confusion later on. *Did I mean to set the local variable or the global variable?* To make your intentions clear, always use different names.

Reusing the same variable name inside different functions is perfectly fine. Because local variables are created when they are first seen inside a function, and are destroyed when the function finishes, there is no name conflict with local variables of the same name used in different functions.

Python's rule for handling global/local name conflicts like this are quite simple. It always assumes that you are using local variables within a function. If you truly want to use a global variable within a function—and I strongly urge you not to—you can do so by first giving a global statement to tell Python that you want to use a global variable. Here is an example of this highly discouraged approach:

```
def myFunction():
    global someVariable    # tell Python that you are using a global variable
    someVariable = someVariable + 1

someVariable = 20
myFunction()
print(someVariable)
```

Running this code results in printing the value 21. But if you want to affect a global variable using a function, it would be better to write that type of code this way:

```
def myFunction(aVariable):
    aVariable = aVariable + 1  # change a local (parameter) variable
    return aVariable     # and return it

someVariable = 20
someVariable = myFunction(someVariable)  # pass in global, and re-assign
the answer
print(someVariable)
```

# Finding Errors in Functions: Traceback

In Chapter 2, I demonstrated that when an error occurs at runtime, Python outputs an error message called a *traceback*. If a runtime error happens inside of a function, it is often difficult to find and fix because a function may be called from many places in a program. Further, different argument values are typically passed in with different calls.

Let's work through a simple example that generates a runtime error in a function. Here is the code of the getGroceries program from earlier in this chapter, except this version contains an extra line that causes a runtime error.

```
def separateRuns():
    print('****************')
    print(someUndefinedVariable)    # will cause a run time error
    print()        #blank line

def getGroceries():
    print('milk')
    print('flour')
    print('sugar')
    print('butter')
    separateRuns()      # call another function

# Main code starts here:
getGroceries()
```

The main code calls the getGroceries function. That function prints a few things and then calls the separateRuns function. Inside that function is a line that tries to print the value of someUndefinedVariable. Because this variable was never defined, it triggers a runtime error. When a runtime error occurs in a function, Python presents information about how the program got to the line of code that caused the error. Let's look at what Python tells us for this example.

```
>>>
milk
flour
sugar
butter
****************

Traceback (most recent call last):
  File "/Learn to Program with Python/Chapter 4 - User-Defined Functions/
  Kalb Code Chapter4/Traceback.py", line 15, in <module>
    getGroceries()
  File "/Learn to Program with Python/Chapter 4 - User-Defined Functions/
  Kalb Code Chapter4/Traceback.py", line 12, in getGroceries
    separateRuns()      # call another function
```

```
File "/Learn to Program with Python/Chapter 4 - User-Defined Functions/
Kalb Code Chapter4/Traceback.py", line 4, in separateRuns
  print(someUndefinedVariable)   # will cause a run time error
NameError: global name 'someUndefinedVariable' is not defined
>>>
```

As you saw earlier, the actual error is printed on the last line of this output. So the first thing to do is to read that line to see what the error was. In this traceback, we additionally see a trail of "electronic breadcrumbs" that tells us how we got to the line that caused the error. The term *traceback* refers to the sequence of calls that were made to get into the function where the error occurred. (In other programming languages, this is often referred to as a *stack trace*.)

We read the traceback information from the top down. In this example, the top line says that we were at line 15 in `<module>`. This means that our source line number 15 of the main code made a call. The next line in the traceback tells us that line 15 of the code made a call to the `getGroceries` function. The next traceback line says that in line 12 of our code, which is inside the `getGroceries` function, we made a call to the `separateRuns` function. The last traceback line says that in line 4 of our code, which is inside the `separateRuns` function, there was an error in the `print` statement.

In most development environments, a line number precedes each line of code. With a setup like that, finding the lines mentioned in a traceback is easy. Unfortunately, IDLE does not work this way. Instead, IDLE shows the line number of the current line (wherever the cursor is) in the bottom-right corner of the editor window. Therefore, to truly understand a traceback in IDLE, you may have to do a lot of clicking in lines and looking down to the bottom-right corner to find line numbers associated with lines of your code (see Figure 4-2).

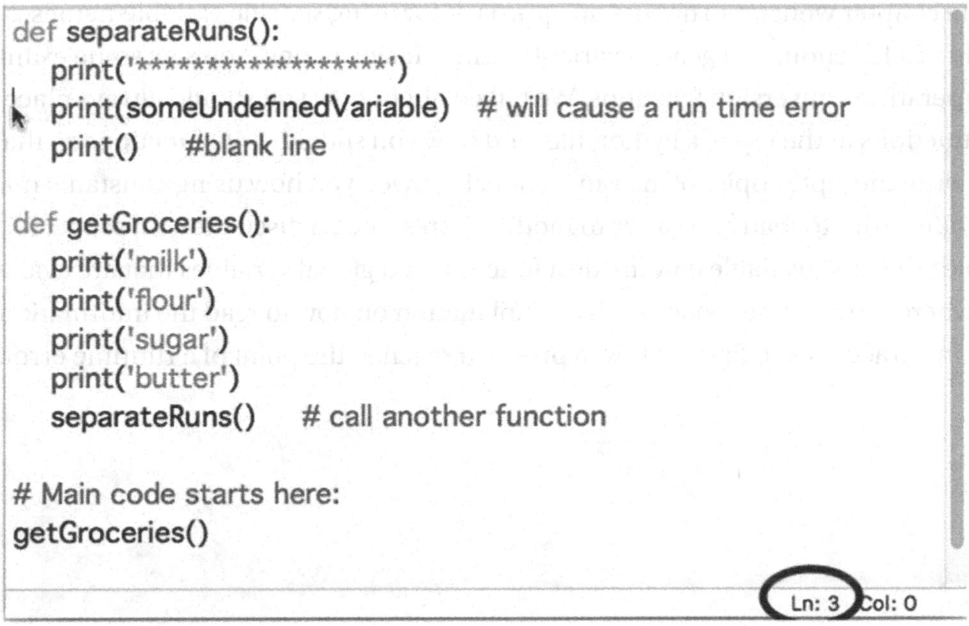

```
def separateRuns():
    print('*******************')
    print(someUndefinedVariable)   # will cause a run time error
    print()     #blank line

def getGroceries():
    print('milk')
    print('flour')
    print('sugar')
    print('butter')
    separateRuns()     # call another function

# Main code starts here:
getGroceries()
```

Ln: 3  Col: 0

***Figure 4-2.*** *The current line number is shown in the bottom right of the editor window*

The example shown in Figure 4-2 is extremely simple and is only used to illustrate the information that is available in a traceback. When programs get large, code often involves many different calls to functions, and the path of execution can go through many layers of function calls. The information provided in a traceback becomes invaluable in tracking down the sequence of code that led to a runtime error.

# Summary

In this chapter, you learned about what happens on the other side of a function call: how to create a user-defined function. You saw how following a recipe presents a good analogy for building software. We defined and built our first function. Then we learned how to receive the data that is passed into a function. We built a number of example functions so we could understand how data is passed with a function call using arguments, and how that data is received in the function using parameters. Then we discussed how a function can give back an answer or answers using a return statement.

The chapter went on to discuss an approach for using specific variable names outside of a function, and general variable names inside of one. You saw some examples of temperature conversion functions. We talked about how you should always place your functions at the top of a Python file, and how you should write functions so that you never write multiple copies of the same code. I showed you how using constants makes your code easier to read and easier to modify. I presented a discussion on scope: local variables that are available only inside a function and global variables that are available everywhere. The chapter ended with an explanation on how to read the information found in a traceback to find out how a program reached the point of a runtime error.

## CHAPTER 5

# if, else, and elif Statements

All the code we have looked at so far has essentially been *linear*. That is, execution of the code starts from the top and goes straight through to the bottom. The only change to this linear nature of execution is when we make a function call. Doing that transfers control to the function, but all the code inside a function also goes straight through from top to bottom. But one of the most powerful things about code is the ability to make a decision and to take a path based on that decision.

This chapter discusses the following topics:

- Flowcharting
- The if statement
- Comparison operators
- Examples of if statements
- Nested if statements
- The else statement
- Using if/else inside a function
- The elif statement
- Using many elif statements
- Example grading program
- Sample program: absolute value
- Programming challenges
- Conditional logic

103

© Irv Kalb 2018
I. Kalb, *Learn to Program with Python 3*, https://doi.org/10.1007/978-1-4842-3879-0_5

- The logical not operator

- The logical and operator

- The logical or operator

- Booleans in if statements

- A program to calculate shipping

In the real world, we ask questions and take actions based on the answers to those questions. Here are some examples formatted using an if/then style:

- If I am hungry, then I will eat.

- If today is Monday, then I will go to work.

- If I am tired, then I will go to sleep.

- If I want to meet my friend at 8:00 and it takes 30 minutes to get there, then I should leave by 7:30.

- If I have to go far and I own a working car, then I will use my car.

- If I have a choice between pizza and liverwurst, then I will choose pizza.

# Flowcharting

To demonstrate questions and answers like these, and the actions that are taken as a result, we'll use a technique called *flowcharting*. A *flowchart* is a representation of all the possible paths through a process. A typical flowchart has a starting point, one or more ending points, and two main types of components: actions (usually shown as rectangles) and decisions (typically shown as diamonds). Figures 5-1 and 5-2 are two examples of processes that have been diagrammed using flowcharts.

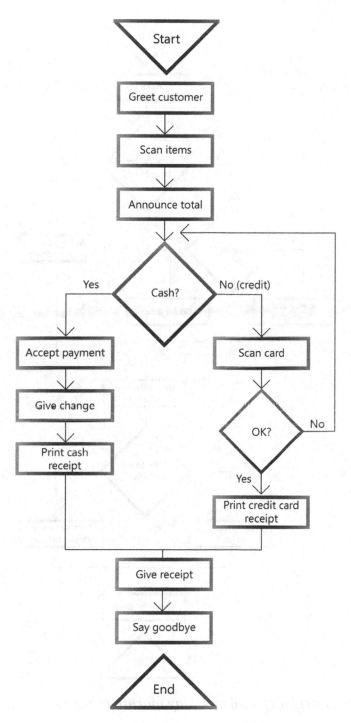

***Figure 5-1.*** *Flowchart for store checkout*

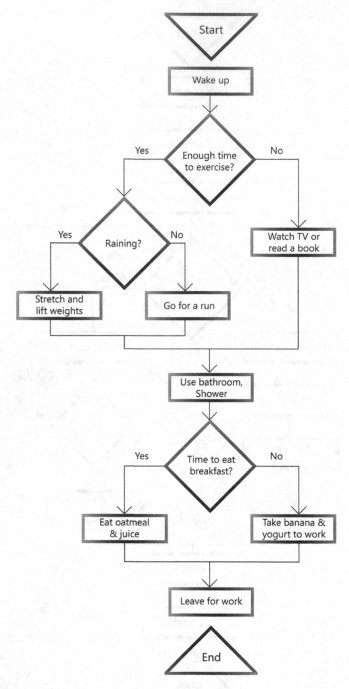

**Figure 5-2.** *Flowchart for typical weekday morning routine*

The flowchart shown in Figure 5-1 shows the process of checking out at a store. The main question that is asked is: *Cash?* If you are paying in cash, then you follow the path on the left. Otherwise, it's assumed that you are paying with a credit card and you take the path on the right. If your credit card scan fails, then you go back and choose to pay in cash or try another credit card.

The flowchart shown in Figure 5-2 shows a typical weekday morning routine. In this flowchart, you first decide whethe there is time to exercise or not. If so, then you follow one branch or another, depending on whether it is raining or not. Later, there is a decision box to determine whether there is time to eat breakfast.

The details of these flowcharts are not really important—they are simple examples. What is important is to see the use of decision diamonds. Each of the questions in these diamonds is a yes/no question. The process follows a different path based on the answer to each question. We will use flowcharts like these to demonstrate statements that control the flow of execution within Python programs.

# The if Statement

A decision box in a flowchart is implemented by an if statement in Python. Using an if statement, a programmer can essentially ask a yes/no question, and if the answer is yes, then some code will run. Figure 5-3 shows the flowchart of an if statement.

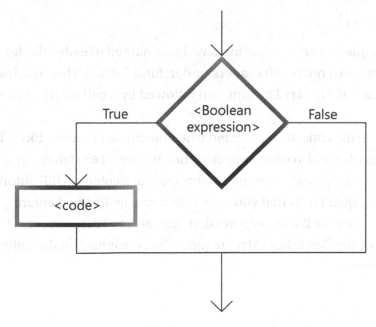

***Figure 5-3.*** *Flowchart of if statement*

And here is the syntax of the `if` statement in Python:

```
if <Boolean expression>:      # notice the colon at the end of the line
    <indented block of code>  # any number of indented lines
```

Inside this specification, you see `<Boolean expression>`. Think of a Boolean expression as a question that can only have two possible answers: yes or no, true or false, one or zero, and so on. Specifically, a Boolean expression is one that yields a Boolean value of only `True` or `False`. For example:

```
if authorsFirstName == 'Irv':
    teachingPython = True
    print('Pay attention to his wisdom')
    respectPoints = respectPoints + 10
```

Let's assume we have a variable named `authorsFirstName` that (not surprisingly) contains the first name of the author of this book. In this example, we are comparing that variable to the string `'Irv'`. That is my first name, so this comparison evaluates to a Python value of `True`. And because the result is `True`, all the indented lines of code will run. Here is another example:

```
if nReadersUnderstandingPython == 0:
    fireIrv()
    getNewAuthor()
```

In this example, we are comparing a variable named `nReadersUnderstanding` `Python` to 0. If it turns out that 0 readers understand Python, then the indented code will run, and we call the `fireIrv` function followed by a call to the `getNewAuthor` function.

Notice that all the code to be executed when the Boolean expression is `True` is indented. This is identical to what happens when we use a `def` statement to create a function. When you type an `if` statement (that ends in a colon), IDLE automatically indents any subsequent lines that you type. When you are finished entering lines that should execute when the Boolean expression evaluates to `True`, you press the Backspace key (Windows) or the Delete key (Mac) to move the cursor back to the indent level of the matching `if` statement.

# Comparison Operators

It is important to note that when comparing for equality, Python requires two equals signs (==), which is often called the *comparison operator*. When reading code out loud, this operator is pronounced as "equals equals"—as in, "if myVariable equals equals 5 …". Remember that the single equals sign (=) is called the *assignment operator*. If you try to use a single equals sign inside an if statement, Python will generate an error. Here is an example:

```
myVariable = 1
if myVariable = 1:      # This is an error, needs to be equals equals
    print('The value of myVariable is one.')
```

If you try to run this code, you will get an error message that says, "There is an error in your program: invalid syntax." In the source window, IDLE will highlight the single equals sign in the if statement, showing that this is where the error occurred.

In addition to the equals equals operator, there are a number of additional operators you can use in if statements for comparisons. Table 5-1 lists and explains these operators.

*Table 5-1. Operators to Use in if Statements*

| Operator | Meaning | Example |
|---|---|---|
| == | Equals | if a == b: |
| != | Not equals | if a != b: |
| < | Less than | if a < b: |
| > | Greater than | if a > b: |
| <= | Less than or equal to | if a <= b: |
| >= | Great than or equal to | if a >= b: |

# Examples of if Statements

Let's look at some examples of these operators used in short snippets of code with if statements.

In the first example, we might be writing code for a game of blackjack. Here we compare the total value of the cards in the dealer's hand against the total value of the cards in the player's hand to see if the player won:

```
if dealersTotal < playersTotal:
    print('You win')
```

In the following example, we are checking a to see whether a person's age is greater than or equal to 18. If so, we set two other variables to True to signify and remember that the person is allowed to vote and is considered an adult:

```
if age >= 18:
    allowedToVote = True
    consideredAnAdult = True
```

In the next snippet, we are checking to see whether the user has enough money to buy a gallon of gas. If so, we call a function to purchase one gallon of gas and reduce the amount of money the user has by the cost of one gallon of gas:

```
if cashInWallet > costOfGasPerGallon:
    purchaseGallonOfGas(1)
    cashInWallet = cashInWallet - costOfGasPerGallon
```

Anyone who has tried to log in to an account on a web site should understand this next snippet. When you provide a password, a program checks to see whether the password you entered matches the password you gave when you set up the account. If not, you are presented with an error message, as follows:

```
if userPassword != savedPassword:
    giveErrorMessageAboutPassword()
```

In the following snippet, we ask the user a question using a call to input. When the user answers the question, the response is put into the answer variable. In the if statement, we check if the user entered the word *yes*:

```
answer = input('Are you ready (yes or no)? ')
if answer == 'yes':
    print('OK, here we go.')
```

# Nested if Statement

When a Boolean expression in an if statement evaluates to True, then the indented block of code runs. But the indented block of code can contain another if statement. And if the Boolean expression in an indented if statement also evaluates to True, then the indented code block associated with that if statement will run. For example:

```
# Purchases at a gas station
totalGasPurchase = priceOfGas * nGallons
amountLeftOver = startingAmountOfMoney - totalGasPurchase

# See if we have enough money to buy a Powerball lottery ticket
if amountLeftOver > 2:
    feeling = evaluateEmotions()
    if feeling == 'lucky':
        buyPowerballTicket()
        amountLeftOver = amountLeftOver - 2
```

In this example, we calculate how much we are spending on gas at a gas station. After paying for the gas, the first if statement checks to see if we have more than two dollars left over. If so, then the indented block of code runs. In that block, we call a function to determine our overall emotional state. We then use a nested if statement that asks another question: whether we feel lucky. If so, then the indented block of code associated with that if statement runs. We call a function to buy a Powerball ticket and adjust the amount of money that we have left. You can nest if statements as many times as you need to. However, too much nesting makes code difficult to read.

# The else Statement

When you ask a question that has only two answers (yes or no, true or false, 1 or 0, and so on), you often want to do one thing if you get one answer and do something different if you get the other answer. As we saw in the earlier flowcharts, taking separate branches like this is very common. In an if statement, we often want to execute different blocks of code based on whether the answer to a Boolean expression is True or False. Figure 5-4 shows a flowchart of this.

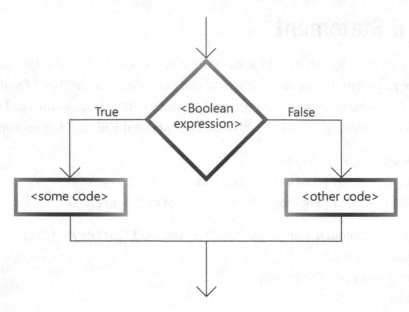

**Figure 5-4.** *Flowchart of* `if/else`

As you saw earlier, in a simple `if` statement, if the Boolean expression evaluates to `True`, the code block on the left side will run. The new piece is that if the Boolean expression evaluates to `False`, the code block on the right side will run. The additional piece is implemented by the use of an `else` statement. Here is the syntax of an `if/else`:

```
if <Boolean expression>:
    <some indented code>
else:   # Notice the colon here too
    <other indented code>
```

The `else` statement and the block of code associated with it are commonly known as an `else` clause. The `else` clause is optional. Similar to the `if` statement, the `else` statement must have a trailing colon. The colon always tells IDLE that the programmer is providing an indented line or block of lines. In this case, the indented code runs only if the original Boolean expression in the `if` statement evaluated to `False`.

Here is a simple example. Let's say we are building a math game and are asking a question: *What integer comes after 4?* The obvious correct answer is 5. The following shows how we can use an `if/else` to evaluate the user's response:

```
#assume the correct answer to question is 5
if answerToQuestion == 5:
    print('You got it')
```

112

```
    print('You are a genius')
else:
    print('Nope')
    print('Time to go back to kindergarden')
```

In this code, if the answer is correct, the block of code associated with the `if` statement will run. If the answer is incorrect, the block associated with the `else` statement will run.

Now let's build an interactive version:

```
usersAnswer = input('What is 6 + 3? ')  # Get the user's answer
usersAnswer = int(usersAnswer)    # convert to an integer
if usersAnswer == 9:
    print('Yessiree Bob')
    print('You are a genius')
else:
    print('Sorry, that is not correct')
    print('The correct answer was 9')
```

We added code at the top to ask the user a question with a call to `input`. Then we used the `int` function to take the answer the user typed in (which comes in as a string) and convert it into an integer.

Next is a simple example that will print the cost of purchasing some number of widgets:

```
COST_PER_WIDGET = 7.49    # Constant price of one widget
nWidgets = input('How many widgets do you want to buy? ')
nWidgets = int(nWidgets)    # convert to an integer
if nWidgets == 1:
    print('One widget will cost you $', COST_PER_WIDGET)
else:
    cost = nWidgets * COST_PER_WIDGET
    print(nWidgets, 'widgets will cost you $', cost)
```

In this snippet, we take different paths, depending on whether the user wants to purchase one widget or multiple widgets. For multiple widgets, we do a simple multiplication and output a message with proper wording.

Here is an example that will execute different code, depending on a person's age:

```
if age < 21:
    okToOrderBeer = False
    print('Sorry, you are too young!')
else:
    okToOrderBeer = True
    beerOrder = input('What kind of beer do you like to drink? ')
```

In this example, we check a variable named age to see if the user is allowed to order a beer. If the value of age is under 21, we print a message saying that the person is too young. We remember this fact by setting the Boolean variable okToOrderBeer to False. Otherwise, we set the Boolean variable to True and ask the user what kind of beer they want.

Next, we have another example of deciding what type of company to apply to:

```
if gpa >= 3.5:
    applyToWorkAtTopLevelCompany()
else:
    if gpa > 3.0:
        applyToWorkAtMediumLevelCompany()
    else:
        applyToWorkAtLowLevelCompany()
```

In this snippet, we decide what type of company to apply to, depending on the value of our grade point average. Notice that if our GPA is less than 3.5, then the code executes the else clause. The else clause contains a nested if/else.

# Using if/else Inside a Function

if statements and if/else statements can be used inside functions. Let's work through an example. In this example, we'll write the beginnings of a "Spaminator" program. That is, we want to start writing a program that will build the header line for a message to be sent to any number of people. In order to make the message appear personalized, if we believe the person is male, we want to address the message to Mr. <name>. If we believe the person is female, we will address the letter to Ms. <name>. To implement this, we'll build a function that accepts a name and a gender—'m' for male, 'f' for female—and returns the header of the greeting as a string:

```
def createHeader(fullName, gender):

    if gender == 'm':
        title = 'Mr.'
    else:
        title = 'Ms.'
    header = 'Dear ' + title + ' ' + fullName + ','  # use concatenation
    return header

# A few test calls to the function
print(createHeader('Joe Smith', 'm'))
print(createHeader('Susan Jones', 'f'))
print(createHeader('Henry Jones', 'm'))
```

The following is the resulting output:

```
Dear Mr. Joe Smith,
Dear Ms. Susan Jones,
Dear Mr. Henry Jones,
```

In this program, the calls that pass in a gender of 'm' return a header that contains Mr., and every call that passes in a gender of 'f' returns a string that contains Ms..

# The elif Statement

Sometimes a question has more than two answers, and you want to do different things based on each possible answer. As a simple example, in our Spaminator program, imagine we have a name for which we are unsure whether the gender is male or female. Maybe we want to send a message to someone named Chris Smith, but we don't know if Chris Smith is male or female. If we don't know the gender, we would want to address our message to "Mr. or Ms. Chris Smith." In our call to the function with a name like this, we could pass in the name and a question mark '?' to indicate that we do not know the gender of this person.

Given the current code, if we passed in a question mark as the gender, the program would check for male, fail that test, assume female, and print, "Dear Ms. Chris Smith." The problem is that the function needs to check for one of *three* possible values: male, female, or *unknown*, each with its desired outcome.

It turns out that you often need to check for three, four, five, or any number of different cases. To handle this, Python gives us another addition to the if statement, called the elif statement. elif is a made-up word that came from taking the words *else if* and smashing them together—so it really means *else if*. To see how this works, take a look at the flowchart shown in Figure 5-5.

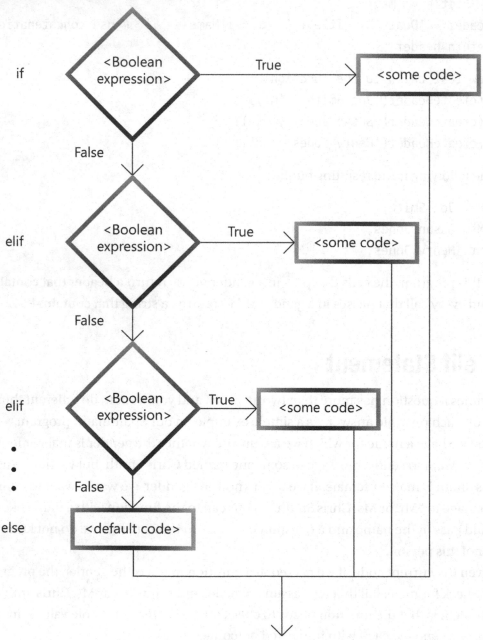

***Figure 5-5.*** *Flowchart of* if/elif/else

The basic idea is that you can ask multiple Boolean questions, and when there is a match (that is, a Boolean expression evaluates to True), then the block of code associated with that case is executed. Here is what the syntax looks like in Python:

```
if <Boolean expression>:
    <some code>
elif <Boolean expression>:
    <some code>
elif <Boolean expression>:
    <some code>
# as many elif's as you need ...
else:
    <some default code>
```

Once one of the Boolean expressions evaluates to True, then the indented code below it runs. When that block is finished, control is passed to the first statement beyond the if/elif/else.

Let's take a look at what the createHeader function would look like using an if/elif/else:

```
def createHeader(fullName, gender):

    if gender == 'm':
        title = 'Mr.'
    elif gender == 'f':
        title = 'Ms.'
    else:    #not sure, could be male or female
        title = 'Mr. or Ms.'
    header = 'Dear ' + title + ' ' + fullName + ',' # use concatenation
    return header

print(createHeader('Joe Smith', 'm'))
print(createHeader('Susan Jones', 'f'))
print(createHeader('Henry Jones', 'm'))
print(createHeader('Chris Smith', '?'))  # Not sure if this is male or female
```

Notice that the values passed in for the gender in the first three calls were 'm' or 'f'. But in the last call, we did not know the gender. In this call, we passed in a question mark. (Actually, anything other than 'm' or 'f' would work fine.) This is the resulting output:

```
Dear Mr. Joe Smith,
Dear Ms. Susan Jones,
Dear Mr. Henry Jones,
Dear Mr. or Ms. Chris Smith,
```

# Using Many elif Statements

Imagine what the code would look like if there were six genders to check instead of just two. In that case, we could have an if statement check for male, an elif to check for female, and four more elif statements to check for the other genders. If the gender was still unrecognized (that is, it did not match any of the genders we were checking for), then we would have an else clause to catch that as the default case.

Here is a good example that uses an if/elif/else construct with a number of different checks. In this function, we pass in a temperature, and the function returns a string that describes the appropriate clothing to wear for that temperature:

```python
def whatToWear(temperature):
    if temperature > 90:
        clothes = 'swim suit'
    elif temperature > 70:
        clothes = 'shorts'
    elif temperature > 50:
        clothes = 'long pants'
    else:
        clothes = 'thermal underwear and long pants'

    return 'Put on ' + clothes

print(whatToWear(100))
print(whatToWear(40))
print(whatToWear(71))
```

When we run this code, we get the following output:

```
Put on swim suit
Put on thermal underwear and long pants
Put on shorts
```

The code runs through each test in the `if` and `elif` statements, looking for the first one that evaluates to `True`. When one test results in a `True`, the indented code block beneath that test will run. Then execution will jump down to the first statement after the `if`/`elif`/`else` statements. If none of the tests results in an answer of `True`, then the code block associated with the `else` will execute. This way, the `else` block serves as a "catchall." In this case, when we passed in a value of 40, all the `if` and `elif` tests resulted in a `False`, so the code of the `else` block ran.

Here is a great example of where you might use an `if`/`elif`/`elif`/ ... /`else` construct. Imagine you are writing a game program. The program could respond to a number of different keys on the keyboard. For example, you might print out a menu of single-letter commands and ask the user to type a letter (and then press Return/ Enter) to continue. The program is designed to do a different action for each letter in the menu. To code something like this, you would use a series of `if`/`elif`/ ... `elif`/`else` comparisons to see which key was pressed, and you would call a different function to do some action based on which key was pressed. In commercial games, the left, right, up, and down arrows are often used to move a character on the screen in the matching direction. The coding to implement this is done using a series of `if`/`elif`/ ... `elif`/ `else` statements.

---

**Note**    If you are familiar with other computer languages, like C or Java, you might recognize this as a `switch`/`case` statement. The people who developed Python saw no need to have two different approaches to do the same thing. Therefore, there is no separate `switch`/`case` construct in Python.

---

# A Grading Program

Here is a real-world example of using if/elif/else statements. Teachers often grade tests, projects, and homework assignments using a number scale of 0 to 100. At the end of the term, the final grading number needs to be converted to a letter grade. Here is a sample function that could be used to do this conversion:

```
#Convert a number score to a letter grade:
def letterGrade(score):
    if score >= 90:
        letter = 'A'
    elif score >= 80:
        letter = 'B'
    elif score >= 70:
        letter = 'C'
    elif score >= 60:
        letter = 'D'
    else:
        letter = 'F'  #fall through or default case
    return letter

grade1 = letterGrade(75)
print(grade1)
grade2 = letterGrade(82)
print(grade2)
print(letterGrade(95))  #call and print in one statement
```

For simplicity, this function only generates full-letter grades—it does not go into plusses and minuses. Adding grades like A–, B+, B–, though, would be a trivial extension that would involve adding more elif lines to check for more values of the variable score.

# A Small Sample Program: Absolute Value

Now I will provide a number of small programming challenges with solutions that involve the use of if/else or if/elif/else constructs. I'll work through the first one with you, and then give you a number of other problems, each building in complexity.

Before attempting to build or fix something, it is always a good idea to think through the approach before actually starting to do any work. This is especially true in computer programming, and there is a special word associated with it: *algorithm.*

---

**Definition**    An *algorithm* is a series of steps to solve a problem.

---

In programming, you should think through your approach and describe it in English before writing any code. In each of the following programming challenges, it should be common practice to think through the problem and develop an appropriate algorithm before turning the algorithm into Python code.

The first program is one that includes a function to calculate the absolute value of a given number. Although *absolute value* may not be an everyday term, it is simply defined as the distance away from zero. That is, the absolute value of 3 is 3. But the absolute value of –3 is also 3. The absolute value function should not print anything; it should just return the absolute value of the starting number.

We'll first come up with an appropriate algorithm. Here is one that will work:

- If the value is positive, then the result is just the starting value.

- If the number is negative, then the result is the starting number multiplied by –1.

That's it. This is a very simple algorithm. Now, let's turn that into code. The approach to writing these small programs is generally to build a function to do the core work, and then build a number of calls to the function, passing in test data to test all paths through the function. Here is the code to implement absolute value:

```
# Absolute Value Program

# Function to generate the absolute value of a number
def absoluteValue(valueIn):
    if valueIn >= 0 :
        valueOut = valueIn
    else:  #must be negative, multiply by minus one to get a positive value
        valueOut = -1 * valueIn
    return valueOut
```

```
#Test cases
result = absoluteValue(10.5)
print('The absolute value of 10.5 is', result)

result = absoluteValue(-8)
print('The absolute value of -8 is', result)
```

The following is the output from running this program:

```
The absolute value of 10.5 is 10.5
The absolute value of -8 is 8
```

This absoluteValue function demonstrates a powerful Python feature. In the first call, we passed in a floating-point number. In the second call, we passed in an integer. The function only has a single parameter variable, valueIn, which is set to the value of whatever argument is passed in. This is a good demonstration of how a variable can have any type, depending on the type of data that is assigned to it.

To extend the main code, we can add an interactive component. That is, we could ask the user to enter a number, use that number in a call to our function, and print the result. Here is a modified version that adds this capability at the end of the main code:

```
#  Absolute Value Program

# Function to generate the absolute value of a number
def absoluteValue(valueIn):
    if valueIn >= 0 :
        valueOut = valueIn
    else:
        valueOut = -1 * valueIn
    return valueOut

#Test cases
result = absoluteValue(10.5)
print('The absolute value of 10.5 is', result)

result = absoluteValue(-8)
print('The absolute value of -8 is', result)

# Get user input and convert to a floating point number
userNumber = input('Enter a number: ')
userNumber = float(userNumber)
```

```
# Call the function with the user's number and print the answer
result = absoluteValue(userNumber)
print('The absolute value of', userNumber, 'is', result)
```

The following is the output from running this program:

```
The absolute value of 10.5 is 10.5
The absolute value of -8 is 8
Enter a number: -123.456
The absolute value of -123.456 is 123.456
```

---

**Note**   Python actually has a full suite of specialized math functions—including one for absolute value—available for Python programmers to use. But building your own functions like this is good practice and furthers your understanding. We'll talk about *packages* like this later.

---

# Programming Challenges

Now it's your turn. I will present a number of detailed challenges for you to implement. Once you understand the specification, think the problem through and develop an algorithm to solve it. Then write the code yourself, using the same style as the absolute value program: build a function and a small number of test cases to demonstrate that your function works correctly. The solution to each problem is provided on the page(s) following each problem.

## Negative, Positive, Zero

Create a program that contains a function called negativePositiveZero. It is passed one numeric (integer or float) parameter. The function should return one of the following string values:

- 'negative' if the number is negative
- 'positive' if the number is positive
- 'zero' if the number is zero

The function should not print anything. Write some main program code to call the function with test values and then print the returned results. For each test, the program should output this:

xxx is negative

or this:

xxx is positive

or this:

xxx is zero

For extra practice, allow the user to enter a value. Use that value in your function call and then print the results.

The algorithm for the negativePositiveZero function is straightforward. Compare to see if the number is less than zero; if not, then compare to see if it is greater than zero; if not, then by default it must be zero. Here is the implementation:

```
# Determine if a number is negative, positive, or zero

# Function to determine negative, positive, or zero
# Returns an appropriate string
def negativePositiveZero(value):

    if value < 0.0:
        answer = 'negative'
    elif value > 0.0:
        answer = 'positive'
    else:   # not negative, not positive, must be zero
        answer = 'zero'
    return answer

#Test cases
result = negativePositiveZero(-25.7)
print('-25.7 is', result)

result = negativePositiveZero(0.0)
print('0.0 is', result)
```

```
result = negativePositiveZero(123.45)
print('123.45 is', result

# Get user input and call the function.
userValue = input('Enter a number: ')
userValue = float(userValue)
userResult = negativePositiveZero(userValue)
print(userValue, 'is', userResult)
```

To code the algorithm, use if/elif/else, where the if and the elif compare for negative and positive, leaving a default of zero. After each test, set a variable appropriately, and at the end of the function return the value of the variable.

# isSquare

Create a program that contains a function called isSquare. The function is passed two parameters that represent the length and the width of a shape. For simplicity, assume that we are talking about a rectangle, where the top and bottom sides are the same width, the left and right sides are the same length, and all angles are 90-degree angles. isSquare should return one of the following:

- True, if the sides represent a square

- False, if the sides do not represent a square

The function should *not* print anything.

Write some main program code to call the function with test values for the length and width of the sides and print the following based on the returned result:

xxx and yyy represent a square

or

xxx and yyy do not represent a square

For extra practice, allow the user to enter values. Use them in your function call and then print based on the results.

Be sure to use different variable names for the user's input and the parameters used in your function.

The algorithm for this function is trivial. Two numbers (length and width) represent a square if they are equal. If not, then the numbers do not represent a square:

```
# Determine if two numbers represent a square

# Function to determine if length and width represent a square
def isSquare(length, width):

    if length == width:
        itsASquare = True
    else:
        itsASquare = False
    return itsASquare

#Test cases
result = isSquare(5, 5)
if result:
    print('5 and 5 represent a square')
else:
    print('5 and 5 do not represent a square')

if isSquare(7.5, 8.5):
    print('7.5 and 8.5 represent a square')
else:
    print('7.5 and 8.5 do not represent a square')

# Get user input, convert to floats and call the function.
userLength = input('Enter a length: ')
userLength = float(userLength)
userWidth = input('Enter a width: ')
userWidth = float(userWidth)
if isSquare(userLength, userWidth):
    print(userLength, 'and', userWidth, 'represent a square')
else:
    print(userLength, 'and', userWidth, 'do not represent a square')
```

The body of the function is a simple if/else statement; then it returns the result.

In the main code, notice that in our first call, we set a `result` variable to the value that is returned from the call. In the second call, we've built the code slightly differently. Because the returned value is a Boolean, we wrote the function call directly in the `if` statement. Both approaches are fine. If we need to remember the result of the call for use in some future statement, we need to assign the answer to a variable. In this small program, we are not using the answer anywhere else, so putting the call inside the `if` statement is perfectly fine.

However, notice that the code that reports the results of each call to the function has a lot of repetition. Whenever you see this kind of repetition, you can generally build another function to get rid of it. Here is a slight rewrite of the previous code to remove redundancy:

```
# Determine if two numbers represent a square

# Function to determine if length and width represent a square
def isSquare(length, width):

    if length == width:
        itsASquare = True
    else:
        itsASquare = False
    return itsASquare

# Intermediate function that checks for a square and prints the result
def printSquare(aLength, aWidth):
    theResult = isSquare(aLength, aWidth)
    if theResult:
        print(aLength, 'and', aWidth, 'represent a square')
    else:
        print(aLength, 'and', aWidth, 'do not represent a square')

#Test cases
printSquare(5, 5)

printSquare(7.5, 8.5)
```

```
# Get user inputconvert to floats and call the function.
userLength = input('Enter a length: ')
userLength = float(userLength)
userWidth = input('Enter a width: ')
userWidth = float(userWidth)
printSquare(userLength, userWidth)
```

In this listing, notice that the isSquare function has not changed at all. But we've introduced a new intermediate function called printSquare. That function calls the isSquare function and does the appropriate printing based on the result. This is a good example of how a function can call another function. Rather than duplicate code as we did in the earlier version, the reporting logic has been moved into the intermediate function. Using this intermediate function allows the main code to become much smaller.

# isEven

Write a program that contains a function called isEven. The function is passed one numeric (integer) parameter. isEven should return as follows:

- True, if the number is even (... , –6, –4, –2, 0, 2, 4, 6, 8, ...)

- False, if the number is odd (... , –5, –3, –1, 1, 3, 5, 7, 9, ...)

Notice that negative integers can be considered even or odd, just like positive integers. Further, 0 is considered even. The function should *not* print anything. Instead, build an intermediate function, as you did for the solution to the isSquare problem.

For each value, the program should output this

```
xxx is even
```

or this:

```
xxx is odd
```

Write your main code with two calls to your function, testing first with an even number and then an odd number. Then allow the user to enter a value and use that value in a call to your intermediate function so that it prints the results.

Be sure to use different variable names for the user's input and the parameters used in your function(s).

The algorithm here is a little tricky. When we look at an integer, it is probably obvious to us whether the number is even or odd, but we need a way to allow the computer to figure this out for a given number. If you have trouble trying to come up with an algorithm, think about how you would explain to a 5-year-old child how you know if a number is even or odd. You have to break down the problem into very simple steps.

The algorithm here works like this: a number is even if it is evenly divisible by 2.

The question then becomes how "evenly divisible by 2" can be implemented in Python. Remember the modulo operator—the percent sign (%)? The modulo operator gives us the remainder of a division. If we take a number and use modulo 2 on it, we can get the remainder after dividing by 2. If the remainder is 0, then the original number was evenly divisible by 2—therefore it was even. Otherwise, the remainder must have been 1 and the original number was odd:

```python
# Determine if a given integer is even or odd:

# Function to determine if a number is even or odd
def isEven(valueIn):
    remainder = valueIn % 2
    if remainder == 0:
        return True
    else:
        return False

def printEvenOrOdd(someValue):
    if isEven(someValue):
        print(someValue, 'is even')
    else:
        print(someValue, 'is odd')

#Test cases
printEvenOrOdd(10)
printEvenOrOdd(11)

# Get user input and convert to an integer
userNumber = input('Enter an integer: ')
userNumber = int(userNumber)

# Pass in the user's number
printEvenOrOdd(userNumber)
```

The modulo operator allows us to construct code that is quite small. We're using an intermediate function to call the isEven function and print the results.

# isRectangle

Write a program that contains a function called isRectangle. The function is passed four parameters representing the length of each of the four sides of a shape in the order of left, top, right, and bottom. You should assume that all angles are 90-degree angles. isRectangle should return this:

- True, if the sides represent a rectangle

- False, if the sides do not represent a rectangle

The function should *not* print anything.

For each set of four numbers, the program should output this

```
<side1>, <side2>, <side3>, and <side4> represents a rectangle
```

or this:

```
<side1>, <side2>, <side3>, and <side4> do not represent a rectangle
```

Write some main program code to call the function with test values for the four sides. Use test values like 5, 6, 5, 6, which do represent a rectangle, and some other values like 5, 6, 7, 8, which do not represent a rectangle. Then allow the user to enter four values. Use those values in a call to your intermediate function that prints the results.

Be sure to use different variable names for the user's input and the parameters used in your function(s).

The algorithm for this function goes like this: if the left side is equal to the right side, and if the top is equal to the bottom, then it is a rectangle; otherwise, the numbers do not represent a rectangle:

```
# Determine if the four side lengths represent a Rectangle or not:

# Function to determine if four sides represent a Rectangle
# Is a rectangle if left is the same as the right
# and top is the same as the bottom
def isRectangle(left, top, right, bottom):
    if left == right:
```

```
    if top == bottom:
        return True
return False

def printRectangle(someLeft, someTop, someRight, someBottom):
    if isRectangle(someLeft, someTop, someRight, someBottom):
        print(someLeft, someTop, someRight, someBottom, 'represents a
        rectangle')
    else:
        print(someLeft, someTop, someRight, someBottom, 'does not
        represent a rectangle')

#Test cases
printRectangle(5, 6, 5, 6)
printRectangle(5, 6, 7, 8)

# Get user input and call the function.
userLeft = input('Enter the left: ')
userLeft = int(userLeft)
userTop = input('Enter the top: ')
userTop = int(userTop)
userRight = input('Enter the right: ')
userRight = int(userRight)
userBottom = input('Enter the bottom: ')
userBottom = int(userBottom)

printRectangle(userLeft, userTop, userRight, userBottom)
```

The implementation is done with a nested if statement. First, check whether the left is equal to the right. If it passes that test, another if statement checks whether the top is equal to the bottom. If it passes that test, True is returned. Placing a return statement in the middle of a function is fine, and if/when it executes, no lines in the function after the return statement will run. The function is finished at that point, and control passes back to the caller.

If we get all the way to the last return statement, we'll return a value of False to say that the numbers do not represent a rectangle.

# Conditional Logic

So far, all the comparisons we have shown in `if` statements have used a single operator (`==`, `!=`, `>`, `<`, `<=`, `>=`). But sometimes it is convenient to have Boolean expressions where we can perform multiple comparisons within a single `if` statement. To create expressions that can contain multiple comparisons, there are three logical operator keywords: `not`, `and`, and `or`.

# The Logical not Operator

We'll start with the simplest one: the `not` operator. Remember that a Boolean can only have a value of `True` or `False`. The `not` operator takes a Boolean value and reverses it. If a Boolean value is `False`, applying the `not` operator changes the value to `True`. If the value is `True`, `not` changes the value to `False`. The `not` operator is often used in `if` statements to make things clear.

The `not` operator is entered directly in front of any Boolean variable or expression. If it is used with a simple variable, no parentheses are needed. If you want to apply a `not` operator to a more complicated expression, you should put parentheses around the expression to create a grouping and place the `not` operator in front of the parentheses. The following are examples:

```
if not open:
    # closed

if not broken:
    # working

# Here is a typical use in an if statement
if not(width == length):
    # not a square

# can use it in an assignment statement:
alive = not dead

# using not to reverse the output of a function:
isOdd = not isEven(value)
```

Table 5-2 is what is called the *truth table* for the not operator. It shows what happens when you apply the not operator to an input Boolean value. The truth table for not is extremely simple.

***Table 5-2.***  *Truth Table for the not Operator*

|     | Input | Result |
| --- | ----- | ------ |
| not | True  | False  |
| not | False | True   |

# The Logical and Operator

The and operator works between two Boolean values. It allows you to do multiple comparisons within a single if statement. The indented block of code following the if statement will only execute if the expressions on *both sides* of an and operator evaluate to True. Here are some examples:

```
if (age >= 12) and (height >= 48):
    # OK to get on roller coaster at amusement park

if (location == 'Hamburger Restaurant') and (nDollars > 4):
    # can buy a hamburger and fries

if (x >= 5) and (x =< 10):
    # x is between 5 and 10

# assume three Boolean variables, each set appropriately
if learningPython and studyingHard and workingThroughExamples:
    # can become a professional Python programmer
```

Table 5-3 is the truth table for the and operator. It shows what happens when two Boolean expressions are put together with and.

**Table 5-3.** *Truth Table for the and Operator*

| Input1 | | Input2 | Result |
|--------|-----|--------|--------|
| False | and | False | False |
| False | and | True | False |
| True | and | False | False |
| True | and | True | True |

Notice that you get a result of False in every case *except* when both inputs are True. Here's another way to think about it: the result is True only when *all* input values are True.

To work through the application of this table, think about the first coding example:

```
if (age >= 12) and (height >= 48):
    # OK to get on roller coaster at amusement park
```

The if statement evaluates the comparisons on either side of the and operator. The only way that the person can get on the roller coaster is if it is true that they are 12 or older *and* it is true that they are at least 48 inches tall. If either comparison evaluates to False, or if both evaluate to False, then the result of the and is False, and the person is not allowed to get on the ride.

Earlier in this chapter, there was a programming challenge to write code to see whether the four sides of a shape represented a rectangle. Using the and operator, the check for a rectangle can be written in a more natural and clearer way:

```
def isRect(left, top, right, bottom):
    if (left == right) and (top == bottom):
        return True
    else:
        return False
```

# The Logical or Operator

The or operator also works between two Boolean values, and it also allows you to do multiple comparisons in a single if statement. The indented block of code following the if statement will execute if *either* side of an or operator evaluates to True. Here are some examples:

```
if (nDollars > 4) or dateIsPaying:
    # can get ice cream sundae
```

```
if (studyingHoursPerDay > 4) or payOffTeacherForGoodGrade:
    # you will do well in class (JOKE!)
```

```
if (userCommand == 'q') or (userCommand == 'quit'):
    # quit the program
```

```
if (age > 65) or disabled:
    # can get government benefits
```

Table 5-4 is the truth table for the or operator. It shows what happens when two Boolean expressions are put together with or.

***Table 5-4.*** *Truth Table for the or Operator*

| Input1 | | Input2 | Result |
|--------|-----|--------|--------|
| False  | or  | False  | False  |
| False  | or  | True   | True   |
| True   | or  | False  | True   |
| True   | or  | True   | True   |

Notice that the result is True in every case *except* when both inputs are False. Another way to think about it is this: the result is True when *any* input value is True.

---

**Note**    Where Python uses the English words for the logical operators and, or, and not, other computer languages, like C and Java, use symbols: && means and, || means or, and ! means not. The use of simple English words for these operators makes Python code more readable for novices.

---

# Precedence of Comparison and Logical Operators

Chapter 2 talks about the order of operations with the standard math operations of addition, multiplication, subtraction, and division. With the introduction of a number of comparison operators and three logical operators, the rules of precedence get even more complicated. Consider the following if statement that contains many logical operators and comparison operators. This if statement is intended to determine whether you are eligible to buy a house in California's Silicon Valley:

```
if not inJail and cash >= 1000000 or haveHighPayingJob and downPayment >=
90000:
    # Can buy a house in Silicon Valley
```

But this is rather confusing. Does or have priority over and? When is the not operator applied? Does the code compare downPayment >= 90000? Or does the logical and operation of haveHighPayingJob and downPayment happen first?

Similar to our discussion about the order of operations for math operators, we can eliminate all these questions by using parentheses to force the order of comparison and logical operators. Adding a set or sets of parentheses makes your intentions clear by creating groupings:

```
if not(inJail) and ((cash >= 1000000) or (haveHighPayingJob and
(downPayment >= 90000)):
    # Can buy a house in Silicon Valley
```

In an if statement, the extra parentheses affect the order of evaluation. With the addition of parentheses, the meaning of the preceding complicated if statement becomes clear. As long as you are not in jail, and either you have a million dollars in cash or you have a high-paying job *and* a down payment of 90,000 dollars, then congratulations—you can buy a house in Silicon Valley!

# Booleans in if Statements

There is one additional note on using Booleans in if statements. Very often, programmers use a Boolean variable to remember the result of an early calculation or setting. Then later, the code tests the Boolean to see which piece of code should run.

For example, consider a program where we need to know if the user is an adult female. We might ask the user at the start of the program about their age and gender. Once we have the user's responses, we might set a Boolean this way:

```
if (age > 21) and (gender == 'f'):
    adultFemale = True
else:
    adultFemale = False
```

Then, later in the program, we might want to make some comment or recommendation if the user is an adult female. Now that we have this information captured in a single Boolean variable, we can use that variable in our next if statement. Many beginning programmers write something like this:

```
if adultFemale == True:
    # Make some special comment/recommendation
```

And that works fine. However, comparing a Boolean to True is not necessary. The following is exactly equivalent:

```
if adultFemale:
    # Make some special comment/recommendation
```

There is nothing wrong with the first form—comparing a Boolean to True. If it is clearer to you, feel free to write it that way. But as you get more comfortable working with Booleans, you will come to recognize that the second approach, of just using the Boolean alone, is even simpler.

# Program to Calculate Shipping

Let's take many of the concepts we have learned in this chapter and put them all together to build a program. The idea is that we have a company that sells widgets. A user fills out a form or answers a set of questions, supplying the number of widgets to purchase and the country to ship to. The program should generate the cost to ship that particular number of widgets to that country. The cost is dependent on both the country to ship to and the number of widgets. The company is set up to ship to either the United States or Canada only. If the user is requesting a shipment to any other country, the company has to decline the order. The costs are outlined in Table 5-5.

137

**Table 5-5.** *Shipping Costs Based on Country and Quantity*

| United States | | Canada | |
|---|---|---|---|
| Quantity | Cost | Quantity | Cost |
| <= 50 | 6.25 | <= 50 | 8.25 |
| <= 100 | 9.50 | <= 100 | 12.50 |
| <= 150 | 12.75 | <= 150 | 18.75 |
| Otherwise | 15.00 | Otherwise | 25.00 |

The key to this program is to build a function that calculates the shipping costs. When it is called, it expects to be passed two pieces of data: the country to ship to and the number of widgets purchased. The function will return a resulting shipping cost. Essentially, we need a way to take the data in Table 5-5 and turn it into code. We'll start with an outline of the code:

```
NOT_YET = 'We don't ship there yet'

#  Function to determine shipping cost, based on country and quantity
def calculateShipping(country, nWidgets):

    if (country == 'USA') or (country == 'US') or (country == 'United
    States'):
        # Calculate costs for US

    elif country == 'Canada':
        # Calculate costs for Canada

    else:
        # We do not ship anywhere else
        shippingCost = NOT_YET  #  special value to say that we don't ship
        to this country

    return shippingCost
```

In this first pass at the code, we made a decision to look at the table by considering the country first. (We could have broken up the problem by looking at the number of widgets first and then at the country, but the former approach seems more logical.) The user types in their country, so our code allows for any of three acceptable spellings or shortened names for the United States. Next, we check whether the user's country is Canada. If the country is not the United States or Canada, execution will go into the else clause. There we assign a special value of the constant NOT_YET to indicate that we do not ship to the given country. The caller has to check for and deal with this special value. If the function returns NOT_YET, then the calling code must tell the user that we cannot ship to that country.

Now let's build up the rest of the calculateShipping function:

```python
NOT_YET = 'We don't ship there yet'

#  Function to determine shipping cost, based on country and quantity
def calculateShipping(country, nWidgets):

    if (country == 'USA') or (country == 'US') or (country == 'United States'):
        if nWidgets < 50:
            shippingCost = 6.25
        elif nWidgets < 100:
            shippingCost = 9.50
        elif nWidgets < 150:
            shippingCost =12.75
        else:
            shippingCost = 15.00

    elif country == 'Canada':
        if nWidgets < 50:
            shippingCost = 8.25
        elif nWidgets < 100:
            shippingCost = 12.50
        elif nWidgets < 150:
            shippingCost = 18.00
        else:
            shippingCost = 25.00

    else:
        # We do not ship anywhere else
        shippingCost = NOT_YET  #  special value to say that we don't ship
        to this country

    return shippingCost
```

The additional code is implemented for the United States and Canada as a nested if/elif/else statement. For those two countries, we check the number of widgets ordered and assign the appropriate value to the shippingCost variable. At the end of the function, we return the calculated cost. Finally, we write the main code that asks a number of questions to the user, as follows:

```
# Get user input then call the above function

userWidgets = input('How many widgets are you buying? ')
userWidgets = int(userWidgets) # convert to integer

userCountry = input('What country are you shipping to? ')
# Other questions about the shipment here

# Call the function to see how much it will cost to ship
amountForShipping = calculateShipping(userCountry, userWidgets)
if amountForShipping == NOT_YET:
    print('Sorry, we do not ship to', userCountry)
else:
    print('It will cost $', amountForShipping, 'to ship your package')
    # more code here to process the shipment
```

The main code gets information from the user, uses that information in a call to the function, and then gets back the amount it costs to ship. Notice that the main code contains a check (using an if statement) to see if we get a valid value for shipping. If so, we tell the user the cost of shipping, and the program can proceed. If we get back our special constant, we know that we cannot ship to the given country, and we print an appropriate message. By having all the shipping calculations inside a function, we could later modify the function to add more countries to ship to, without making any changes to the calling code.

# Summary

The chapter began with flowcharting to introduce the concept of branching. Then I showed you how decision boxes in flowcharts are implemented by if statements, if/ else statements, and if/elif/else statements. I gave many examples of how you can use nested if statements, if statements inside of functions, and if statements with multiple elif branches. If you took the challenges, you got some good practice by writing relatively simple functions with if statements in them.

Next, I introduced the three logical operators: and, or, and not. I showed you the truth table for each of these operators and demonstrated how we can use these operators to create more complex but often more natural if statements.

The chapter concluded with a good example of using nested if/elif/else statements in a program to calculate shipping.

# CHAPTER 6

# Loops

In this chapter, we'll build a Guess the Number program. The computer will pick a random number between 1 and 20, and the user will have five attempts to guess the number. For every incorrect guess, the computer will let the user know if the correct answer is higher or lower than the user's guess. If the user doesn't guess the answer in five attempts, the program will tell the user what the number was.

To learn how to build a game like this, this chapter covers the following topics:

- User's view of the game

- Loops

- `while` statement

- First loop in a real program

- Increment and decrement

- Running a program multiple times

- Python's built-in packages

- Generating a random number

- Simulating flipping a coin

- Other examples of using random numbers

- Creating an infinite loop

- A new style of building a loop: `while True` and `break`

- Asking if the user wants to repeat: the empty string

- Pseudocode

- Building our Guess the Number program

- Playing a game multiple times

143

© Irv Kalb 2018
I. Kalb, *Learn to Program with Python 3*, https://doi.org/10.1007/978-1-4842-3879-0_6

- Error checking with try/except

- continue statement

- Building error-checking utility functions

- Coding challenge

# User's View of the Game

Rather than start with the code, let's start by showing what the program looks like from the user's point of view:

```
>>>
Welcome to my Guess the Number program.
Guess my number between 1 and 20
You have 5 guesses.

Take a guess: 5
Your guess is too low
Take a guess: 7
Your guess is too high
Take a guess: 6
You got it in 3 guesses

Play again? Press y to continue or press ENTER to quit: y
Take a guess: 12
Your guess is too low
Take a guess: 18
Your guess is too high
Take a guess: 15
Your guess is too low
Take a guess: 16
Your guess is too low
Take a guess: 17
You got it in 5 guesses

Play again? Press y to continue or press ENTER to quit: y
Take a guess: 10
```

```
Your guess is too low
Take a guess: 11
Your guess is too low
Take a guess: 12
Your guess is too low
Take a guess: 13
You got it in 4 guesses

Play again? Press y to continue or press ENTER to quit: y
Take a guess: 1
Your guess is too low
Take a guess: 2
Your guess is too low
Take a guess: 3
Your guess is too low
Take a guess: 4
Your guess is too low
Take a guess: 5
Your guess is too low
You didn't get it in 5 guesses.
The correct answer was: 11

Play again? Press y to continue or press ENTER to quit:
```

From the output, you can probably figure out how some of the code works. You already know how to get the user's guesses using a call to `input`. You also know how to compare the user's guess to the randomly chosen target number using an `if/elif/else` statement. And you know how to keep track of the number of guesses by setting a variable to 0, and adding 1 to it every time the user makes a guess. But in order to build the full program, we need to learn a few more things about programming and how to implement these things in Python.

# Loops

In the output of the program, you can see how the user was allowed to make multiple guesses. Also, the user is allowed to play the game multiple times. In order to build code with these types of repetitions, we need to introduce a new concept called a *loop*.

145

**Definition**   A *loop* is a block of code that is repeated until a certain condition is met.

Figure 6-1 shows the flowchart of a loop.

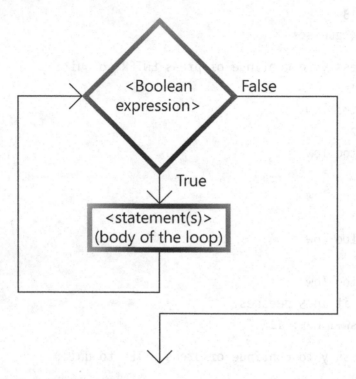

***Figure 6-1.*** *The flowchart of a loop*

To understand how this works, let's start with a silly real-life example:

I am hungry

while hungry

take a bite of food

chew

swallow

if thirsty:

take a drink

go back to the point of checking if I am still hungry

eat dessert!

In this example, we repeatedly take a bite of food, chew, swallow, and if we are thirsty, take a drink. This process keeps going as long as we are still hungry. When we eventually reach the point where we are no longer hungry, the loop finishes and we eat dessert.

Here is a second silly real-life example of a loop:

```
ask son to take out garbage
anger is non-existent, perfectly calm
while son has not taken out the garbage
    increase anger level by a bit
    tell son to take out the garbage
    wait 2 minutes
    go back to checking if garbage has been taken out
```

In this example, as long as my son has not taken out the garbage, my anger level continues to go up.

# The while Statement

In Python (as with many languages), a loop is implemented with a while statement. This is the generic form of the while statement:

```
while <Boolean expression>:   # as long as the expression evaluates to True
    <indented block of code>
```

Notice that this syntax is very similar to an if statement. The while statement contains a Boolean expression followed by a colon. After the while statement is an indented block of code. Again, similar to an if statement, the block of code can be as short or as long as needed. The block of code is often referred to as the *body* of the loop. The while statement and the indented block together are called a while loop. As long as the Boolean expression in the while statement evaluates to True, the statements in the body of the loop are repeated. When executing the while statement, if the Boolean expression evaluates to False, the body of the loop is skipped, and execution continues with the first statement after the body of the loop.

Again, similar to what happens when you type an if statement, when you type a while statement with a trailing colon, IDLE automatically indents for you to allow you to build the body of the loop. When you are finished entering the statement(s) that make up the body of the loop, you can press Backspace (Windows) or the Delete (Mac) key to move the indenting level back four spaces.

Let's start with a silly Python example. In the following code, we'll ask the user to type the letter *a*, and we'll keep asking until the user types an *a*:

```
looping = True
while looping == True:
    answer = input("Please type the letter 'a': ")
    if answer == 'a':
        looping = False   # we're done
    else:
        print("Come on, type an 'a'!)")

print("Thanks for typing an 'a'")
```

Before the loop starts, we set a Boolean variable named looping to True. The Boolean expression in this while statement compares the Boolean to the value True. We could also have written it as follows:

```
looping = True
while looping:
```

This would work the same way, because comparing a Boolean to True is the same as just the value of the Boolean itself.

At the end of the loop, execution automatically goes back to the while statement at the top of the loop. As long as the looping variable has a value of True, the lines of code in the indented block will be repeated. Therefore, when we want the loop to end, something inside the loop must affect the value of that expression. In this loop, when the user types the letter *a*, we set looping to False. When control goes back to the while statement, because the Boolean expression is now False, we exit the loop. For this reason, the Boolean expression in the while statement is often called the *exit condition*—the condition under which you can exit the loop.

But it is interesting to consider what would happen if we never set looping to False. If we never have any code that changes the exit condition, then we would create what is called an *infinite loop*—a loop that runs forever (or until you quit IDLE or shut down your computer).

## ONE INFINITE LOOP

Did you know that when Apple built its corporate headquarters, it paid homage to software developers? The current headquarters is a series of six buildings. When the buildings were built, an oval road was built to allow cars to navigate around the buildings. The official address of Apple is One Infinite Loop Drive in Cupertino, California.

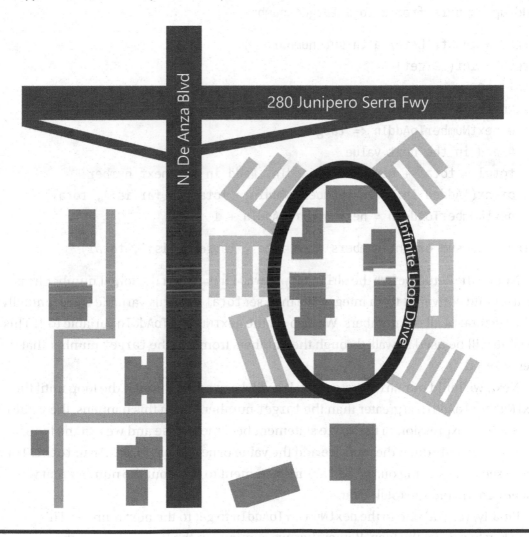

# First Loop in a Real Program

Let's build a simple program using a loop. The program asks the user for a target number. The goal of the program is to calculate the sum of the numbers from 1 through the target number. For example, if the user enters 4, then we want to calculate $1 + 2 + 3 + 4$, and report the answer of 10:

```
#Add up numbers from 1 to a target number

target = input('Enter a target number: ')
target = int(target)
total = 0
nextNumberToAddIn = 1
while nextNumberToAddIn <= target:
    # add in the next value
    total = total + nextNumberToAddIn  #add in the next number
    print('Added in:', nextNumberToAddIn, 'Total so far is:', total)
    nextNumberToAddIn = nextNumberToAddIn + 1

print('The sum of the numbers from 1 to', target, 'is:', total)
```

Notice the setup before the while loop starts. First, we get the target number from the user and convert it to an integer. We then set total to 0; this variable will eventually hold the total of all the numbers. We also set the nextNumberToAddIn variable to 1. This variable will be used to walk through the numbers from 1 to the target number that the user entered.

Next, we build our while statement. We will keep going through the loop until the nextNumberToAddIn is greater than the target number. When this happens, the value of the Boolean expression in the while statement becomes False and we exit the loop.

Every time through the loop, we add the value of nextNumberToAddIn to total. Then, just to see what's going on, we add a print statement to print out the number that was just added in, and the total so far.

Finally, we add one to the nextNumberToAddIn to get to the next number. This is the key to exiting the loop. Remember, we continue in the loop as long as the nextNumberToAddIn is less than or equal to the target number.

Here is a sample run of the program with an input of 4:

```
Enter a target number: 4
Added in: 1 Total so far is: 1
Added in: 2 Total so far is: 3
Added in: 3 Total so far is: 6
Added in: 4 Total so far is: 10
The sum of the numbers from 1 to 4 is: 10
>>>
```

# Increment and Decrement

The previous code contained the following statement:

```
nextNumberToAddIn = nextNumberToAddIn + 1
```

That line takes the current value of `nextNumberToAddIn`, adds 1 to it, and puts the resulting value back into the same variable. The operation of increasing the value of a variable this way is extremely common. In fact, it has a special name: increment.

---

**Definition**    An *increment* is when a variable adds to itself.

---

By default, when we say *increment*, we mean add 1 to the variable, but you can increment by any amount. Counting by 2 is done by incrementing a variable by 2 in a loop.

In many cases, you use this type of statement to count the number of times through a loop, or to count the number of attempts to do something until there is a success or failure.

This example statement is the standard way of incrementing a variable:

```
counter = counter + 1
```

However, there is also another syntax you can use:

```
counter += 1
```

151

This line uses a new operator: the *plus-equals* operator. These two lines do exactly the same thing and give the exact same result. The plus-equals operator is commonly used by C programmers. In this book, we will use the first syntax because it uses the simple assignment operator.

Imagine if you worked for NASA and were asked to write the code to count down for a rocket launch. For that code, you would want to start with a large number and count down by ones. There is a similar word to describe this action: decrement.

---

**Definition**    A *decrement* is when a variable subtracts from itself.

---

Again, by default, when we use the word *decrement* by itself, it is implied that we want to count down by 1. But just like incrementing, you can decrement by any amount. Here is an example using the standard assignment statement syntax:

```
counter = counter - 1
```

But decrementing also has an alternative syntax using the minus-equals operator:

```
counter -= 1
```

And again, in this book, we use the first syntax.

In building our guessing game, to keep track of how many guesses the user has made, we'll use a counter and increment it with each guess.

# Running a Program Multiple Times

Let's say we want to be able to run a program over and over again. For example, in the earlier program, where we asked the user for a target number and we added up all the numbers up to that target, we may want to allow the user to be able to do this multiple times. From the user's point of view, the whole program would run, and then the user is asked if they want to try again. If the answer to that question is yes, then the user would see the program start again, ask for another target number, and calculate the new total. This loop would continue until the user's answer to the question asking if they want to go again is no.

There are a few ways to do this, but one simple approach is to place the core of the program inside a function. Then we build a loop. In the body of the loop, we call the function, and at the end of the loop, we ask the user if they want to go again. Here's the code:

```
# Calculate total - repeated

def calculateSum(target):
    total = 0
    nextNumberToAddIn = 1
    while nextNumberToAddIn <= target:
        # add in the next value
        total = total + nextNumberToAddIn
        #increment
        nextNumberToAddIn = nextNumberToAddIn + 1
    return total

answer = 'y'  # start off with the value 'y' to go through the first time
while answer == 'y':
    usersTarget = input('Enter a target number: ')
    usersTarget = int(usersTarget)
    thisTotal = calculateSum(usersTarget)  # call our function and get back
    the answer
    print('The sum of the numbers 1 to', usersTarget, 'is:', thisTotal)

    answer = input('Do you want to try again (y or n): ')
print('OK Bye')
```

Notice that with this structure, all the core calculations (in this case, generating the sum) are done inside of a function, and the function returns the answer. The main code concerns itself mostly with interacting with the user and calling the function.

Alternatively, if you want to run the whole program a certain number of times, you could modify the looping condition to count the number of times through a loop:

```
nTimes = 0  # initialize a counter
while nTimes < 3:
    usersTarget = input('Enter a target number: ')
    usersTarget = int(usersTarget)
    thisTotal = calculateSum(usersTarget)
    print('The sum of the numbers 1 to', usersTarget, 'is:', thisTotal)
    nTimes = nTimes + 1   # increment the counter

print('OK Bye')
```

153

This version allows the user loop to run exactly three times, without the need to ask the user if they want to go again. Notice that with this change, there is no modification needed in the function.

# Python's Built-in Packages

Let's get back to our Guess the Number program. The next thing we need to do is generate a random number. The question that arises is: how can a computer, which does everything exactly the same way every time a program runs, generate a random number? To answer this question, we have to learn a little more about how the Python language is put together; specifically, we need to understand Python *packages*.

In order to keep programs small, the base Python language only has a small number of keywords (`if`, `elif`, `else`, `while`, `def`, and a few more) and built-in functions (`int`, `str`, `input`, and so on).

Python also has some built-in prewritten packages of code that are available to programmers. (In other computer languages, each of these packages might be called a *library*.) The packages are installed on the hard disk of your computer when you install Python. Altogether, they comprise what is called the Python Standard Library.

There are also external packages written by programmers all over the world, who make their code available to other programmers. To get an external package, you need to download it from the Internet. For example, one of these packages is called PyGame. PyGame contains code that allows Python programmers to build games that use graphics in a window, use a mouse as a pointing device, play sounds, and much more. There are thousands of such packages available.

Figure 6-2 shows a diagram that should help explain these three categories.

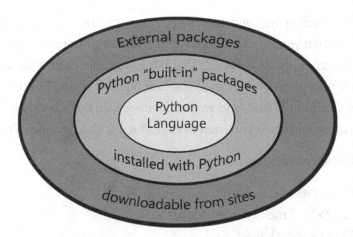

***Figure 6-2.*** *Base Python language, Python Standard Library, and external downloadable packages*

# Generating a Random Number

One built-in package is called the random package. It contains a large number of functions that allow programmers to generate and use random numbers. Because this is one of Python's built-in packages, you already have it on your computer; there is no need to download anything. But because the developers of Python want to keep Python programs as small as possible, you don't get access to this package in the same way that you have immediate access to the built-in functions we discussed earlier.

When you want to use a built-in package, you need to *tell* Python that you want to use it. You have to explicitly ask Python to include a package in your program. The way you do that is to use the import statement, which looks like this:

```
import <packageName>
```

In this case, to import the random package, we would use the following statement:

```
import random
```

Let's take a quick look at the `random` package using the Shell. Bring up IDLE and enter the preceding line. When you press Enter or Return, nothing should happen. The fact that nothing happens is a good thing. It implies that IDLE was able to find the `random` package and its contents are now available to you. If you had typed it wrong or attempted to import a package that IDLE could not find, you would have seen an error message. Here's an example of what you would see if you tried to import a package that does not exist:

```
>>> import NonExistentPackage

Traceback (most recent call last):
  File "<pyshell#2>", line 1, in <module>
    import NonExistentPackage
ImportError: No module named NonExistentPackage
>>>
```

When you write a program that uses an `import` statement, you typically place any `import` statement(s) at the top of your code. If you want to see the documentation of all the functions that are available in this package, you can call the built-in `help` function and pass in the name of the package, like this:

```
help(random)
```

If you do this, you will get screens and screens worth of documentation. In you are truly interested in the details of all the functions, feel free to read through this documentation. There are a large number of functions that you can call in the `random` package. For now, we are interested in one specific function named `randrange`.

The purpose of `randrange` is to generate a random integer number within a given range. `randrange` is interesting because the range itself can be specified in a number of different ways, with different numbers of arguments. Using the most straightforward form, we'll call the `randrange` function specifying the range as two integers. Here is the way we call it:

```
random.randrange(<lowValue>, <upToButNotIncludingHighValue>)
```

You start by specifying the name of the package—in this case, the word `random`. After the package name, you type a period (generally read as "dot"). After the dot, you specify the function you want to call; in this case, you type `randrange` to say that you want to use that specific function. In the preceding line, `randrange` expects to be called with two arguments: a low-end value and a high-end value. The low-end value *is* included in the range, but the high-end value is *not* included in the range. The way that we say this is, "up to but not including" the high-end value. (We'll see this "up to but not including" concept many times in Python.)

The function returns an integer within the specified range. The most typical way to use randrange is in an assignment statement, where you save the returned value in a variable, like this:

```
<resultVariable> = random.randrange(<lowValue>, <upToButNotIncludingHighValue>)
```

Here are some examples:

```
#random between 1 and 10
aRandomNumber = random.randrange(1, 11)

#random between 1 and 52, to pick a card number from a deck
anotherRandomNumber = random.randrange(1, 53)
```

The important thing to remember (which may seem very odd) is that the second argument needs to be one more than the top end of your intended range. That's because the number you specify here is *not* included in the range.

As an alternative syntax, you can call randrange with only a single argument: the "up to but not including" high end. If you make this call with only the one argument, randrange assumes that the low end of your range is zero:

```
#random between 0 and 8
myRandomNumber = random.randrange(9)  # same as random.randrange(0, 8)
```

# Simulation of Flipping a Coin

Now it's time for a good example program that uses random numbers. We will simulate flipping a coin some number of times. The program will run in a loop. Each time through the loop, we randomly generate a 0 or 1. Then we'll do a mapping. That is, we'll say that if we randomly get a 0, that means tails. If we get a 1, that means heads. When the loop finishes, we report the results:

```
# Coin flip program
import random

nFlips = 0  # to count the number of flips
nTails = 0  # to count the number of flips that came up as tails
nHeads = 0  # to count the number of flips that came up as heads
```

157

```
maxFlips = input('How many flips do you want to do? ')
maxFlips = int(maxFlips)

while nFlips < maxFlips:
    # Randomly choose 0 or 1, because a coin flip can only result in one of
      two answers
    # (heads or tails)
    zeroOrOne = random.randrange(0, 2)

    # If we get a zero, say that was a heads
    # If we get a one, we say that was a tails
    if zeroOrOne == 0:
        nTails = nTails + 1
    else:
        nHeads = nHeads + 1

    nFlips = nFlips + 1

print()
print('Out of', nFlips, 'coin tosses, we had:', nHeads, 'heads, and',
nTails, 'tails.')
```

Notice that we didn't randomly pick heads or tails directly. We randomly picked from a range that encompasses all possible outcomes, and then mapped the numeric answer to the outcomes we were looking for. In this case, there are only two possible outcomes, so we get random values of 0 or 1, map 0 to tails, and 1 to heads.

# Other Examples of Using Random Numbers

Another example of this approach is if we were writing a program to play the game of rock-paper-scissors. In this case, there are three possible choices. To make a random choice, we would generate a random number between 0 to 2 (or 1 to 3, or in fact, any range of three consecutive numbers), and use the resulting number to make our choice:

```
import random

choiceNumber = random.randrange(0, 3)  # to get a 0, 1, or 2
if choiceNumber == 0:
```

```
    randomChoice = 'rock'
elif choiceNumber  == 1:
    randomChoice == 'paper':
else:  # not zero and not one, must be 2
    randomChoice == 'scissors'
```

Here we use an if/elif/else statement to account for all possible numbers generated by calling random.randrange, and we set another variable to a string representing the actual choice.

At the beginning of the Chapter 2, just to get your feet wet with Python, I showed a sample program. It was a simulation of the Magic 8-Ball children's toy. Let's revisit the portion of that code that selected a random answer:

```
randomAnswer = random.randrange(0, 8)  # pick a random number between 0 and 7

if randomAnswer == 0:
    print('It is certain.')
elif randomAnswer == 1:
    print('Absolutely!')
elif randomAnswer == 2:
    print('You may rely on it.')
elif randomAnswer == 3:
    print('Answer is foggy, ask again later.')
elif randomAnswer == 4:
    print('Concentrate and ask again.')
elif randomAnswer == 5:
    print('Unsure at this point, try again.')
elif randomAnswer == 6:
    print('No way, dude!')
else:    # must be 7
    print ('No, no, no, no, no.')
```

Now it should be obvious how this works. We generate a random number between 0 and 7 using random.randrange, and then we use an if/elif ... elif/else to pick a message to print, based on the random number that was chosen.

# Creating an Infinite Loop

When we introduced the `while` statement, we said that as long as the Boolean expression evaluates to `True`, the `while` statement would continue to loop. The loop only stops when the Boolean expression evaluates to `False`. Any loop can be built using this structure.

Earlier, we said that the Boolean expression in the `while` statement is called the *exit condition*—that is, the test for exiting the loop is done in the `while` statement. So far, we've shown that the way to handle this is to write some test, typically in an `if` statement, where you determine whether you are ready to exit the loop. If you are ready to exit, you set some variable to a known value that will later be checked in the Boolean expression of the `while` statement. Here is an example:

```
looping = True
while looping:
    <statement(s)>
    if <found exit condition?>:
        looping = False      # found the exit condition at this point
    else:
        <continuing statement(s) inside the loop>
```

In effect, you have found the exit condition, but you can't exit the loop until execution goes back to the `while` statement. Unfortunately, this style often makes it more difficult to write the continuing part of the loop that follows. The code that you run if the exit condition has not been reached must get indented.

If you need to detect and handle multiple exit conditions, each `if` statement would set the same variable (that is later checked in the `while` statement), and the code that continues the normal execution gets indented further. This excessive indenting makes it difficult to write and even more difficult to read through the normal path through the loop.

Fortunately, there is another way to build a `while` loop.

# A New Style of Building a Loop: while True, and break

Earlier I talked about how you might accidentally create an infinite loop. I said that as long as nothing changed the value of the Boolean expression in the `while` statement, the loop would run forever. Therefore, the simplest way to create an infinite loop is like this:

```
while True:
    <statement(s)>
```

That loop would run forever. Python provides another statement called the break statement, which is made up of just the word break. If your code is running in a while loop, and a break statement is reached, control is immediately transferred to the first statement past the last line of the loop. With the addition of the break statement, we can now think differently about writing loops. Rather than checking for the exit condition in the while statement, we can check for an exit condition anywhere in the body of the loop. If we find an exit condition, we use a break statement to exit out of the loop right at that point. The flowchart in Figure 6-3 shows how this works.

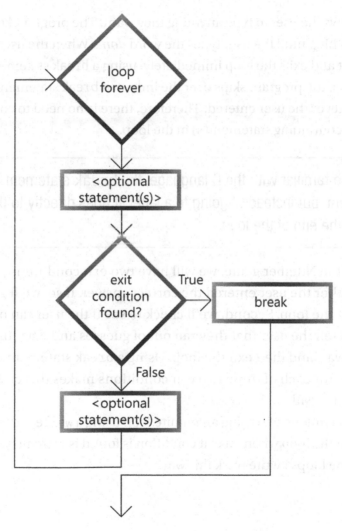

***Figure 6-3.*** *Flowchart of a loop using a break statement*

Here is a simple example:

```
while True:  # loop forever
    line = input("Type anything, type 'done' to exit: ")
    if line == 'done':
        break  # transfers control out of the loop

    print('You entered:', line)

print('Finished')
```

This code allows the user to type anything they want. The program keeps asking the user to type something until the user types the word *done*. When the user types *done*, the program detects it and exits the loop immediately, using a break statement. If the user types anything else, the program skips over the indented break statement and prints out a copy of whatever the user entered. Therefore, there is no need to code an else statement for the continuing statement(s) in the loop.

---

**Note**  If you are familiar with the C language, the break statement is effectively a goto statement, but instead of going to a label, it goes directly to the first statement past the end of the loop.

---

In our Guess the Number game, we will have two exit conditions. First, we'll check to see whether the user entered the correct answer. If so, we'll give some feedback and exit the loop. Second, we'll check to see if the user ran out of guesses. In this case, we'll tell the user that they ran out of guesses and what the randomly chosen number was, and then exit the loop. Using a break statement at the appropriate point for each of these two exit conditions makes this code easier to write and clearer to read.

This general technique of writing an infinite loop using a while True statement and using break to exit the loop when an exit condition is found is extremely effective and clear. Almost all the loops I write work this way.

# Asking If the User Wants to Repeat: the Empty String

We are almost ready to build our Guess the Number game. In the demonstration version of the game, you may have noticed that once a round of the game was over (because the user either got the right answer or ran out of guesses), the program asked if the user wanted to play again. Now we have learned all statements needed to build a game with repetition like that. For example, we can build our game loop this way:

```
while True:
    # do whatever, e.g., play a round of a game

    # now ask the user if they want to go again
    goAgain = input('Press Return/Enter to quit, or anything else to
    continue: ')
    if goAgain == '':  # check for no entry
        break  # user said they want to quit

print 'Finished'
```

This code may seem a little odd, so I'll explain how this works. When the user types any response to the question posed by the call to input, whatever characters the user types are assigned into the goAgain variable. If the user enters the string as **yes**, then goAgain is assigned the string 'yes'. If the user just enters the letter **y**, then goAgain is set to the string 'y'.

But if the user just presses the Return key (Mac) or the Enter key (PC), then input still returns the characters the user typed. In this case, the user did not type any characters, so the result of the call is a special string called the *empty string*—a string with no characters in it. It is represented as two single quotes ('') or the two double quotes (""), which we read as "quote quote." The empty string is essentially the equivalent of zero as a number—a number with no value. Therefore, if the user types no characters, the goAgain variable is set to the empty string. We use an if statement to check for this case, and if we find that the user did not type any characters, then we exit the loop using a break statement.

# Pseudocode

Now we have enough information to write our game. But rather than jump right into the code, let's talk about how the program is going to work. We'll come up with an overall approach before writing the actual code.

---

**Definition**   *Pseudocode* is an English-like description of an algorithm in a made-up computer language.

---

Very often, programmers develop an algorithm and write the algorithm in pseudocode before writing it in a real computer language. This allows programmers to think through the approach to the overall structure of a solution without having to worry about the detailed syntax of a computer language.

As a demonstration, here is the pseudocode for one round of our Guess the Number program:

```
Show introduction
Choose random target
Initialize a guess counter

Loop forever
    Ask the user to for a guess
    Increment guess counter
    If user's guess is correct, congratulate user, we're done
    If user's guess is too low, tell user
    If user's guess is too high, tell user
    If reached max guesses, tell correct answer, we're done.
```

We can take this pseudocode and turn each statement into a comment inside IDLE. We can use the comments essentially as an outline inside the code of the program.

# Building the Guess the Number Program

We are finally ready to build our full game. This is our first significant program. It requires quite a few lines of code. Rather than write all the code from top to bottom and test the entire program, we'll write small portions at a time and test as we go. This is a standard technique for writing larger programs. Writing or changing too many things at once makes the development process difficult because if an error shows up, it may not be clear which line of code is the culprit, and there could be logic errors that need to be addressed.

For this program, we'll start by writing only the user's guess and comparison logic code. It can be difficult to build and test a program that has randomization in it, because the code typically takes different branches on each run. So, to start building our program, let's start by hard-coding a target number of 10. Later, we'll modify the code to pick the target number randomly:

```
# Guess the Number  (version 1)

# Show introduction
# Choose random target
target = 10     # start with a known value

# Initialize a guess counter

# Loop forever
# Ask the user to for a guess
userGuess = input('Take a guess: ')
userGuess = int(userGuess)

# Increment guess counter
# If user's guess is correct, congratulate user, we're done
if userGuess == target:
    print('You got it!')

# If user's guess is too low, tell user
elif userGuess < target:
    print('Your guess was too low.')

# If user's guess is too high, tell user)
else:
    print('Your guess was too high.'

#If reached max guesses, tell answer correct answer, we're done.
```

Checking the user's response is essentially a three-way branch: the answer is correct, the answer is too low, or the answer is too high. We implement this using an if/elif/else. Then we test this code to ensure that all branches work correctly:

```
>>> ============================== RESTART ==============================
>>>
Take a guess: 5
Your guess was too low.
>>> ============================== RESTART ==============================
>>>
Take a guess: 15
Your guess was too high.
>>> ============================== RESTART ==============================
>>>
Take a guess: 10
You got it!
>>>
```

Next, we'll add code to keep track of the number of guesses and allow the user to make multiple guesses:

```
# Guess the Number  (version 2)

# Show introduction
# Choose random target
target = 10     # start with a known value
# Initialize a guess counter
guessCounter = 0

# Loop forever
while True:
    # Ask the user to for a guess
    userGuess = input('Take a guess: ')
    userGuess = int(userGuess)

    # Increment guess counter
    guessCounter = guessCounter + 1
```

```
# If user's guess is correct, congratulate user, we're done
if userGuess == target:
    print('You got it!')
    print('It only took you', guessCounter, 'guess(es).')
    break

# If user's guess is too low, tell user
elif userGuess < target:
    print('Your guess was too low.')

# If user's guess is too high, tell user
else:
    print('Your guess was too high.')

# If reached max guesses, tell answer correct answer, we're done.
if guessCounter == 5:
    print('Sorry, you did not get it in 5 guesses')
    print('The number was:', target)

print('Thanks for playing.')
```

In this version, we keep track of the number of guesses by introducing a new variable: guessCounter. We initialize it to zero at the top. Next, we add a while True so that the user can take multiple guesses. We then indent all the lines below that to turn these lines into the body of the loop. IDLE provides a quick way to do this all in one shot. You start by selecting a number of lines of code (using click and drag or click and Shift-click). With a selection highlighted, click the Format menu. The first item is Indent Region with a shortcut key of Control+] (Windows) or Command+] (Mac). Selecting this option from the menu or pressing the appropriate shortcut key will move all the selected lines in one level of indenting. Notice that the next option, Format ➤ Dedent Region, moves all selected code in the opposite direction.

With the while True in place, we have an infinite loop. Every time through the loop, we increment our guess counter. The loop needs to handle two exit conditions. First, if the user guesses the correct answer, we tell the user and execute a break statement to leave the loop. Second, if the user reaches the maximum number of guesses, we give the user feedback and exit the loop with another break statement.

We'll run two tests on this code. First, we'll test to make sure that the code still works when you get the correct answer. We'll check to ensure that the guess counter works correctly, and that this exit condition gets you out of the loop:

```
>>>
Take a guess: 5
Your guess was too low.
Take a guess: 15
Your guess was too high.
Take a guess: 10
You got it!
It only took you 3 guess(es).
Thanks for playing.
>>>
```

Now we'll run it again. In this run, we know the correct answer is 10, so we'll give five incorrect answers to ensure that the code testing for the number of guesses and the second exit condition work correctly:

```
>>>
Take a guess: 1
Your guess was too low.
Take a guess: 1
Your guess was too low.
Take a guess: 1
Your guess was too low.
Take a guess: 1
Your guess was too low.
Take a guess: 1
Your guess was too low.
Sorry, you did not get it in 5 guesses
The number was: 10
Thanks for playing.
>>>
```

Now that the core code seems to be working well, we'll finally add in the randomization code. We'll also finish the program by building the introduction and add some constants to make it more flexible:

```python
# Guess the Number  (version 3)

import random

MAX_GUESSES = 5  # maximum number of guesses allowed
MAX_RANGE = 20 # highest possible number

# Show introduction
print('Welcome to my Guess the Number program.')
print('Guess my number between 1 and', MAX_RANGE)
print('You will have', MAX_GUESSES, 'guesses.')

# Choose random target
target = random.randrange(1, MAX_RANGE + 1)

# Initialize a guess counter
guessCounter = 0

# Loop forever
while True:
    # Ask the user to for a guess
    userGuess = input('Take a guess: ')
    userGuess = int(userGuess)

    # Increment guess counter
    guessCounter = guessCounter + 1

    # If user's guess is correct, congratulate user, we're done
    if userGuess == target:
        print('You got it!')
        print('It only took you', guessCounter, 'guess(es).')
        break

    # If user's guess is too low, tell user
    elif userGuess < target:
        print('Your guess was too low.')
```

```
    # If user's guess is too high, tell user
    else:
        print('Your guess was too high.')

    # If reached max guesses, tell answer correct answer, we're done.
    if guessCounter == MAX_GUESSES:
        print('Sorry, you did not get it in', MAX_GUESSES, 'guesses.')
        print('The number was:', target)
        break

print('Thanks for playing.')
```

Because we wanted to choose a random number, we started by importing the random package. After that, we created two constants: MAX_GUESSES and MAX_RANGE. Using constants like these makes the code more readable than having "magic numbers" (in this case, 5 and 20) in the code. The meanings of these constants are much clearer, and their values are now changeable in a single place. We added a simple introduction that uses those constants. When calling random.randrange to generate the random number, we added 1 to the MAX_GUESSES value. We did that because this argument needs to be an "up to but not including" value. In this case, we want to get a number in the range of 1 to 20, so we need to pass in values of 1 and 21.

The program now implements one round of playing the game:

```
>>>
Welcome to my Guess the Number program.
Guess my number between 1 and 20
You will have 5 guesses.
Take a guess: 15
Your guess was too low.
Take a guess: 18
Your guess was too low.
Take a guess: 20
Your guess was too high.
Take a guess: 19
You got it!
It only took you 4 guess(es).
Thanks for playing.
>>>
```

# Playing a Game Multiple Times

In most computer games, when one round of the game is over, you get the option to play again. In the output at the beginning of this chapter, I showed this option for our Guess the Number game. On a conceptual level, playing a game multiple times can be thought of as each round of the game in a loop. That is, we can build an outer loop to play multiple games, and an inner loop that plays a round within each game.

There are two possible implementations. If the game is simple enough, you can build a loop within a loop. Here is the pseudocode:

```
#
Playing multiple games loop
    Play multiple rounds of the current game
        Play a round or move within a game
    Ask if the user wants to play again, if not, exit
```

The implementation would consist of an outer while loop and another inner while loop that plays a single round. After the end of the inner loop, we ask the user whether they want to play again. If they do, the outer loops runs again, and the game restarts.

The other approach is to take the code that implements one round and put that inside a function. Then the main code can be a simple loop that calls the function to play a round of the game.

Let's build that second version. We'll move all the code dealing with one round into a function called playOneRound:

```
# Guess the Number   (version 4)

import random

MAX_GUESSES = 5  # maximum number of guesses allowed
MAX_RANGE = 20 # highest possible number

# Show introduction
print('Welcome to my Guess the Number program.')
print('Guess my number between 1 and', MAX_RANGE)
print('You will have', MAX_GUESSES, 'guesses.')
```

```python
def playOneRound():
    # Choose random target
    target = random.randrange(1, MAX_RANGE + 1)

    # Initialize a guess counter
    guessCounter = 0

    # Loop forever
    while True:
        # Ask the user to for a guess
        userGuess = input('Take a guess: ')
        userGuess = int(userGuess)

        # Increment guess counter
        guessCounter = guessCounter + 1

        # If user's guess is correct, congratulate user, we're done
        if userGuess == target:
            print('You got it!')
            print('It only took you', guessCounter, 'guess(es).')
            break

        # If user's guess is too low, tell user
        elif userGuess < target:
            print('Your guess was too low.')

        # If user's guess is too high, tell user
        else:
            print('Your guess was too high.')

        # If reached max guesses, tell answer correct answer, we're done.
        if guessCounter == MAX_GUESSES:
            print('Sorry, you did not get it in', MAX_GUESSES, 'guesses.')
            print('The number was:', target)
            break
```

```
#main code
while True:
    playOneRound()  # call a function to play one round of the game
    goAgain = input('Play again? (Press ENTER to continue, or q to quit):
')
    if goAgain == 'q':
        break

print('Thanks for playing.')
```

We've taken all the code to play a single round of the game and moved it inside a function (using the Format ➤ Indent Region to indent all this code). Then we built the main code, which consists of a loop that calls the function to play one round and asks the user whether they want to play again. This approach yields code that is very simple and clear.

# Error Detection with try/except

In any program that asks the user to enter a number, there is a possibility that the user might make a mistake. For example, when asked for a number (integer or float), the user might type one or more letters. If the user enters something that is not a number and your program then attempts to use either the int or float built-in function to try to convert the user's input to a number, Python generates an error. Here is a simple example done in the Shell:

```
>>> userInput = input('Please enter a number: ')
Please enter an integer: xyz
>>> userInput = int(userInput)    # convert user's input to an integer

Traceback (most recent call last):
  File "<pyshell#4>", line 1, in <module>
    userInput = int(userInput)
ValueError: invalid literal for int() with base 10: 'xyz'
```

When this type of error happens, the program crashes. It is much better to detect an error like this and inform the user of the error rather than having Python generate an error message and have the program exit.

Python provides a mechanism for doing this type of error checking, but it takes a little getting used to. Here's the theory. Before we run some code that *might* cause an error (in this case, trying to convert a number to an integer), we ask Python to watch what's going on. If an error occurs while Python is in this watching mode, you can tell Python to run an additional block of code. In that block, you can print out a message of your choosing, which tells the user more information about what went wrong and maybe how to fix it.

The error checking is implemented in Python with a try/except block. Here's what it looks like:

```
try:
    <statement(s) that may cause an error>
except:
    <statement(s) to execute IF an error occurs>

else:    #optional, often not needed
    <statement(s) to execute if NO error occurs>
```

In our Guess the Number program, if we wanted to ensure that the user entered a valid number, we could do it with a try/except block like this:

```
userGuess = input(' Take a guess: ')
try:
    userInput = int(userInput)
except:
    print('The number you entered was not an integer')
```

As a general rule, the try block should be built to cover as few statements as possible. As in the given example, ideally a try block should only contain one statement.

Let's modify our program to replace the single call to input with the preceding code and see how it works. The good news is that our code now detects (or *catches*) the user's error and prints an appropriate error message. The bad news is that after printing an error message, the code keeps going and tries to use the value of our variable userInput assuming that it is an integer, and fails a little later. Specifically, it fails when trying to compare the randomly chosen target integer to the string the user entered. Therefore, we need one more statement to allow us to do some error correction.

# The continue Statement

When we detect some error condition in a loop, we typically want to transfer control back to the while statement at the top of the loop, without executing the rest of the code inside the loop. To do that, we can execute a new statement called a continue statement, as shown in Figure 6-4.

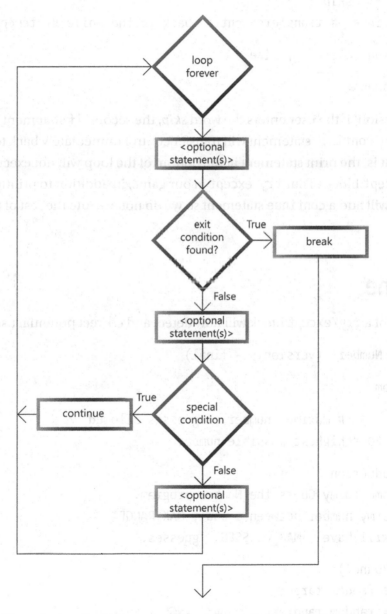

***Figure 6-4.*** *Flowchart of a loop using a break and a* continue *statement*

This is an example:

```
while True:  # loop forever
    line = input("Type anything, type 'done' to exit: ")
    if line == 'done':
        break  # transfers control out of the loop

    if line == 'skip':
        continue  # transfers control back to the while statement

    print 'You entered:', line

print 'Finished'
```

In this version, if the user enters the word *skip*, the second `if` statement will find a match, and the `continue` statement will transfer control immediately back to the top of the loop—that is, the print statement at the bottom of the loop will not execute.

In the except block of our `try/except` in our game, in addition to printing an error message, we will add a `continue` statement so we do not execute the rest of the code in the loop.

# Full Game

The addition of a `try/except` block will now detect and correct potential user errors:

```
# Guess the Number  (version 5 - final)

import random

MAX_GUESSES = 5  # maximum number of guesses allowed
MAX_RANGE = 20 # highest possible number

# Show introduction
print 'Welcome to my Guess the Number program.'
print 'Guess my number between 1 and', MAX_RANGE
print 'You will have', MAX_GUESSES, 'guesses.'

def playOneRound():
    # Choose random target
    target = random.randrange(1, MAX_RANGE + 1)
```

```
# Initialize a guess counter
guessCounter = 0

# Loop forever
while True:
    # Ask the user to for a guess
    userGuess = input('Take a guess: ')

    # Check for potential error
    try:
        userGuess = int(userGuess)
    except:
        print 'Hey, that was NOT an integer!'
        continue  # transfer control back to the while

    # Increment guess counter
    guessCounter = guessCounter + 1

    # If user's guess is correct, congratulate user, we're done
    if userGuess == target:
        print 'You got it!'
        print 'It only took you', guessCounter, 'guess(es).'
        break

    # If user's guess is too low, tell user
    elif userGuess < target:
        print 'Your guess was too low.'

    # If user's guess is too high, tell user
    else:
        print 'Your guess was too high.'

    # If reached max guesses, tell answer correct answer, we're done.
    if guessCounter == MAX_GUESSES:
        print 'Sorry, you did not get it in', MAX_GUESSES, 'guesses.'
        print 'The number was:', target
        break
```

```
# main code
while True:
    playOneRound()  # call a function to play one round of the game
    goAgain = input('Play again? (Press ENTER to continue, or q to quit):
')
    if goAgain == 'q':
        break

print 'Thanks for playing.'
```

We added a try/expect block make sure the user enters an integer. Notice that using this structure, user errors are not counted as actual attempts.

# Building Error-Checking Utility Functions

Using try/except, we can build a set of reusable utility functions to get a number from the user. The idea is to have two functions (one for integers, one for floats) that ask the user to enter a number, ensure that the user has entered a valid number, and return the number to the caller. If the user types something that is not a number, then we show an error and ask the user to enter a number again. When the user types a valid number, the function returns the number that the user entered:

```
def getIntegerFromUser(prompt):
    while True:
        number = input(prompt)
        try:
            number = int(number)
        except:
            print('That is not an integer, please try again.')
            continue
        #  everything OK
        return number

def getFloatFromUser(prompt):
    while True:
        number = input(prompt)
```

```
    try:
        number = float(number)
    except:
        print('That is not a float, please try again.')
        continue
    # everything OK
    return number

myInteger = getIntegerFromUser('Please enter an integer: ')
print(myInteger)

myFloat = getFloatFromUser('Please enter a float: ')
print(myFloat)
```

Those two functions are almost identical. The only difference is that the first one is used when you want the user to enter an integer, and the second one expects a float. You call either function and pass in a prompt string containing any wording you want to ask the user to enter a number. The function starts a loop and keeps going through the loop as long as the user does *not* enter a valid number. Inside the loop, we pose the prompt string that the caller passes in. Then we have a try block where we attempt to convert the user's string to a number. If that fails, control is sent to the except block. There we print out the error message and then execute a continue statement. This passes control back to the while statement, and that starts the loop over.

# Coding Challenge

It's time for you to write some code. In this challenge, I ask you to make a more powerful version of the getIntegerFromUser function. In addition to ensuring that the user has entered a valid number, add code to test and ensure that the user has entered a number within a range of two integers.

Let's name this function getIntegerInRange. It should be built to expect the following parameters: prompt, lowEnd, upToButNotIncludingHighEnd. The code should be modified to add a second check to make sure that the number is within the given range. If the user enters an invalid response (not an integer, or the number is not in the range), the user should be given an appropriate error message and be prompted to enter a number again. This process should continue until the user enters a valid integer.

As with previous challenges, once you understand what is being asked, close the book and write and test the code using a sample call to the function.

Here is the solution:

```
# Ask the user to enter an integer within a given range

def getIntegerInRange(prompt, lowEnd, includedHighEnd):
    while True:
        number = input(prompt)
        try:
            number = int(number)
        except:
            print('That is not an integer, please try again.')
            continue

        if (number < lowEnd) or (number > includedHighEnd):
            print ('The number you entered is not in between', \
                    lowEnd, 'and', includedHighEnd)
        else:
            #Everything OK
            return number

# Ask user to give a number between -5 and 20
myInteger = getIntegerInRange('Please enter an integer: ', -5, 21)
print('The number you entered was: ', myInteger)
```

There are many different ways to write this function. The approach shown here is to first calculate the largest integer included in the range and save that in a variable. (This will make the rest of the code clearer.) Then we have the same code as the earlier version, where we ask the user to enter a number and attempt to convert their response to an integer. After that test, we added a new test. We check to see whether the value of the number entered is outside the given range. If so, we print an error message and execute a `continue` statement to transfer control back to the `while` statement, and we go around the loop again. Notice that we do not need a `try/except` here because there is no conversion error—a simple `if` statement will do. When we pass both tests, the function returns the value of the number entered by the user.

Here is a test run with four invalid entries before entering a valid integer in the range:

```
>>>
Please enter an integer: abcd
That is not an integer, please try again.
Please enter an integer: 123.45
That is not an integer, please try again.
Please enter an integer: -123
The number you entered is not in the range of -5 to 20
Please enter an integer: 21
The number you entered is not in the range of -5 to 20
Please enter an integer: 7
The number you entered was:   7
>>>
```

Incorporating error detection like that makes your code more robust by reducing the frustration that users may experience if they enter an invalid response. The general approach is to build a function that contains a while loop. Inside the loop, you check for invalid responses and only return once the user has supplied a valid answer.

# Summary

In this chapter, we worked our way through building the Guess the Number program. To implement the game, you learned about the concept of a *loop*, which is implemented in Python using a while statement. I discussed the concepts of incrementing and decrementing variables to do simple counting. You learned how to use loops to construct programs that are run multiple times.

I discussed the concept of a built-in package, which is brought into your program with an import statement. As a useful example of a built-in package, I talked about the random package and specifically made calls to the randrange function inside that package to generate random numbers. I showed you how to use a random number to choose from a selection, building an example of a simulation of flipping a coin.

Then I showed you a different way to build and exit from a loop. Using while True builds an infinite loop, but you can check for an exit condition and leave a loop using a break statement. I also introduced the continue statement that can be helpful in recovering from user errors.

We built loops where we asked the user whether they wanted to run through the program multiple times. In doing so, you saw how to check for no user input using the empty string.

We eventually went through the process of building our game. We started with a pseudocode description of the algorithm and then built up and tested various pieces of the game.

Finally, I discussed how we could catch user errors using a `try/except` block. We then generalized this concept by building some reusable functions to ensure that the user enters a valid number.

# CHAPTER 7

# Lists

Prior to this chapter, we've talked about four types of data: integer, float, string, and Boolean. But imagine that you want to represent a lot of data—for example, the names of all the students in a class, or better yet, the names of all students in a school, or city, or state. So far, our definition of a variable allows us to only represent a single piece of data. Therefore, if we wanted to represent a group of students' names, we would do something like this:

```
student1 = 'Joe Schmoe'
student2 = 'Sally Smith'
student3 = 'Henry Jones'
student4 = 'Betty Johnson'
student5 = 'Chris Smith'
```

Every time we get a new student, we need to create a new variable to represent that student's name. But more importantly, every time we add a new variable, we have to modify every piece of our code that operates on all students. As you might guess, this becomes unmanageable very quickly. In this chapter, I introduce a new data type that allows us to store, access, retrieve, and manipulate collections of data.

This chapter discusses the following topics:

- Collections of data

- Lists

- Elements

- Python syntax for a list

- Empty list

- Position of an element in a list: index

- Accessing an element in a list

- Using a variable or expression as an index in a list

© Irv Kalb 2018
I. Kalb, *Learn to Program with Python 3*, https://doi.org/10.1007/978-1-4842-3879-0_7

- Changing a value in a list

- Using negative indices

- Building a simple Mad Libs game

- Adding a list to our Mad Libs game

- Determining the number of elements in a list: the `len` function

- Programming challenge 1

- Using a list argument with a function

- Accessing all elements of a list: iteration

- `for` statements and `for` loops

- Programming challenge 2

- Generating a range of numbers

- Programming challenge 3

- Scientific simulations

- List manipulation

- List manipulation: an inventory example

- Pizza toppings example

# Collections of Data

Representing a group of students is just one of many examples in the real world where groups of data are stored. Here are some more examples of collections of related data:

- Computer games that keep a high-scores leader board

- Browser programs that maintain your bookmarked sites

- Credit card companies that remember all the purchases you made with your credit card

- All the contacts and phone numbers in your phone

- The members of a team

- The teams in a tournament

- Books in a library

- Names of clubs at a school

# Lists

Rather than using individually named variables to represent a group of related data, most programming languages allow you to represent this type of data using a single name. In Python, it is called a *list*. A list is a new data type.

---

**Definition**    A *list* is an ordered collection of data that is referred to by a single variable name. (In most other computer languages, the same concept is called an *array*.)

---

This is a shopping list made up of all strings:

```
'apples'
'bananas'
'cherries'
'dates'
'eggplant'
```

This is a list of test scores:

```
99
72
88
82
54
```

# Elements

There is a special name for each thing in a list.

---

**Definition**    An *element* is a single member of a list. (It is also known as an *item* in the list.)

---

Let's look at our shopping list again:

```
'apples'
'bananas'
'cherries'
'dates'
'eggplant'
```

Each string in the list is an element of the list: `'apples'` is an element, `'bananas'` is an element, and so on.

# Python Syntax for a List

Let's see how this looks in Python. When we make a list, like a shopping list on paper, we typically write the elements vertically, one per line. In a computer language, we need some special syntax to indicate that we are talking about a list. In Python, we use the square bracket characters, [ and ]. A list is represented by an open square bracket, the elements separated by commas, and a closing square bracket, as follows:

```
[<element>, <element>, ... <element>]
```

Just like any other type of data, a list is created using an assignment statement. That is, you write single variable name followed by an equals sign, and then you define your list.

```
<myListVariable> = [<element>, <element>, ... <element>]
```

A list can essentially have any number of elements. The actual number of elements is limited only by the amount of memory available. Here are some examples:

```
shoppingList = ['apples', 'bananas', 'cherries', 'dates', 'eggplant']

scoresList = [24, 33, 22, 45, 56, 33, 45]
```

A list can also be created using a mix of data types:

```
mixedList = [True, 5, 'some string', 123.45]
```

Note that we are showing variable names that represent a list in the form of <name>List. This is not required, but a name in this form clearly indicates that the variable represents a list rather than an individual piece of data. We will use this naming convention throughout the rest of this book.

A list is a new data type. To show that a list is a standard data type in Python, let's create a list, print it, and use the type function to find out which data type it is:

```
>>> mixedList = [True, 5, 'some string', 123.45]
>>> print(mixedList)
[True, 5, 'some string', 123.45]
>>> print(type(mixedList))
<class 'list'>
>>>
```

So, a list is of type list, independent of the type of data of its contents. A list is unusual because it is made up of multiple pieces of data, where each one can be of any data type.

## Empty List

Although a list can have any number of elements, there is also a special list that is made up of no elements. This is known as the *empty list*:

```
>>> someList = []   # set a list variable to the empty list - no elements
>>> print(someList)
[]
>>>
```

You can think of the empty list relative to other lists, like zero in comparison to other numbers. We will use this later by creating an empty list and then adding elements to it on the fly.

## Position of an Element in a List: Index

You've seen that we can create a list with the square bracket syntax, and we can print a list using the print statement, but the power of a list comes from the ability to use the individual elements in the list. Therefore, we need a way to *reference* (get at) any individual element of a list. Let's look at our example shopping list again:

```
>>> shoppingList = ['apples', 'bananas', 'cherries', 'dates', 'eggplant']
>>> print(shoppingList)
['apples', 'bananas', 'cherries', 'dates', 'eggplant']
>>>
```

You can think of any physical list, like a shopping list, as a numbered list. That is, we could assign a consecutive integer to each element, and reference any element in our shopping list using that number. In fact, that identifying number has a clear definition.

---

**Definition**    An *index* is the position (or number) of an element in a list. (It is sometimes referred to as a *subscript*.)

---

An index is always an integer value. Because each element has an index (number), we can reference any element in the list by using its associated number or position in the list.

To us humans, in our shopping list, apples is element number 1, bananas is element number 2, and cherries is element number 3. This is the way that we typically think of numbering things:

Sample shoppingList:

| Human<br>Number | Element |
|---|---|
| 1 | 'apples' |
| 2 | 'bananas' |
| 3 | 'cherries' |
| 4 | 'dates' |
| 5 | 'eggplant' |

In Python (and most other computer languages), the elements in a list are also numbered consecutively—but the counting starts at zero. That is, all lists start at an index of zero. The indices for the preceding list are 0, 1, 2, 3, and 4. 'apples' is element number 0, 'bananas' is element number 1, and up to 'eggplant', which is element 4:

| Python<br>Index | Element |
|---|---|
| 0 | 'apples' |
| 1 | 'bananas' |
| 2 | 'cherries' |
| 3 | 'dates' |
| 4 | 'eggplant' |

This list has five elements, but they are numbered 0 to 4.

---

**Caution**   This concept of starting a count at zero is very important, and until you wrap your head around it, it will cause you much grief!

---

# Accessing an Element in a List

Now we have a way to represent a list of data in a single variable: enclosing the list in brackets, separating elements by commas. But we need some way to *get at* the individual elements in the list. The way we do that is to use the following syntax:

```
<listVariable>[<index>]
```

This syntax results in the value of the element in the list at the given index. Let's assume a list of numbers defined with this assignment statement:

```
numbersList = [20, -34, 486, 3129]
```

We can access each element in the numbersList as follows:

```
numbersList[0]     # would evaluate to 20
numbersList[1]     # would evaluate to -34
numbersList[2]     # would evaluate to 486
numbersList[3]     # would evaluate to 3129
```

I'll demonstrate this in the Shell using our shopping list with some simple print statements:

```
>>> shoppingList = ['apples', 'bananas', 'cherries', 'dates', 'eggplant']
>>> print(shoppingList)
['apples', 'bananas', 'cherries', 'dates', 'eggplant']
>>> print(shoppingList[2])
cherries
>>> print(shoppingList[4])
eggplant
>>> print(shoppingList[0])
apples
>>>
```

Here are some suggestions for how to read a list variable with an index value. Let's say you see something like this:

```
myList[2]
```

Rather than read it as "myList bracket 2 bracket," it is probably clearer if you read it as any of the following:

- myList element 2
- The element in position 2 of myList
- Element 2 of myList
- The third element of myList
- myList sub 2 ("old school" reference to subscripts)

The first one—"myList element 2"—is probably the most straightforward.

# Using a Variable or Expression as an Index in a List

An index can also be written as a variable or an expression. In fact, most of the time, we access elements in a list this way. The following is a simple code snippet that demonstrates this approach. We'll ask the user to enter an integer and will use that value as an index to our shopping list:

```
>>> shoppingList = ['apples', 'bananas', 'cherries', 'dates', 'eggplant']
>>> myIndex = input('Enter an index: ')
Enter an index: 3
>>> myIndex = int(myIndex)    # convert to integer
>>> myElement = shoppingList[myIndex]    # use as an index into the list
>>> print('The element at index', myIndex, 'is', myElement)
The element at index 3 is dates
```

Let's show this as a simple program with a loop. We'll use concepts from Chapter 6 to allow the user to run the program multiple times:

```
shoppingList = ['apples', 'bananas', 'cherries', 'dates', 'eggplant']

while True:
    myIndex = input('Enter a number to use as an index: ')
```

```
    if myIndex == ":
        break
    myIndex = int(myIndex)
    myElement = shoppingList[myIndex]

    print('The element at index, myIndex, 'is', myElement)

print('Bye')
```

Entering any value between 0 and 4 gives us the appropriate answer:

```
Enter a number to use as an index: 0
The element at index 0 is apples
Enter a number to use as an index: 1
The element at index 1 is bananas
Enter a number to use as an index: 2
The element at index 2 is cherries
Enter a number to use as an index: 3
The element at index 3 is dates
Enter a number to use as an index: 4
The element at index 4 is cggplant
```

Now run it again, but this time let's see what happens if we enter 100 as the index:

```
Enter a number to use as an index: 100

Traceback (most recent call last):
  File "/Learn to Program with Python/Chapter 7 Lists/Kalb Chapter 7 Code/
  IndexAsVariable.py", line 10, in <module>
    myElement = shoppingList[myIndex]
IndexError: list index out of range
```

Again, when you get a runtime error or a traceback, you should read the last line first. It tells you which type of error occurred. This error message says, "Index Error: list index out of range." It is extremely clear. You tried to access an element that is outside the valid range of the list indices. There is no element 100, so when you try to use that as an index, you get an error. Python has built-in range checking to ensure that you are using a valid number when you attempt to index into a list.

**Note**    Many other languages do not do range checking. If you use an out-of-range index in one of those languages, the code accesses a part of the memory of the computer that is not part of the list, and retrieves some arbitrary value found there. Sometime later, when you attempt to use the value, the program may crash mysteriously. Tracking down errors like that can be extremely difficult.

# Changing a Value in a List

So far, I've shown list index references on the right-hand side of an assignment statement. This is how you *get* (or *retrieve*) a value from a list. You can also *set* a value in a list—that is, replace the current contents of an element in a list by putting the list variable with its index on the left-hand side of an assignment, like this:

```
>>> shoppingList = ['apples', 'bananas', 'cherries', 'dates', 'eggplant']
>>> shoppingList[2] = 'cucumbers'
>>> print(shoppingList)
['apples', 'bananas', 'cucumbers', 'dates', 'eggplant']
>>>
```

This changes the value of an element at the given index to a new value. Notice that element 2 was 'cherries' but has been changed to 'cucumbers'.

Now you know how to change the value of a given element. Shortly, I'll show you how to change the number of elements in a list. Python people talk about lists as being *mutable*, which means changeable.

# Using Negative Indices

In addition to indices starting at 0 and going up to the number of elements minus 1, there is another way to index elements in a list. Python allows you to use negative integers as indices to a list. A negative index means to count backwards from the end, the end being the number of elements in the list. Here are the positive and equivalent negative indices for a list of five elements:

```
0        -5        <element>
1        -4        <element>
2        -3        <element>
3        -2        <element>
4        -1        <element>
```

Let's demonstrate with our shopping list:

```
>>> shoppingList = ['apples', 'bananas', 'cherries', 'dates', 'eggplant']
>>> print(shoppingList[-1])
eggplant
>>> print(shoppingList[-2])
dates
>>> print(shoppingList[-3])
cherries
```

When using a negative number as an index, Python takes the number of elements in the list and then adds the negative amount to get the positive index. Using our shopping list as an example, element –2 is 5 (the number of elements in the list) minus 2, which equals 3, for a value of 'dates'. Negative indexing is rarely used, but the main way to use it is to use –1 as an index as a quick way of getting to the last element in a list.

# Building a Simple Mad Libs Game

Let's build an old, popular game: Mad Libs. We'll start by getting input from the user, just like in a real Mad Libs game, and use the user's responses in our story. The starting version of this game has nothing to do with lists, but once we build the base game, we'll modify it to use lists.

The starting version of this program is all about strings. Remember that when we want to add strings together, it is called *concatenation*. And the concatenation operator is the plus sign between strings. Just as we can add a long group of numbers, we can also concatenate multiple strings. In this version of Mad Libs, our story is just one sentence that is built using concatenation. Our one-sentence story will be as follows:

<name> <verb> through the forest, hoping to escape the <adjective> <noun>.

```
# MadLib (version 1)

while True:
    name = input('Enter a name: ')
```

```
    verb = input('Enter a verb: ')
    adjective = input('Enter an adjective: ')
    noun = input('Enter a noun: ')

    sentence = name + ' ' + verb + ' through the forest, hoping to escape
    the ' + adjective + ' ' + noun + '.'
    print()
    print(sentence)
    print()

    # See if the user wants to quit or continue
    answer = input('Type "q" to quit, or anything else (even Return/Enter)
    to continue: ')
    if answer == 'q':
        break

print('Bye')
```

The program asks the user to enter the four parts of speech and then concatenates the sentence and prints it. Here's what our program looks like when it runs:

```
>>>
Enter a name: Weird Al Yankovic
Enter a verb: screams
Enter an adjective: orange
Enter a noun: dinosaur

Weird Al Yankovic screams through the forest, hoping to escape the orange
dinosaur.

Return/Enter to continue, "q" to quit:
Enter a name: The Teenage Mutant Ninja Turtles
Enter a verb: burped
Enter an adjective: frilly
Enter a noun: Frisbee
```

The Teenage Mutant Ninja Turtles burped through the forest, hoping to escape the frilly Frisbee.

Return/Enter to continue, "q" to quit: q
Bye
>>>

# Adding a List to Our Mad Libs Game

Now, we'll change the program. Rather than have the user enter a name, we'll build a pool of names and select one randomly for the user. The pool of predetermined names will be built as a list. We could use any names for our list, but to make our Mad Libs game fun, our list will look like this:

```
namesList = ['Weird Al Yankovic', 'The Teenage Mutant Ninja Turtles',
          'Supergirl', \
             'The Stay Puft Marshmallow Man', 'Shrek', 'Sherlock Holmes', \
             'The Beatles', 'Powerpuff Girl', 'The Pillsbury Doughboy']
```

Next, we want to choose a random name from this list. This particular list has nine elements in it. In order to select a random element from the list, we need to generate a random index between 0 and 8 (remember, list indices start at zero). In Chapter 6, we learned that to generate a random number, we use the randrange function in the random package:

```
import random
```

```
randomIndex = random.randrange(<lowerLimit>, <upToButNotIncluding>)
```

Again, our goal is to select a random number to use as an index of an element in the list. With our list of nine names, we would call random.randrange, passing in a 0 and a 9. It would return a random integer of 0 to 8 (up to but not including 9). The resulting program would look like this:

```
# MadLib (version 2)
```

```
import random
```

```
namesList = ['Weird Al Yankovic', 'The Teenage Mutant Ninja Turtles',
          'Supergirl', \
             'The Stay Puft Marshmallow Man', 'Shrek', 'Sherlock Holmes', \
             'The Beatles', 'Powerpuff Girl', 'The Pillsbury Doughboy']
```

```
while True:
    nameIndex = random.randrange(0, 9)  # Choose a random index into the
                                              namesList
    name = namesList[nameIndex]  # Use the index to choose a random name
    verb = input('Enter a verb: ')
    adjective = input('Enter an adjective: ')
    noun = input('Enter a noun: ')

    sentence = name + ' ' + verb + ' through the forest, hoping to escape
    the ' + adjective + ' ' + noun + '.'
    print()
    print(sentence)
    print()

    # See if the user wants to quit or continue
    answer = input('Type "q" to quit, or anything else (even Return/Enter)
    to continue: ')
    if answer == 'q':
        break

print('Bye')
```

In this version, we added the list of names and we replaced the code that asked the user for a name with code that randomly picks a name from the list provided.

# Determining the Number of Elements in a List: The len Function

The list of names could contain any number of names. Rather than hard-code an integer for the number of names in our list, we would ideally want to write code that would be able to work for any number of elements in the list. Therefore, we need a way to find out how many elements are in a list. Python has a built-in function for this, called len (short for *length*).

```
len(<listVariable>)
```

To find the length of a list—that is, the number of elements in a list—you call the len function and pass in the variable name that holds the list:

```
>>> shoppingList = ['apples', 'bananas', 'cherries', 'dates', 'eggplant']
>>> nElements = len(shoppingList)
>>> print('There are', nElements, 'items in our shopping list.')
There are 5 items in our shopping list.
>>>
```

There are five elements in our shopping list, but again, the elements are numbered 0 to 4. If we want to use random.randrange to choose a random element, we certainly want to use 0 as the low-end value because indices always start at 0. But random.randrange also requires an <upToButNotIncludingHighEnd> value. The len of a list is perfect for use as the high end with this call because it gives you one more than the last index to the list. Let's incorporate the len function into our Mad Libs program:

```
# MadLib (version 3)

import random

namesList = ['Weird Al Yankovic', 'The Teenage Mutant Ninja Turtles',
             'Supergirl', \
             'The Stay Puft Marshmallow Man', 'Shrek', 'Sherlock Holmes', \
             'The Beatles', 'Powerpuff Girl', 'The Pillsbury Doughboy',
'Sam-I-Am']
nNames = len(namesList)  # find out how many names are in the list of names

while True:
    nameIndex = random.randrange(0, nNames)  # Choose a random index into
the namesList
    name = namesList[nameIndex]  # Use the index to choose a random name
    verb = input('Enter a verb: ')
    adjective = input('Enter an adjective: ')
    noun = input('Enter a noun: ')

    sentence = name + ' ' + verb + ' through the forest, hoping to escape
    the ' + adjective + ' ' + noun + '.'
    print()
```

```
    print(sentence)
    print()

    # See if the user wants to quit or continue
    answer = input('Type "q" to quit, or anything else (even Return/Enter)
    to continue: ')
    if answer == 'q':
        break

print('Bye')
```

Notice that in this version, we've added another name to our list of names. But we also used the len function to set a variable, nNames, to the number of elements in our list of names. Finally, we used that variable in our call to randrange. Using this approach, we can put as many names in our list as we want, and the code will adjust at runtime for us.

# Programming Challenge 1

Similar to the modification to use a list of names, let's modify the program to include a list of verbs, a list of adjectives, and a list of nouns. The program should randomly choose a name, a verb, an adjective, and a noun. You can put as many elements as you want into each list, and the program should create and print a fully randomized Mad Lib.

Here is our Mad Libs program using lists for names, verbs, adjectives, and nouns. I have tried to choose silly words to generate humorous sentences:

```
# MadLib (version 4)

import random

namesList = ['Weird Al Yankovic', 'The Teenage Mutant Ninja Turtles',
             'Supergirl', \
             'The Stay Puft Marshmallow Man', 'Shrek', 'Sherlock Holmes', \
             'The Beatles', 'Powerpuff Girl', 'The Pillsbury Doughboy',
             'Sam-I-Am']
nNames = len(namesList)  # find out how many names are in the list of names
verbsList = ['screamed', 'burped', 'ran', 'galumphed', 'rolled', 'ate',
'laughed', 'complained', 'whistled']
```

```
nVerbs = len(verbsList)
adjectivesList = ['purple', 'giant', 'lazy', 'curly-haired', 'wireless
electric', 'ten foot tall']
nAdjectives = len(adjectivesList)
nounsList = ['ogre', 'dinosaur', 'Frisbee', 'robot', 'staple gun', 'hot dog
vendor', 'tortoise', 'rodeo clown', 'unicorn', 'Santa hat', 'garbage can']
nNouns = len(nounsList)

while True:
    nameIndex = random.randrange(0, nNames)  # Choose a random index into
    the namesList
    name = namesList[nameIndex]  # Use the index to choose a random name
    verbIndex = random.randrange(0, nVerbs)
    verb = verbsList[verbIndex]
    adjectiveIndex = random.randrange(0, nAdjectives)
    adjective = adjectivesList[adjectiveIndex]
    nounIndex = random.randrange(0, nNouns)
    noun = nounsList[nounIndex]

    sentence = name + ' ' + verb + ' through the forest, hoping to escape
    the ' + adjective + ' ' + noun + '.'
    print()
    print(sentence)
    print()

    # See if the user wants to quit or continue
    answer = input('Type "q" to quit, or anything else (even Return/Enter)
    to continue: ')
    if answer == 'q':
        break
print('Bye')
```

This code generated the following sample output—without any suggestions from the user:

The Pillsbury Doughboy burped through the forest, hoping to escape the giant Frisbee.

Type "q" to quit, or anything else (even Return/Enter) to continue:

Sam-I-Am complained through the forest, hoping to escape the wireless electric ogre.

Type "q" to quit, or anything else (even Return/Enter) to continue:

The Beatles ate through the forest, hoping to escape the lazy staple gun.

Type "q" to quit, or anything else (even Return/Enter) to continue:

The Beatles laughed through the forest, hoping to escape the ten foot tall unicorn.

Type "q" to quit, or anything else (even Return/Enter) to continue:

The Stay Puft Marshmallow Man galumphed through the forest, hoping to escape the giant unicorn.

Type "q" to quit, or anything else (even Return/Enter) to continue: q
Bye

# Using a List Argument with a Function

In the prior code, you may have noticed a pattern. For each of the four lists (nounsList, verbsList, adjectivesList, and nounsList), we have built essentially the same code. Whenever we wanted to select a random element, we chose a random index and then found the element at that index. Although this clearly works, whenever we see essentially the same code repeated, it is a signal that it is probably a good candidate to turn into a function. In this case, rather than repeat the same set of operations four times, we'll build a single function to select a random element from a list and call it four times:

```python
# MadLib (version 5)

import random

def chooseRandomFromList(aList):
    nItems = len(aList)
    randomIndex = random.randrange(0, nItems)
    randomElement = aList[randomIndex]
    return randomElement

namesList = ['Weird Al Yankovic', 'The Teenage Mutant Ninja Turtles',
             'Supergirl', \
             'The Stay Puft Marshmallow Man', 'Shrek', 'Sherlock Holmes', \
             'The Beatles', 'Powerpuff Girl', 'The Pillsbury Doughboy',
             'Sam-I-Am']
verbsList = ['screamed', 'burped', 'ran', 'galumphed', 'rolled', 'ate',
'laughed', 'complained', 'whistled']
adjectivesList = ['purple', 'giant', 'lazy', 'curly-haired', 'wireless
electric', 'ten foot tall']
nounsList = ['ogre', 'dinosaur', 'Frisbee', 'robot', 'staple gun', 'hot dog
vendor', 'tortoise', 'rodeo clown', 'unicorn', 'Santa hat', 'garbage can']

while True:
    name = chooseRandomFromList(namesList)
    verb = chooseRandomFromList(verbsList)
    adjective = chooseRandomFromList(adjectivesList)
    noun = chooseRandomFromList(nounsList)

    sentence = name + ' ' + verb + ' through the forest, hoping to escape
    the ' + adjective + ' ' + noun + '.'
    print()
    print(sentence)
    print()
```

```
    # See if the user wants to quit or continue
    answer = input('Type "q" to quit, or anything else (even Return/Enter)
    to continue: ')
    if answer == 'q':
        break

print('Bye')
```

In this version, we've built a small function called chooseRandomFromList. It is designed to expect to have one parameter passed in when it is called. It is expected to be passed in a list. The aList parameter variable takes on the value of the list passed in. We used a very generic name here because we do not know what the contents of the list are, and inside the function, we do not care. The function uses the len function to see how many items are in the list, chooses a random index, finds the element at that index, and returns that element. From the main code, we now call the function four times, passing in four different lists. This version of the code generates the same type of Mad Libs sentences as the earlier version, but it is easier to read and is less prone to errors.

It turns out that Python actually provides this exact functionality with a built-in function in the random package. The function is called choice. To get a randomized selection from a list, you make a call like this:

```
random.choice(<list>)
```

Here is a simple example:

```
>>> optionsList = ['rock', 'paper', 'scissors', 'lizard', 'Spock']
>>> anOption = random.choice(optionsList)
>>> print(anOption)
paper
>>>
```

# Accessing All Elements of a List: Iteration

Using bracketing syntax such as someList[someIndex], we have a way to access any element in a list. But we need a way to access *all* elements in a list. As a simple example, let's say we just wanted to print out the value of all the elements of a list. We can write this:

```
print(myList)
```

And that works fine. But it prints the list in the Python list syntax (including the square brackets and commas), and prints all elements horizontally. What if we wanted to print one element per line? Or what if the list contains numbers and we want to add them up? We need some way to get at all the elements of a list, but one at a time. That's called iteration.

---

**Definition**   *Iterate* means to traverse through, or visit all elements of a list.

---

Using code that we already know, we can build a loop using a while statement to get the job done. The following is some code to print our shopping list, one item per line. (This is for demonstration purposes only—it is *not* the best way.)

```
shoppingList = ['apples', 'bananas', 'cherries', 'dates', 'eggplant']
nItems = len(shoppingList)
myIndex = 0  # start with an index for the zero'th element
while myIndex < nItems:
    print(shoppingList[myIndex])
    myIndex = myIndex + 1  # increment the index
```

The idea here is to create a myIndex variable that starts at zero. Each time through the loop, we use that variable as an index, get the element at that position, and print it. Then we increment the variable, preparing for the next time through the loop. The code produces the correct result but seems a little "clunky." You have to remember a lot of details and get them all right to make this loop work correctly.

# for Statements and for Loops

The people who designed Python came up with a better way to handle iterating through a list. As long-time programmers, they noticed that this pattern of looping and doing something with each element of a list happens quite often. So they came up with an additional statement and a new type of loop that gives you an extremely simple way to iterate through a list. It is called the for statement. Here is the generic form:

```
for <elementVariable> in <list>:
    <indented statement(s)>
```

The for statement is made up of new keyword, for, a variable name, another new keyword, in, and then the list you want to iterate through. The statement ends with a colon. After the colon is an indented block of statement(s) called the *body* of the loop. Together, the for statement and the indented block are called a for loop.

The key to the for loop is the <elementVariable>. Here's how it works. The for statement causes the body of the loop to execute once for every element in the <list>. Each time through the loop, the variable you specify as <elementVariable> is set to the value of the next element in the list.

When you see a for statement, think of it as saying, "for each element in the list." Notice the new in keyword, which makes the for statement very English-like and readable. For example, let's say you saw a for statement like this:

```
for name in namesList:
```

You could read it as, "for each name in the list namesList"—that is, it would iterate through namesList, and in each iteration would set the variable name to the next name in the namesList.

The flowchart of a for loop is shown in Figure 7-1.

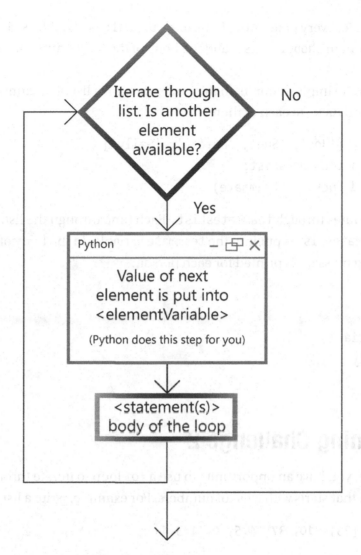

**Figure 7-1.** *The flowchart of a for loop*

Notice that you do not need to use any index to get the value of each element in your list. The for loop does that for you automatically. It takes care of the tedious bookkeeping. This syntax is extremely elegant and simple.

Let's build a simple example. Suppose you want to print out your shopping list with one item per line:

```
shoppingList = ['apples', 'bananas', 'cherries', 'dates', 'eggplant']
for anItem in shoppingList:
    print(anItem)
```

In this example, every time through the loop, the `anItem` variable is given the value of the next element in `shoppingList`, and the body of the loop prints each element on a separate line.

Here is another simple example. In this code, we have a list of teammates, and we want to say, "Good luck," to each of them:

```
teammatesList = ['Joe', 'Sue', 'Marcia', 'Sally']
for teammate in teammatesList:
    print('Good Luck ' + teammate)
```

This code iterates through `teammatesList`. Each time through the list, the next element of `teammatesList` is put into the `teammate` variable. In the body of the loop, a separate greeting message is printed for each person:

```
Good Luck Joe
Good Luck Sue
Good Luck Marcia
Good Luck Sally
>>>
```

# Programming Challenge 2

In this challenge, you have an opportunity to use a `for` loop to iterate through a list. Write a program that starts with a list of numbers. For example, write a list like this:

```
numbersList = [23, -10, 37, 4.5, 0, 123.4]
```

Then use a `for` loop to add all the numbers in the list. Print the total.

Here is the solution:

```
# Calculate the total of numbers in a list

numbersList = [23, -10, 37, 4.5, 0, 123.4]

total = 0
for number in numbersList:
    total = total + number

print('The total of all numbers is:', total)
```

The key to writing this code is to create a variable with a name like `total` and initialize it to zero. Then build a `for` loop to iterate through the list of numbers. Every time through the loop, the `number` variable is given the value of the next number in the list. In the body of the loop, add each value to the previous total. At the end, print the total:

```
>>>
The total of all numbers is: 177.9
```

# Generating a Range of Numbers

There are many situations where you would like to have a consecutive ordered sequence of integer numbers. For example, imagine you are doing some math, such as adding up the numbers from 1 to $n$. To help with problems like this, Python has a built-in function called `range` that creates an ordered sequence of integers. The typical way of calling the `range` function is like this:

```
range(<lowEnd>, <upToButNotIncludingHighEnd>)
```

The `range` function generates a collection of numbers that includes the `<lowEnd>` value and goes consecutively up to, but does not include, the value of `<upToButNotIncludingHighEnd>`. This approach to defining a range of numbers is identical to the way that `random.randrange` works.

---

**Note**    Because `range` is very often used with lists, you can call the `range` function with a single argument instead of two arguments. When called this way, the single argument represents only the high end of the range. The low end of the range defaults to be zero. For example, specifying `range(25)` is identical to specifying `range(0, 25)`, and will both create a collection of numbers from 0 to 24. To make things explicitly clear, we always use the `range` function with two arguments.

---

The interesting use case for the `range` function is in a `for` statement. Remember that a `for` statement is designed to let you easily iterate through a collection, typically through a list. The `range` function works seamlessly in a `for` statement. Here is a good example:

```
for number in range(0, 10):
    print(number)
```

This for statement iterates through a collection of numbers from 0 to 9. Every time through the loop, it assigns the next value to the variable number. This code would print the numbers 0 to 9, each on a separate line.

# Programming Challenge 3

This challenge gives you practice in using the range function in a for loop. The challenge is to write a program that allows the user to enter an integer. The program should calculate and print the total of all integers from 1 up to and including the user's number. For example, if the user enters 3, then the program should add up 1 + 2 + 3 and print the total of 6. If the user enters 10, then the program should calculate the total of 1 + 2 + 3 + ... + 10, and output a total of 55.

This is a solution to the challenge:

```python
# Calculate the total of numbers up to a number entered by the user

usersNumber = input('Please enter an integer: ')
usersNumber = int(usersNumber)
highEndOfRange = usersNumber + 1

total = 0
for number in range(1, highEndOfRange):
    total = total + number

print('The total numbers from 1 to', usersNumber, 'is', total)
```

This uses a similar approach to adding up a list of numbers as used in the previous coding challenge (by starting a total at zero and then adding each number). But in this challenge, the numbers to be added are not predefined. Instead, you must generate the numbers using a call to the range function. In order to get the proper upper bound for the call to range, you have to add one to the user's number, because the value of highEndOfRange is not included in the range itself. Here is the output of a few runs of this program:

```
>>>
Please enter an integer: 3
The total numbers from 1 to 3 is 6
```

```
>>> ============================== RESTART ==============================
>>>
Please enter an integer: 10
The total numbers from 1 to 10 is 55
>>> ============================== RESTART ==============================
>>>
Please enter an integer: 100
The total numbers from 1 to 100 is 5050
>>> ============================== RESTART ==============================
>>>
Please enter an integer: 1000
The total numbers from 1 to 1000 is 500500
>>>
```

**Note**   In Python 2, the `range` function worked differently. It created and returned a list. If the requested range was large, the list might have taken up a considerable amount of memory. In Python 3, the `range` function does not return a list. Instead, `range` has become a new type called a generator. A *generator* creates the next number in the sequence every time a new number is needed. Therefore, when using `range` in Python 3 in a `for` loop, there is a good chance that your loop may run faster than the equivalent code in Python 2. (The Python 2 `xrange` function is the equivalent of the Python 3 `range` function.)

# Scientific Simulations

In the scientific community, computers are often used to simulate the outcome of a large number of trials. In each trial, one or more pieces of data are given randomized values from all possible values. The scientists then look at the result of many trials to see if they can identify patterns.

Consider a simulation of rolling dice. In our simulation, we will perform many rounds of rolling two six-sided dice and then we will count the number of times that the dice generate *doubles* (that is, when both dice show the same value or *face*).

First, let's do a little math to see what we would expect for an answer. In each round, the first die can have any value from 1 to 6, and so can the second die. Figure 7-2 is a chart showing all possible rolls of two dice.

|  |  | Die 2 | | | | |
|---|---|---|---|---|---|---|
|  | 1 | 2 | 3 | 4 | 5 | 6 |
| 1 | Doubles |  |  |  |  |  |
| 2 |  | Doubles |  |  |  |  |
| 3 |  |  | Doubles |  |  |  |
| 4 |  |  |  | Doubles |  |  |
| 5 |  |  |  |  | Doubles |  |
| 6 |  |  |  |  |  | Doubles |

(Die 1 labels the rows, Die 2 labels the columns)

***Figure 7-2.*** *Possible rolls of two dice*

In this chart, the left side shows the possible faces for the first die. The top shows the possible faces for the second die. Out of the 36 possible combinations, 6 of them result in a doubles. That means that we should expect 6/36ths or 1/6th or 16.6666666 percent of rolls to be doubles.

Here's the code for doing this simulation. We'll ask the user to enter the number of rounds, and for each round, we'll simulate rolling two dice:

```
# Dice: count doubles in user-defined number of rounds

import random

# simulate rolling a six-sided die and return its value
def rollOneDie():
    # generate a random numbers between 1 and 6
    thisFace = random.randrange(1, 7)
    return thisFace

nDoubles = 0
```

```
maxRounds = input('How many rounds do you want to do? ')
maxRounds = int(maxRounds)

for roundNumber in range(0, maxRounds):
    die1 = rollOneDie()
    die2 = rollOneDie()

    if die1 == die2:
        nDoubles = nDoubles + 1

percent = (nDoubles * 100.0) / maxRounds
print('Out of', maxRounds, 'you rolled', nDoubles, 'doubles, or',
percent, '%')
```

In this program, the user specifies a number of rounds to roll two dice. As an example, let's say that the user wants to run ten rounds of dice rolls. We take the 10 the user gives us, convert it to an integer, and use it in a call to the range function. Passing 0 and 10 to range builds a collection of the numbers from 0 to 9. This is an example of zero-based counting; 0 through 9 is ten numbers, so the code will run through the loop ten times. The roundNumber variable is given the value of the next number in the collection, but we never use that variable anywhere in this loop. (If we wanted to report the result of every round, we could print that value each time through the loop.) The key concept here is that we are using the range function to help us go through the loop the correct number of times. In essence, the for loop is acting as a counter for us.

In each round (every time through the loop), we call the rollOneDie function twice. rollOneDie does what its name implies and simulates the rolling of a single die. We assign the answers to two different variables: die1 and die2. If these two variables have the same value, then we had a doubles, and we increment the count of doubles. When the loop is finished, we do a calculation of percentage (multiplying by 100.0 ensures that this will be a floating-point calculation), and we print the answer.

Here is the output of a sample run:

```
>>>
How many rounds do you want to do? 1000
Out of 1000 you rolled 158 doubles, or 15.8 %
>>>
```

If we want to run our simulation again, we would have to run the program again. Instead, let's make a modification to the code to allow the user to continue to enter different values for the number of rounds:

```python
# Dice - count doubles in user-defined number of rounds ... repeated

import random

# simulate rolling a six-sided die and return its value
def rollOneDie():
    # generate a random numbers between 1 and 6
    thisFace = random.randrange(1, 7)
    return thisFace

while True:
    nDoubles = 0

    maxRounds = input('How many rounds do you want to do? (Or ENTER to
    quit): ')
    if maxRounds == '':
        break
    try:
        maxRounds = int(maxRounds)
    except:
        print('Please enter an integer number.')
        continue  #  go back to the while statement

    for roundNumber in range(0, maxRounds):
        die1 = rollOneDie()
        die2 = rollOneDie()

        if die1 == die2:
            nDoubles = nDoubles + 1

    percent = (nDoubles * 100.0) / maxRounds
    print('Out of', maxRounds, 'you rolled', nDoubles, 'doubles, or',
    percent, '%')

print('OK Bye')
```

In this version, the code has been modified so that the main portion is now inside a larger while loop. Each time through the outer while loop, we ask the user how many rounds they want to do. The program also has a try/except to ensure that the value the user enters is an integer. The program keeps running simulations until the user presses Enter (Windows) or Return (Mac) to exit.

Here is the output of a run where we entered increasingly larger values:

```
>>>
How many rounds do you want to do? (Or ENTER to quit): 1000
Out of 1000 you rolled 164 doubles, or 16.4 %
How many rounds do you want to do? (Or ENTER to quit): 10000
Out of 10000 you rolled 1690 doubles, or 16.9 %
How many rounds do you want to do? (Or ENTER to quit): 100000
Out of 100000 you rolled 16638 doubles, or 16.638 %
How many rounds do you want to do? (Or ENTER to quit): 1000000
Out of 1000000 you rolled 166751 doubles, or 16.6751 %
How many rounds do you want to do? (Or ENTER to quit): 10000000
Out of 10000000 you rolled 1666941 doubles, or 16.66941 %
How many rounds do you want to do? (Or ENTER to quit):
OK Bye
>>>
```

There are two interesting things to note here. First, these simulations run quite quickly. Even with the last one, where we did ten million rounds, the program took only a matter of seconds. Second, notice that the more rounds we ran, the more accurate the answer was—the closer it got to the predicted value of 16 .6666666.

Python is becoming more and more popular in the scientific community because of these two reasons. Very often, scientists set up random simulations like this and then run them a large number of times to test out theories. Further, the random distribution of results is extremely even. The fact that we get a result very close to 16.666666 demonstrates this.

# List Manipulation

Let's go back to our example of a shopping list one more time, but this time consider what happens to a shopping list in a typical house. Right after a shopping trip, you might put up a new, empty shopping list on the refrigerator. As you notice that you are running low on groceries, you add items to the list. So maybe you add three items to your list one day, add two more the next day, and another the following day. Later, you move a box of cereal in your pantry and discover a hidden box of crackers that was on your list. You go back to the list and cross off crackers. If your list becomes long, you probably want to see if an item already appears in the list before adding it. You may also want to count the number of occurrences of an item to see if it appears more than once.

Python provides many built-in operations that allow you to manipulate and search through lists. The syntax of these operations is a little different from what we have seen before. This is the general syntax:

```
<listVariable>.<operation>(<any argument(s)>)
```

---

### THE "OBJECT" IN COMPUTER SCIENCE

In the world of computer science, there is an important concept called an *object*. My definition of an object is: *data—and code that acts on that data—over time.* Although objects are beyond the scope of this book, I can tell you that internally in Python, all lists are implemented as objects. The *data* (from my definition) is the content of the list—the collection of elements. The *code* (from my definition) is the operations that act on any list. These list operations are available on any list just because they are lists. In this sense, each list object "knows" how to do each of these operations. Generically, the code of every object is provided by functions, but these functions go by another name. When functions are applied to an object, they are called *methods of an object.* This is the syntax used to call a method of an object:

```
<object>.<method>(<any argument(s)>)
```

That is why the syntax of the list operations in Table 7-1 look the way they do.

---

*Table 7-1.*  *The Built-In List Operations*

| Operation | Description |
| --- | --- |
| `<list>.append(<thing>)` | Add `<thing>` to the end of a list |
| `<list>.count(<thing>)` | Returns the number of times `<thing>` was found in the `<list>` |
| `<list>.extend(<otherList>)` | Appends all elements in `<otherList>` to `<list>` |
| `<list>.index(<thing>)` | Returns the first index in the `<list>` where `<thing>` is found |
| `<list>.insert(<thing>, <index>)` | Inserts `<thing>` into the `<list>` at position `<index>` |
| `<list>.pop()` | Remove and return the last element from a `<list>` |
| `<list>.pop(<index>)` | Remove and return the element from a `<list>` at the given `<index>` |
| `<list>.remove(<thing>)` | Find first occurrence of `<thing>` in a `<list>` and remove it |
| `<list>.reverse()` | Reverse the position of all the elements in a `<list>` |
| `<list>.sort()` | Sort elements in a `<list>` from low to high |

The full documentation on all list operations can be found in the official Python documentation at `https://docs.python.org/3/tutorial/datastructures.html` in section 5.1.

The keyword in can also be used as an operator with a list:

`<value> in <listVariable>`

This syntax defines a Boolean expression that will generate a True if the value is found in the list, and a False if the value is not found. This type of expression can be used in an if statement or a while loop. The keywords not in can be used to reverse the result.

# List Manipulation Example: an Inventory Example

Consider an adventure game where you wander around a landscape. Games like this often allow you to maintain an inventory. At the start of the game, you have nothing, or an empty inventory. As you move about the environment, you find different items and can add them to your inventory. Later in the game, you may find yourself in a situation where you need to use something in your inventory to get out of a tricky situation. Here is an example of some code that can simulate these actions—first, let's build up an inventory from scratch:

```
>>> inventoryList = []  # start as an empty list.
>>>
>>> inventoryList.append('treasure')
>>> print(inventoryList)
['treasure']
>>>
>>> inventoryList.append('magic stones')
>>> print(inventoryList)
['treasure', 'magic stones']
>>>
>>> inventoryList.append('potion')
>>> print(inventoryList)
['treasure', 'magic stones', 'potion']
>>>
```

We started with an empty list and as we found items, we appended them to the list. Our list now has three elements. Later in the game, we learn that in order to kill a dragon, we need to throw some magic stones at it:

```
>>> print('magic stones' in inventoryList)
True
>>>
>>> indexOfStones = inventoryList.index('magic stones')
>>> itemToThrow = inventoryList.pop(indexOfStones)
>>> print(inventoryList)
['treasure', 'potion']
>>> print(itemToThrow)
magic stones
>>>
```

216

First, we check to ensure that we have the magic stones in our inventory by using the in operator. Seeing that we have the stones, we check to see where the magic stones live in our inventory by using the index operation. Once we have the index of where they are found, we use the pop operation to remove the magic stones from our inventory list and put them in a variable so that we can then throw the stones at the dragon.

# Pizza Toppings Example

Let's wrap up this chapter by building a program that creates and modifies a list, one that uses many built-in list operations, while loops, and for loops.

In this sample program, you own a pizzeria. Customers are allowed to get any toppings on their pizza that they want. Your program needs to cater to their wishes. The program will handle the following operations:

- a *or* add: Adds a topping

- c *or* change: Changes a topping

- o *or* order: Orders the current pizza

- q *or* quit: Quits the program

- r *or* remove: Removes a topping

- s *or* startover: Starts the current pizza over

Here is the pseudocode of our program:

```
Function To Show Pizza Toppings
    If there are no toppings, say there are none
    Else
        print each topping on a separate line

Print Welcome message, instructions, and large form of menu
Loop forever
    Show short form of menu
    Ask the user what they want to do:
    If "add"
        ask user what topping to add, add it
    Else if "change"
```

```
        find topping to change
        ask user what topping to change to, change it
    Else if "order"
        Show pizza being ordered
        Thank user
        Ask if they want to order another
        If yes, start over
        Else quit
    Else if "remove"
        Ask user what topping to remove
        Remove that topping if found
    Else if "startover"
        Reset to starting state
    Else
        Tell user we did not understand

    Show the current pizza
```

Based on that approach, we can write the code in Python. A key concept driving this program is that we will maintain the user's topping choices as a Python list. Each section of the code uses some different list operation to manipulate that list. This is the longest program we have seen so far. If you read through the code slowly to see how it matches the pseudocode, it should not be too hard to follow:

```python
# Pizza toppings program

# Function to show the list of toppings
def showPizzaToppings(theList):
    print()
    if len(theList) == 0:
        print('Your pizza has no toppings.')
    else:
        print('The toppings on your pizza are:')
        print()
        for thisItem in theList:  # iterate through the list, print each item
            print('   ' + thisItem)
    print() # blank line
```

```
# main code
print('Welcome to my Pizzeria, where you get to choose your toppings.')
print('When prompted, enter the first letter or the full word of what you
want to do.')
print()
print('---- Operations ----')
print('a/add          Add a topping')
print('c/change     Change a topping')
print('o/order        Order the pizza')
print('q/quit           Quit')
print('r/remove      Remove a topping')
print('s/startover    Start over')
print()

toppingsList = [ ]  # begin as an empty list
while True:

    print('What would you like to do?')
    menuChoice = input('   add, change, order, quit, remove, startover: ')

    if (menuChoice == 'a') or (menuChoice == 'add'):  # add a topping
        newTopping = input('Type in a topping to add: ')
        toppingsList.append(newTopping)  # append adds to the end of a list

    elif (menuChoice == 'c') or (menuChoice == 'change'):  # change a
    topping
        oldTopping = input('What topping would you like to change: ')
        if oldTopping in toppingsList:  # is it in the list
            index = toppingsList.index(oldTopping)  # find out where it is
            in the list
            newTopping = input('What is the new topping: ')
            toppingsList[index] = newTopping   # set a new value at that index
        else:
            print(oldTopping, 'was not found.')
```

```
    elif (menuChoice == 'o') or (menuChoice == 'order'):  # order the pizza
        showPizzaToppings(toppingsList)
        print()
        print('Thanks for your order!')
        print()
        another = input('Would you like to order another pizza (y/n) ? ')
        if another == 'y':
            toppingsList = [ ]  # reset to the empty list
        else:
            break

    elif (menuChoice == 'q') or (menuChoice == 'quit'): # quit
        break

    elif (menuChoice == 'r') or (menuChoice == 'remove'):  # remove a
    topping
        delTopping = input('What topping would you like to remove: ')
        if delTopping in toppingsList:  # check to see if the topping is in
        our list
            index = toppingsList.index(delTopping)  # find out where it is
            toppingsList.pop(index)    # remove it
            # The code above only removes the first occurrence of the
            topping.
        else:
            print(delTopping, 'was not found')

    elif (menuChoice == 's') or (menuChoice == 'startover'):  # reset to no
    toppings
        print("OK, let's start over.")
        toppingsList = [ ]  # reset to the empty list

    else:
        print("Uh ... sorry, I'm not sure what you said, please try again.")

    showPizzaToppings(toppingsList)  # show the list of toppings on the pizza

print()
print('Goodbye')
```

The key to this program is the toppingsList list variable in the main section of the code. It starts off as the empty list to represent a pizza with no toppings on it. The user can then add toppings to the pizza, and in response, the program uses the append operation to add to the end of the list. For a change operation, we first use the in operator to ensure that the topping to be changed exists in the list of toppings. If so, we replace the old topping with the new topping by using the index of where the old topping was found. Ordering winds up resetting the toppingsList back to the empty list. Should the user ask to remove a topping, the program checks to see if that topping is in the list, and if so, finds the index of the topping and uses the pop operation to remove that topping. Starting over simply resets to the empty list.

At the top of the program is a small function that prints the list of toppings. If there are none, the function prints that. Otherwise, it uses a for loop to iterate through the list of the pizza toppings and prints each one on a separate line. The output of a typical run could look like this:

```
Welcome to my Pizzeria, where you get to choose your toppings.
When prompted, enter the first letter or the full word what you want to do.

---- Operations ----
a/add            Add a topping
c/change         Change a topping
o/order          Order the pizza
q/quit           Quit
r/remove         Remove a topping
s/startover      Start over

What would you like to do?
add, change, order, quit, remove, startover: add
Type in a topping to add: mushrooms

The toppings on your pizza are:

   mushrooms

What would you like to do?
add, change, order, quit, remove, startover: a
Type in a topping to add: pineapples

The toppings on your pizza are:
```

    mushrooms
    pineapples

What would you like to do?
    add, change, order, quit, remove, startover: uvwxyz
Uh ... sorry, I'm not sure what you said, please try again.

The toppings on your pizza are:

    mushrooms
    pineapples

What would you like to do?
    add, change, order, quit, remove, startover: add
Type in a topping to add: bacon

The toppings on your pizza are:

    mushrooms
    pineapples
    bacon

What would you like to do?
    add, change, order, quit, remove, startover: change
What topping would you like to change: bacon
What is the new topping: pepperoni

The toppings on your pizza are:

    mushrooms
    pineapples
    pepperoni

What would you like to do?
    add, change, order, quit, remove, startover: r
What topping would you like to remove: pineapples

The toppings on your pizza are:

    mushrooms
    pepperoni

```
What would you like to do?
    add, change, order, quit, remove, startover: o

The toppings on your pizza are:

    mushrooms
    pepperoni

Thanks for your order!

Would you like to order another pizza (y/n) ? n

Goodbye
>>>
```

# Summary

In this chapter, you learned how to store, access, retrieve, and manipulate ordered collections of data called *lists*. You learned that lists are made up of elements, and each element has a position known as its *index*. Lists are defined in Python using the square brackets with elements separated by commas. We can refer to an individual element in a list by using the bracket syntax and specifying the index of the element we want. An index can be a constant, a variable, or an expression.

We built a fun Mad Libs game and then modified it to use lists. The program chose random words from a number of lists. We used the len function to find out how many elements are in a list. You saw how to use a list as an argument in a function call.

Then we explored the topic of iteration—the ability to visit all elements of a list. To do this, we used a for statement and built a for loop. We used iteration to sum up the numbers in a list. We found that the range function can be used to generate a list of consecutive integers, and is often used in for loops. We demonstrated how the range function can be used to run a loop through a set number of iterations.

Finally, we introduced a number of list-manipulation operations that can be used modify and search through the contents of a list. We ended with a demonstration program that maintains a list of pizza toppings as a list and uses these list manipulation operations to do so.

# CHAPTER 8

# Strings

Other than using them to nicely format output, we haven't talked much about strings. In this chapter and the next two chapters, we get heavily into strings. I'll show you how to manipulate them and find smaller strings within larger strings.

We started using strings in Chapter 1 with this statement:

```
print('Hello World')
```

Later, we talked about how you get input from the user as a string, and how to convert that input into a number:

```
>>>
>>> age = input('Please enter your age: ')
Please enter your age: 24
>>> age = int(age)
>>>
```

Then I showed you how to concatenate strings, like this:

```
>>>
>>> string1 = 'Hello'
>>> string2 = 'there'
>>> greeting = string1 + ' ' + string2
>>> print(greeting)
Hello there
>>>
```

This chapter covers the following topics:

- len function applied to strings

- Indexing characters in a string

- Accessing characters in a string

© Irv Kalb 2018
I. Kalb, *Learn to Program with Python 3*, https://doi.org/10.1007/978-1-4842-3879-0_8

- Iterating through characters in a string

- Creating a substring: a slice

- Programming challenge 1: creating a slice

- Additional slicing syntax

- Slicing as applied to a list

- Strings are not changeable

- Programming challenge 2: searching a string

- Built-in string operations

- Examples of string operations

- Programming challenge 3: directory style

# len Function Applied to Strings

Though it may not seem obvious, strings are very similar to lists. Think of a string as a list of characters. That is worth repeating: *think of a string as a list of characters*. Many of the operations you can do with lists, you can also do with strings.

For example, like a list, a string can be any length. To find out how many elements are in a list, you use the len built-in function. But len can also be used on a string:

```
>>> state = 'Mississippi'
>>> theLength = len(state)
>>> print(theLength)
11
>>>
```

# Indexing Characters in a String

Again, if we think of a string as a *list* of characters, then we can think of each character as an *element*. Further, we can use an index to refer to a character in a string the same way we index an element in an array. Remember from the definition, the index is the position of an element. With respect to a string, an index is the position of a character in a string. Given the earlier assignment statement, where we set the variable state to the string 'Mississippi', Figure 8-1 shows the indices of the characters in the string.

0  1  2  3  4  5  6  7  8  9  10

| M | i | s | s | i | s | s | i | p | p | i |

***Figure 8-1.*** *The indices of the characters in the string*

The string in Figure 8-1 has 11 characters. Notice that the characters in a string are numbered (or indexed) identically to the elements in a list. What we humans would think of as the first character (uppercase *M*) in Python is considered the character at index 0. The last character is always found at an index equal to the length of the string minus one. Because there are 11 characters in this string, the last character is found at index 10.

Similar to the indices of a list, you can also use negative indices to access the characters in a string, as shown in Figure 8-2.

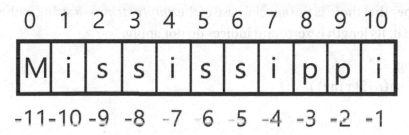

***Figure 8-2.*** *Negative indices of the characters in a string*

You can think of the negative index as the positive index minus the length of the string. For example, the first *p* in Mississippi is at index 8. But it can also be addressed by using –3, because 8 – 11 = –3. In practice, negative indexing is not used very often. Perhaps its most useful purpose is when you want to get the last character in a string; its index is always –1.

## Accessing Characters in a String

As with a list, we can also use the bracket syntax to identify a character at a specific index in a string:

```
>>> print(state[0])
M
>>> print(state[1])
```

```
i
>>> print(state[2])
s
>>>
```

If you try to access a character that is beyond the end of a string, Python will generate an appropriate error message:

```
>>> print(state[1000])   # only has 11 characters

Traceback (most recent call last):
  File "<pyshell#12>", line 1, in <module>
    print(state[1000])
IndexError: string index out of range
>>>
```

Remember that there is the special case of the *empty string*—a string with no characters in it. Its length is zero, and indices do not apply:

```
>>> myString = "
>>> print(len(myString))
0
>>>
```

# Iterating Through Characters in a String

Similar to the way we iterate through all elements of a list, we often want to iterate through all characters in a string. And similar to the while loop that I first showed to iterate through a list, we could build an identical while loop to iterate through a string:

```
# Iterate through a string
# This is the WRONG approach, just showing a concept!

state = 'Mississippi'
myIndex = 0
while myIndex < len(state):
    print(state[myIndex])
    myIndex = myIndex + 1
```

This code would correctly print all characters in the string, one per line. But just like when visiting all elements in a list, the for statement allows you to easily loop through (or iterate through) all characters in a string. Figure 8-3 is the same flowchart of a for loop that we saw earlier, but this time applied to iterating through the characters in a string.

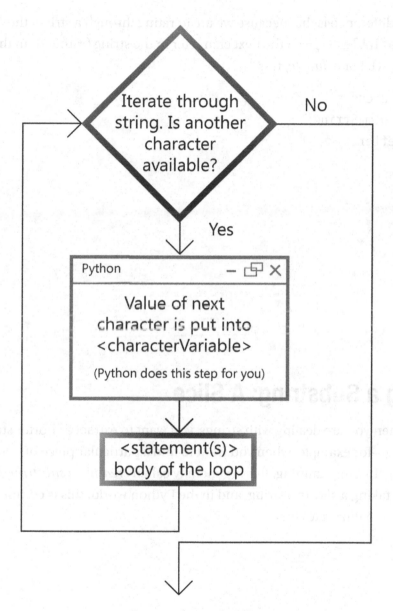

***Figure 8-3.*** *The flowchart of a* for *loop iterating through a string*

This syntax and the operation are identical to the for loop used to iterate through a list:

```
for <characterVariable> in <string>:
    <indented statement(s)>
```

The only difference is that because we are iterating through a string, the <characterVariable> is given the next character in the string (rather than the next element in a list). For example, this

```
myString = 'abcdefg'
for letter in myString:
    print(letter)
```

prints this:

```
a
b
c
d
e
f
g
```

# Creating a Substring: A Slice

Very often when you are dealing with strings, you want to extract a shorter string from a longer string—for example, when you want to find a particular piece of information within a string. In programming, this is generally called *creating a substring*. In Python, we do this by taking a *slice* of a string, and in the Python world, this is commonly called *slicing*. Figure 8-4 illustrates this.

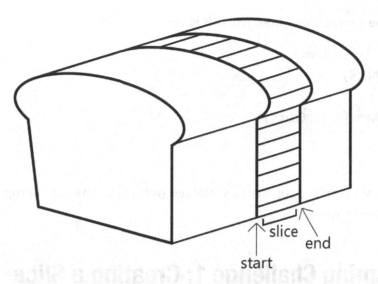

**Figure 8-4.** *Think of a string as a loaf of bread and take a slice of it*

To make a slice of a string, we have to specify the start index and the end index of the slice we want to create. If you think of a string as a loaf of bread, then the analogy of cutting a slice makes this concept very clear. But when you make a slice in a string, Python makes a copy of the characters in the slice. It does not remove those characters from the string.

To specify a slice, Python provides the following syntax:

```
<string>[<startIndex> : <upToButNotIncludingEndingIndex>]
```

Once again, we see this consistent concept of a Python range, where the start value is included and an ending value is not included. The character at `<startIndex>` *is* included as the first character of the substring. But the ending index, `<upToButNotIncludingEndingIndex>`, is the index of the first character that is *not* included in our slice. For example, we could have a string like this:

```
myName = 'Joe Schmoe'
```

To get just the first name, we want to take a slice starting at index 0 (the *J*), through index 2 (the *e*). Therefore, to create a substring that includes just the first name, we would ask for this slice:

```
>>> print(myName[0:3])
Joe
>>>
```

To get the last name, we would use this slice:

```
>>> nChars = len(myName)
>>> print(nChars)
10
>>> print(myName[4 : nChars])
Schmoe
>>>
```

Notice that you can use constants, variables, or expressions in defining the starting or ending value of a slice.

# Programming Challenge 1: Creating a Slice

To see if the concept of a slice is making sense, it's time for a programming challenge. In this challenge, we start with the following string:

```
months = 'JanFebMarAprMayJunJulAugSepOctNovDec'
```

Your job is to write a program that allows the user to enter a month number and print the three-letter abbreviation for that month. For example, if the user enters **1**, the program should print Jan. If the user enters **12**, the program should print Dec.

To get you going in the right direction, I'll give you the "scaffolding" of this assignment and leave the tricky part for you:

```
# Given a month number, find the three letter abbreviation for that month

months = 'JanFebMarAprMayJunJulAugSepOctNovDec'

monthNumber = input('Enter a month number (1-12): ')
monthNumber = int(monthNumber)

# Some code that generates the appropriate start and end indices.

# Generate the appropriate slice
monthAbbrev = months[startIndex : endIndex]
print(monthAbbrev)
```

This program can be done in two or three lines of code. (Do not cheat by using 12 if statements!).

**Hint**   Think about the slice indices that have to be created for Jan and the slice that has to be created for Feb, for Mar, and for Apr. Is there a pattern? Can you write some simple code that generates a solution to this pattern?

To work through a solution, let's start with a chart (see Table 8-1) that shows the mapping between the month number and the start index in our months string.

**Table 8-1.** *Mapping Month Number to the Related Start Index*

| monthNumber | | startIndex |
|---|---|---|
| 1 | Jan | 0 |
| 2 | Feb | 3 |
| 3 | Mar | 6 |
| 4 | Apr | 9 |
| | ... | |
| 12 | Dec | 33 |

The idea is to look for a pattern. If you look at these numbers long enough, you start to recognize that the start index can be calculated by taking the month number, subtracting one from it, and then multiplying the result by three. Writing this in Python looks like this:

```
startIndex = (monthNumber – 1) * 3
```

We can calculate the end index two different ways. We could look in our string and see which character is the end character for each month. (Remember, when making a slice, the end index is the index of the first character that is *not* included.) We could extend the chart as shown in Table 8-2.

**Table 8-2.** *Mapping Month Number to the Related Start and End Index*

| monthNumber | | startIndex | endIndex |
|---|---|---|---|
| 1 | Jan | 0 | 3 |
| 2 | Feb | 3 | 6 |
| 3 | Mar | 6 | 9 |
| 4 | Apr | 9 | 12 |
| | ... | | |
| 12 | Dec | 33 | 36 |

The values in the last column also make logical sense. Because each abbreviation is three letters long, it may now seem obvious that the end index is three more than each start index. Let's write the Python code for that:

```
endIndex = startIndex + 3
```

Now we plug those two lines into our program, and the full solution becomes the following:

```
# Given a month number, find the three letter abbreviation for that month

months = 'JanFebMarAprMayJunJulAugSepOctNovDec'

monthNumber = input('Enter a month number (1-12): ')
monthNumber = int(monthNumber)

startIndex = (monthNumber - 1) * 3
endIndex = startIndex + 3

# Generate the appropriate slice
monthAbbrev = months[startIndex : endIndex]
print(monthAbbrev)
```

Here are a few runs to test our code:

```
>>>
Enter a month number (1-12): 1
Jan
```

```
>>> ============================== RESTART ==============================
>>>
Enter a month number (1-12): 2
Feb
>>> ============================== RESTART ==============================
>>>
Enter a month number (1-12): 12
Dec
>>>
```

# Additional Slicing Syntax

Python also allows additional syntax if you want the slice to start at the first character or end at the last character of a string. You can leave off the starting index of a string like this:

```
<someString>[: <upToButNotIncludingIndex>]
```

This means to create a slice starting at the first character of a given string, and go up to but don't include the character at index <upToButNotIncludingIndex>. Similarly, you can also use this syntax:

```
<someString>[<startIndex> :]
```

This means start at the given index and include all characters through the end of the string.

Finally, you can use this syntax:

```
<someString>[:]
```

That means to make a copy of the whole string. Here are some examples:

```
>>> sample = 'This is a sample string'
>>> print(sample[10:])
sample string
>>> print(sample[:16])
This is a sample
>>> print(sample[:])
This is a sample string
>>>
```

235

# Slicing as Applied to a List

I didn't mention this in the last chapter, but the slicing syntax I have just shown for creating a substring can also be used with a list to create a sublist. The exact same syntax is used:

```
<someList>[<startingIndex> : <upToButNotIncludingIndex>]
```

For example:

```
>>> startingList = [22, 104, 55, 37, -100, 12, 25]
>>> mySubList = startingList[3 : 6]
>>> print(mySubList)
[37, -100, 12]
>>>
```

# Strings Are Not Changeable

There is one big difference between lists and strings. Strings are *not* changeable. Remember that I said that lists are changeable, or *mutable*. In Python terms, strings are *immutable*. You cannot set or change an individual character in a string. For example, let's say you wanted to change a specific character of a string to some other character. Let's try to change the second character of a given string to a different letter:

```
>>> someString= 'abcdefghijkl'
>>> someString[2] = 'x'

Traceback (most recent call last):
  File "<pyshell#18>", line 1, in <module>
    someString[2] = 'x'
TypeError: 'str' object does not support item assignment
>>>
```

This error message happens because strings are not changeable. However, you can always create a new string or reassign a different value to an existing string variable. To change the second character of a string to another value, you have to reassign a string or create a new string. To accomplish our task, we can take this approach:

```
>>> someString= 'abcdefghijkl'
>>> someString = someString[:2] + 'x' + someString[3:]
>>> print(someString)
abxdefghijkl
>>>
```

We've taken our original string, created a slice before the character we want, concatenated the letter we want, and then concatenated another slice starting right after the character we wanted to eliminate. Finally, we assigned the resulting string back into our string variable.

# Programming Challenge 2: Searching a String

In this challenge, I ask you to write a small function called countCharInString. It is passed the following two parameters:

- findChar: A character to find
- targetString: A string to be searched

It should return the number of times findChar is found in targetString.

You can test your function with the following calls:

```
print(countCharInString ('s', 'Mississippi'))  # expect 4

print(countCharInString ('p', 'Mississippi'))  # expect 2

print(countCharInString ('q', 'Mississippi'))  # expect 0
```

Here is a solution:

```
# Count a single char in another string

def countCharInString(findChar, targetString):
    count = 0
    for letter in targetString:    #  for each letter in the target string
        if findChar == letter:     #  if there is a match
            count = count + 1      #  increment the count
```

```
    return count
print(countCharInString ('s', 'Mississippi'))  # expect 4

print(countCharInString ('p', 'Mississippi'))  # expect 2

print(countCharInString ('q', 'Mississippi'))  # expect 0
```

And the following output is what we expect:

```
>>>
4
2
0
>>>
```

# Built-in String Operations

Although it is fun to build these types of functions, it turns out we don't have to. The people who built Python have done all this work for us. In fact, there is a whole set of string manipulation routines built in to Python.

Similar to our discussion of lists in Chapter 7, strings are also internally implemented as objects in Python. Because of that, you use the same syntax we used for list operations to invoke a string operation:

```
<string>.<operationName>(<optionalArguments>)
```

Table 8-3 describes the most commonly used built-in string operations.

***Table 8-3.***  *The Most Commonly Used Built-In String Operations*

| Operation | Description |
|---|---|
| `<string>.count(<substring>)` | Returns the number of times `<subString>` was found in `<string>`. |
| `<string>.find(<subString>)` | Returns the index of the first occurrence of `<substring>` in `<string>`. Returns −1 if `<substring>` is not found. |
| `<string>.index(<subString>)` | Returns the index of the first occurrence of `<substring>` in `<string>`. |
| `<string>.lower()` | Returns a lowercase version of `<string>`. |
| `<string>.lstrip()` | Returns the string with leading (left) whitespace removed. |
| `<string>.replace(<old>, <new>)` | Returns a version of `<string>` where all `<old>` are replaced by `<new>`. |
| `<string>.rstrip()` | Returns the string with trailing (right) whitespace removed. |
| `<string>.startswith(<prefix>)` | Returns True if `<string>` starts with `<prefix>`, otherwise returns `False`. |
| `<string>.strip()` | Returns the string with leading and trailing whitespace removed. |
| `<string>.title()` | Returns a version of `<string>` where the first letter of every word is uppercase, and all other letters are lowercase. |
| `<string>.upper()` | Returns an uppercase version of `<string>`. |

To see the list of all string operations, you can enter this in the Shell:

```
dir('abc')
```

That prints out a list of the names of all string operations. You can ignore the ones that start with one or two underscores. The ones that seem human readable (at the end of the list) are the interesting ones. The full documentation on all string operations can be found in the official Python documentation at `https://docs.python.org/2/library/stdtypes.html` in section 5.6.1.

# Examples of String Operations

In one of our earlier programming challenges, I asked you to write a function to count the number of times a character appears in a target string. Although it's good practice to write functions like this, built-in string operations are available to do much of the work like that for you. For example, the count operation does everything that our function does and more. The count operation finds not only a single character within another string, it finds a substring of any length in a string:

```
>>> myString = 'Ask not what your country can do for you, ask what you can
do for your country.'
>>> print(myString.count('o'))   # how many of the letter o
11
>>> print(myString.count('can do'))
2
>>>
```

Whenever you ask the user for a text-based answer to a question, you can never know whether the user will enter the answer in all lowercase, all uppercase, or some mix of cases. This is a problem because Python string comparisons are case sensitive. An answer of **OK** is not the same as **ok** and is not the same as **Ok**. Therefore, whenever you want to check for a user's text response, it is a good idea to convert the user's answer using either the lower operation (generally preferred) or the upper operation, before comparing their input. For example:

```
>>> userAnswer = input('Type OK if you want to continue: ')
Type OK if you want to continue: OK
>>> if userAnswer.lower() == 'ok':
        # user answered OK, do whatever you need to do to continue
```

Another example is where you ask the user a yes-or-no question. Again, you cannot know in advance whether the user will type **Yes**, or **yes**, or **yES**, or even just the letter **y**. You can use two string operations to handle all of these cases easily:

```
>>> userInput = input('Type yes to continue, no to quit: ')
Type yes to continue, no to quit: yes
>>> userInput = userInput.lower()
>>> if userInput.startwith('y'):
        #  user said yes, continue on with the program.
```

In this example, we take whatever the user types and convert it to lowercase. Then we only look at the first character to see if the user's answer starts with the letter *y*.

# Programming Challenge 3: Directory Style

It's time for the final programming challenge in this chapter. In this challenge, you ask the user to enter their name in the normal first name/last name style. Your job is to convert the name to directory style. Here are the details:

1.  Ask the user to enter their name in the form `<firstName><space>`
    `<lastName>`.

2.  Take the name the user enters and find the index of the space.

3.  Given that index, break up the user's string into a first name and last name.

4.  Create a new string by reassembling the name to be shown in directory style, `<lastName>,<space><lastName>`, and print it.

Here is the solution:

```
# First name last name, produce directory style:
fullName = input('Please enter your full name: ')
indexOfSpace = fullName.index(' ')
firstName = fullName[:indexOfSpace]
lastName = fullName[indexOfSpace + 1:]
print(lastName + ', ' + firstName)
```

This one is fairly straightforward. The key is to find the index of the space. Once you find where the space character is in the string, you can use the slicing syntax to create a slice for the first name (starting at the first character), and a slice for the last name (that goes through the last character).

Often in programming, in order to eliminate potential errors where the program might crash, we use *defensive coding* techniques to ensure that the user provided valid input. In this programming challenge, our original solution assumed that the user entered a single space character in between the names. But what if the user forgot to enter a space, or entered multiple spaces, or entered spaces at the beginning and/or ending of the name? We can check for all these cases without crashing.

Here is another version of the code that has some additional defensive coding to ensure that the program would not crash from these types of errors:

```
# Read in first name last name, produce directory style with error
detection

while True:
    fullName = input('Please enter your full name: ')
    fullName = fullName.strip()      # remove any spaces before or after
    nSpaces = fullName.count(' ')
    if nSpaces == 1:  # OK if there is a single space
        break
    print('Please try again.  Enter your name as first name, space, last name')
    print()

indexOfSpace = fullName.index(' ')

firstName = fullName[:indexOfSpace]
firstName = firstName[0].upper() + firstName[1:]    # Force first letter to
uppercase

lastName = fullName[indexOfSpace + 1:]
lastName = lastName[0].upper() + lastName[1:]    # Force first letter to
uppercase

print(lastName + ', ' + firstName)
```

In addition to checking for incorrect spacing, the code also makes sure that the first letter of the first and last names are uppercase. The following is a sample run, first with an error and then with the user entering the name in all lowercase:

```
>>>
Please enter your full name: joeschmoe
Please try again.  Enter your name as first name, space, last name

Please enter your full name: joe schmoe
Schmoe, Joe
>>>
```

# Summary

In this chapter, you learned to think of a string as a list of characters. You saw how the len function, indexing, and accessing characters in a string are identical to the way we use them in lists. You also learned that a for loop can be used to iterate through all the characters of a string. A new concept of a substring, known as a *slice* in Python, can be created using a new bracketing syntax.

You saw that the main difference between a string and a list is that a string is immutable (not changeable), whereas lists are mutable (easily changeable). I introduced a number of built-in string operations that can be used to manipulate string data.

The next two chapters continue our discussion of strings, with more examples of how strings are used in real-world programs.

# CHAPTER 9

# File Input/Output

In every program we have talked about so far, when the program ends, the computer forgets everything that happened in the program. Every variable you created, every string you used, every Boolean, every list—it's all gone. But what if you want to keep some of the data you generate in a program and save it for when you run the program later? Or maybe you want to save some data so that a different program could use the data you generated.

If you want to keep some information around between runs of a program, you need a way of having what is called *persistent* data—you want the data to remain available on the computer. To do that, you need the ability to write to and read from a file on the computer.

This chapter discusses file input/output, often shortened to *file I/O*, and covers the following topics:

- Saving files on a computer

- Defining a path to a file

- Reading from and writing to a file

- File handle

- The Python os package

- Building reusable file I/O functions

- Example using our file I/O functions

- Importing our own modules

- Saving data to a file and reading it back

- Building an adding game

- Programming challenge 1

© Irv Kalb 2018
I. Kalb, *Learn to Program with Python 3*, https://doi.org/10.1007/978-1-4842-3879-0_9

- Programming challenge 2

- Writing/reading one piece of data to and from a file

- Writing/reading multiple pieces of data to and from a file

- The join function

- The split function

- Final version of the adding game

- Writing and reading a line at a time with a file

- Example: multiple-choice test

- A compiled version of a module

# Saving Files on a Computer

There are many examples of storing data in a file that you are already familiar with. Think about a word processor or spreadsheet program. You create a document in your word processor or spreadsheet application, save it as a file on your computer, and then quit the program. Later, you reopen the word processor or spreadsheet program, reopen the saved file, and all the information you entered is brought back.

In fact, the Python source files that you write work the same way. You open the Python IDLE editor and create a Python source file (a document). As you edit your source code in IDLE, the content is kept in the memory of the computer. When you save it, the content (which is really just a string of text) is written to a file on the computer. You can then quit IDLE. Later, when you come back into IDLE and open the file, the text of your program is read in and displayed. IDLE displays the text, character by character, across each line. Whenever it finds an end-of-line character, it moves down to the first character of the next line. The content is displayed for you, and you can edit again. Whenever you save, the current version of your program is written out to the file—again, as a long string of text.

But as I said at the start of this chapter, when we run a Python program and then stop it or quit IDLE, any data that we have manipulated in the program goes away. In order to save data, we need a way to write data from a running program to a text file, and when we run the program again, be able to read that data back into our program. Python allows programmers to easily write and read files of text. When dealing with files that contain only text, the convention is to name such a file with a .txt extension.

# Defining a Path to a File

When you want to read or write a text file, you must first identify which file you want to write to or read from.

---

**Definition**   A *path* is a string that uniquely identifies a file on a computer. (It is sometimes called a *filespec*, short for *file specification*.)

---

A path is a string. There are two different ways to specify a path: absolute and relative. An *absolute* path is one that starts at the top of the file system on your computer and ends in the name of the file. For example, an absolute path might look like this in Windows:

`C:\MyFolder\MySubFolder\MySubSubFolder\MyFile.txt`

It might look like this on a Mac:

`Macintosh HD/MyFolder/MySubFolder/MySubSubFolderMyFile/MyFile.txt`

However, one of the great things about Python is that it is designed to allow programmers to write portable code, which can be used on different computers and on different operating systems. Because a path on one computer may not match a path on another one (because of different drive letters or drive names, or by being in different folders on different computers), most code that uses absolute paths is not portable.

Therefore, in this discussion, we will use relative paths. Instead of starting at the top of the file system on your computer, a *relative* path starts in the folder that contains your Python source file. We say that the path is *relative to the location of the source file*. That means any file we want to use or create resides either in the same folder as your Python source file or in a folder somewhere below that folder.

To see how this works, let's assume a folder structure like the one shown in Figure 9-1.

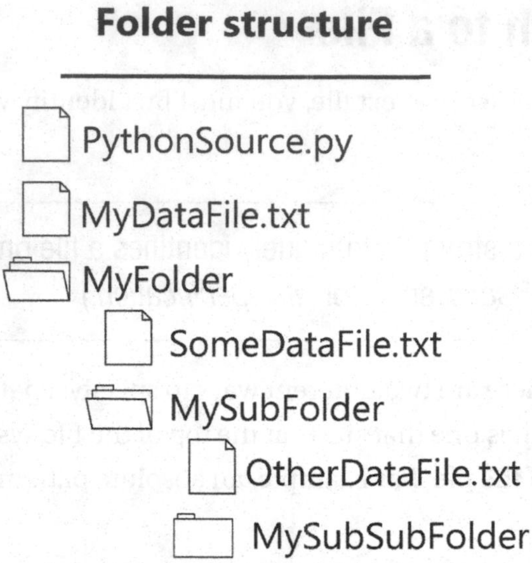

## Folder structure

```
📄 PythonSource.py
📄 MyDataFile.txt
📁 MyFolder
    📄 SomeDataFile.txt
    📁 MySubFolder
        📄 OtherDataFile.txt
        📁 MySubSubFolder
```

*Figure 9-1.*  *Example contents of a folder*

In this example, we have an enclosing folder located anywhere on a computer. In that folder, there is a Python source file named PythonSource.py and a text file called MyDataFile.txt. In addition to these two files, there is also a folder named MyFolder. Within MyFolder, there is another data file called SomeDataFile.txt and a folder called MySubFolder. Within MySubFolder, there is a data file called OtherDataFile.txt and a subfolder. From the point of view of the PythonSource.py file, Figure 9-2 shows the relative paths to the three different data files.

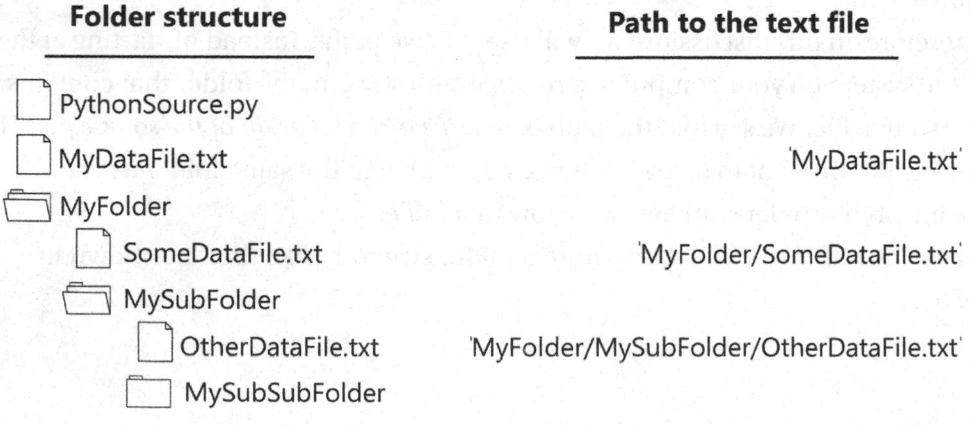

| Folder structure | Path to the text file |
|---|---|
| 📄 PythonSource.py | |
| 📄 MyDataFile.txt | `MyDataFile.txt` |
| 📁 MyFolder | |
|    📄 SomeDataFile.txt | `MyFolder/SomeDataFile.txt` |
|    📁 MySubFolder | |
|       📄 OtherDataFile.txt | `MyFolder/MySubFolder/OtherDataFile.txt` |
|       📁 MySubSubFolder | |

*Figure 9-2.*  *Example contents of a folder with relative paths to text files*

In the simplest case, if you are running a Python program and you want to use a file in the same folder, then the path for the data file is simply the name of the file as a string. In our example, if we were running `PythonSource.py` and we wanted to use the file `MyDataFile.txt`, we would specify the path as this string:

`'MyDataFile.txt'`

However, if you want to use a file that is inside a folder where the Python program lives, then you specify the folder name, a *forward slash* (/)—which is more commonly referred to as simply a *slash*—and then the file name, all as a string. From `PythonSource.py`, we get to `SomeDataFile.txt` by using this path:

`'MyFolder/SomeDataFile.txt'`

To go down two levels of folders and then find a file, specify the name of the first folder, followed by a slash, and then the next subfolder, followed by a slash, and then the name of the file. The following is the path to get to the `OtherDataFile.txt` file from `PythonSource.py`:

`'MyFolder/MySubFolder/OtherDataFile.txt'`

This can go on for any number of levels of subfolders. Just add a slash after every folder name, eventually placing the name of the file at the end. Through testing, we have found that although Windows uses the backward slash (\) as the folder separator character, using the slash (/) as the folder separator character in Python paths works correctly across operating systems. That means using the slash character in paths allows you to build platform-indepent relative paths. That is, this approach allows you to build programs with relative paths on a Mac, and the program will be able to access files in the same relative folders on Windows (and vice versa) without changing code.

# Reading from and Writing to a File

When you want to write to or read from a file, you first need tell the operating system that you want to *open* the file for reading or writing. To read, you read the contents of the file into a string variable. To write, you take the contents of a string variable and write that out to a file. When you are done reading or writing, you close the file.

Reading text from a file requires three steps:

1. Open the file for reading

2. Read from the file (usually into a string variable)

3. Close the file

Writing text to a file requires three similar steps:

1. Open the file for writing

2. Write a string (usually from a string variable) to the file

3. Close the file

# File Handle

Notice that whenever you deal with a file, you first need to open the file. In all operating systems, when a program opens a file, the operating system gives back a *file handle*. Rather than give you a formal definition of what a file handle is, you should think of it like the illustration shown in Figure 9-3.

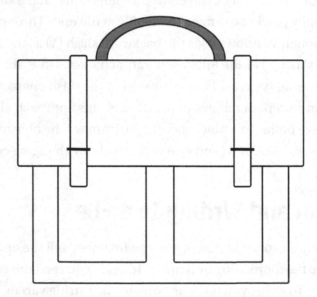

***Figure 9-3.*** *Think of a file on the computer as a bag with a handle*

The bag in Figure 9-3 represents a file. Any time you want to put something into the bag or take something out of it, you have to grab the handle. Similarly, any time you want to read from or write to a file on your computer, you have to use the file handle that the operating system gives you when you open the file. When you are done using the file, you have to close the file using the file handle; this is like releasing the handle of the bag.

The following is the core code needed to read from and write to a file. We will wind up *wrapping* this code into functions for you to use. For now, just pay attention to the basic steps involved.

Here is the code to read from a file:

```
fileHandle = open(filePath, 'r')  # r for reading
data = fileHandle.read()  # read into a variable
fileHandle.close()
# text read in is now in the variable called data
```

And here is the code to write text to a file:

```
# text to be written is contained in the variable textToWrite
fileHandle = open(filePath, 'w')  # w for writing
fileHandle.write(textToWrite)  # write out text from a variable
fileHandle.close()
```

Notice filePath (which is a string) and fileHandle (which is returned by the call to open). We use that file handle in the calls to read, write, and close.

Before attempting to read from a file, there is one more thing you need to do. Obviously, you cannot read from a file that doesn't exist. So, you need to check that the file you want to read from actually exists before you attempt to read from it.

# The Python os Package

In the same way that the random module provides a great deal of code for dealing with random numbers, there is a module that provides information about the operating system. It is called the os module. To use it, you first import it:

```
import os
```

For now, we're only interested in one operation that can tell us whether a file exists. Here's how to use it:

```
exists = os.path.exists(filePath)  #returns a boolean
```

The call to `os.path.exists` returns `True` if the file exists, or `False` if the file does not exist.

---

### OS MODULE

For anyone who is into UNIX, or who wants to write the equivalent of shell scripts (for automation), the os module is extremely important. The os module allows you to do many UNIX commands as Python statements. Here are just a few of the things the os module allows you to do:

- `os.listdir`: Generate a list containing the names of the entries in a directory (folder)

- `os.mkdir`: Make a directory (folder)

- `os.rename`: Rename a file

- `os.walk`: Generate the names of files in a directory (folder)

- `os.getcwd`: Get the current working directory (folder)

- `os.chmod`: Change the mode of a path

For a complete listing and detailed information, check the official Python documentation at `https://docs.python.org/2/library/os.html`.

---

# Building Reusable File I/O Functions

We now have enough information to build three very useful, highly reusable functions. We'll build the following:

- `fileExists`: Returns a Boolean to say whether a file with a given path exists or not

- `writeFile`: Takes a string of data and writes it to a file with a given path

- `readFile`: Reads the contents of a file and returns the contents to the caller

Let's start by creating a new Python source file named `FileReadWrite.py`. We'll put the following code into it:

```python
# FileReadWrite.py
# Functions for checking if a file exists, read from a file, write to a file

import os

def fileExists(filePath):
    exists = os.path.exists(filePath)
    return exists

def writeFile(filePath, textToWrite):
    fileHandle = open(filePath, 'w')
    fileHandle.write(textToWrite)
    fileHandle.close()

def readFile(filePath):
    if not fileExists(filePath):
        print('The file, ' + filePath + ' does not exist - cannot read it.')
        return ''

    fileHandle = open(filePath, 'r')
    data = fileHandle.read()
    fileHandle.close()
    return data
```

These functions provide very nice wrappers for the functionality. For example, now that we have written `fileExists`, we don't need to remember the details of the os module (that you need to use `os.path.exists`). Instead, we have built a simple function with a nice clean name of `fileExists`. We can reuse this function in any of our projects.

`writeFile` is very easy to use. You pass it a file path to write to and a string, and it writes the string to the file. If the file already exists, the older version of the file is completely overwritten by the new text.

The `readFile` function is also very straightforward. You pass in a path to a file, it checks to ensure that the file exists, and if so, does all the work to read all the text from the file and then returns that text to the caller. If the file does not exist, it prints an appropriate error message and returns the empty string to signify that there was no text to read.

# Example Using Our File I/O Functions

Let's work through an example of writing to and reading from a file. We'll start by selecting all the code we just built in FileReadWrite.py by using Command+A (Mac) or Control+A (Windows). Once all of it is selected, copy the code. Now open a new Python file. Paste the code into this new window. Save it with any name you want (be sure that the name ends in .py). Let's call this file TestFileIO.py.

Now we'll write some code to use these functions. The program we want to write will take a sample string, write it out to a file, and read it back in. Add the following after the three functions you pasted into this file:

```python
# Previous code from FileReadWrite pasted here

DATA_FILE_PATH = 'TestData.txt'  # path to the file as a constant

stringToWriteOutToFile = 'abcdefghijkl'   # contents could be anything,
this is just a test
writeFile(DATA_FILE_PATH, stringToWriteOutToFile)

stringReadInFromFile = readFile(DATA_FILE_PATH)
print('Read in: ', stringReadInFromFile)
```

When we save and run this program, we see this output in the Shell:

```
>>>
Read in:  abcdefghijkl
>>>
```

What has happened here is that this code called our writeFile function to write out some text to a file. Then we used the readFile function to read from the same file back in, and saved the text in a different variable. Because we are using the same file path for reading and for writing, we specified the path to the file as a constant.

After running the program, if we look in the folder where this Python source file resides, we now see that a file named TestData.txt is present. Opening that text file in any text editor shows that the contents consist of the string we wrote out.

# Importing Our Own Modules

We could certainly use this approach of copying and pasting these three functions into any program that wants to perform any file I/O. But consider what happens if we find a bug in our FileReadWrite.py file, or if we want to add more functions to help read files in different ways. In either case, we would have to go back into every Python source file that incorporated these three functions and modify the code there to fix the bug and/or add functionality. There is a better way.

You have seen how to use the import statement to make a built-in Python package available to our program. For example, you import the random package with this statement:

```
import random
```

When we import a package this way, we have to explicitly specify the name of the package when we make a call to a function in that package. For example, when we want to get a random number, we write this:

```
value = random.randrange(0, 10)
```

That is very clear. It says that inside the random package, we want to call the randrange function.

In addition to being able to import built-in modules like the random and the os modules, we can use the import statement to import our own Python files. If we are building a program where we need to read from or write to a file, we can import our own FileReadWrite.py file. We can use the same import statement, like this:

```
import FileReadWrite
```

---

**Note**    An important thing to notice is that when you specify a <moduleName> to import, you do *not* specify the .py extension. I explain why it is done this way at the end of this chapter. For now, remember to remove the .py extension when specifying a file to import.

---

After importing this way, you construct a line like this to write to a file:

```
FileReadWrite.writeFile('SomeFilePathToWriteTo', 'some test string')
```

However, there is another syntax available for the `import` statement. This alternative syntax allows you to specifically name which function(s) and/or variable(s) to import. This is what it looks like:

```
from <moduleName> import <functionOrVariableName>,
<optionalFunctionOrVariableName>, ...
```

If you use the `from` syntax, then when you make a call to a function, you do *not* specify the package name, only the function name(s). The advantage is simplicity. For example, if you wanted to make a call to `readFile`, you would write this:

```
from FileReadWrite import readFile

data = readFile('SomePathToAFileToRead')
```

The downside is twofold. First, if you import many source files this way, there is a chance of a name conflict. That is, it is possible that your main program file and one or more of your imported modules have a function or a variable that has the same name. (In that case, whichever one was used last overrides the earlier one(s)). Second, if you import many modules, it may be confusing as to where a function name or a variable name came from, because it could come from one of many different files.

For the sizes of programs used in this book, neither of these should be considered a serious drawback. Most Python programmers use the `from` syntax when importing their own modules.

As an even simpler approach, you can tell Python to import an entire file of code using a line like this:

```
from <moduleName> import *
```

The asterisk (*) means bring in the entire contents of that file. For example, to import the `FileReadWrite` module and read a file, we would write this:

```
from FileReadWrite import *

data = readFile('SomePathToAFileToRead')
```

Using this syntax essentially says to Python, "Bring in the full code of the `FileReadWrite` file as though I had written that code right here." See Figure 9-4.

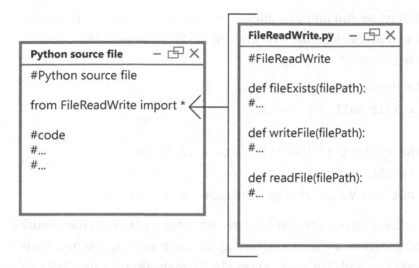

*Figure 9-4.* *Using the from statement to import contents of another file*

If you plan to use most of or all of the code from an external Python file, use the asterisk to bring in the entire file. The case where you should name the functions individually is when the Python file you are importing is extremely large and you are only using a small number of functions.

For our purposes, using the asterisk syntax is fine and ensures that all functions in the external Python file are available to our code.

Building and using external Python files this way allows programmers to split up large programs into a number of files. Having the ability to import these types of Python source files allows you to build up files of reusable code and incorporate this code into multiple programs. Further, finding and fixing a bug in a file like this fixes the bug in every program that imports the file.

# Saving Data to a File and Reading It Back

Now that we have built our three reusable functions in an external file, we can build a sample main program. Our goal is to write a program that counts the number of times it has run. To implement this, the program reads a data file that contains the number of times the program has been run. Every time the program runs, it should read the file, add 1 to the number, and then rewrite the file.

Immediately, we run into a problem: the first time we run the program, there is no file. So, we need to check for the existence of the file right from the outset. Let's first write the approach as pseudocode:

```
If the file does not exist
    Write a file with a 1 in it
Otherwise
    Read the content of the file into a variable
    Add 1 to the variable
    Write out the value of the variable to a file
```

When we feel that our approach solves the problem, we turn the pseudocode into a real Python program. We'll take advantage of the three reusable functions we already built: fileExists, readFile, and writeFile. To make things clear, let's use a constant for the file path:

```python
# Increment test

from FileReadWrite import *

# Here is a constant - the name of the data file that we will use
throughout
DATA_FILE_PATH = 'CountData.txt'

# Main program - reads from file, increments a counter, writes to file

if not fileExists(DATA_FILE_PATH):
    # The file was not found, this is the first time we are running the
    program
    print('First time - creating the data file.')  # for testing
    writeFile(DATA_FILE_PATH, '1')

else:
    # The file was found. We have run this program before
    count = readFile(DATA_FILE_PATH)
    print('Found the file, data read was: ', count)  # for testing
    count = int(count)
    count = count + 1
    textToWrite = str(count)
        writeFile(DATA_FILE_PATH, textToWrite)

print('This was run number:', count)
```

258

Because we already have our reusable functions in `FileReadWrite.py`, we first use an `import` statement to bring in the code of the three functions that are found in that file.

Now let's walk through the logic of the program. The first time the program runs, the data file does not exist. So, we explicitly write out the string `'1'` to our external data file.

Every subsequent time we run the program, the file does exist, and the `else` clause will run. In the code of the `else` block, we read in the contents of the file (which is just a number, as text), we convert what we read into an integer and then increment it to add 1 to the number of times we have run the program. Finally, we convert the number back to a string and write out the new value to the file.

Here is the output of several runs of the program:

```
>>>
First time - creating the data file.
This was run number: 1
>>> ============================== RESTART ==============================
>>>
Found the file, data read was:  1
This was run number: 2
>>> ============================== RESTART ==============================
>>>
Found the file, data read was:  2
This was run number: 3
>>> ============================== RESTART ==============================
>>>
Found the file, data read was:  3
This was run number: 4
>>> ============================== RESTART ==============================
>>>
Found the file, data read was:  4
This was run number: 5
```

As you can see from the output, the code following the `if` ran the first time that the program ran. In every subsequent run, the code following the `else` ran because the program found the data file.

# Building an Adding Game

Let's take these concepts and use them in a real program—a simple adding game for kids. Rather than build a large game in one shot, we'll split it up into four versions, adding complexity as we go.

Let's start by building the core part of the game, where we ask the user to add two integers and then see if the user answers correctly. We'll expand the program to allow for any number of questions and keep score. Then we'll expand it further to write out the score when we exit the program, and then read the score back in when we start up the program again. Finally, we'll modify the program yet again to write out and read back in several pieces of information about the game.

You'll write the first version of the game as a programming challenge.

# Programming Challenge 1

Build a simple adding game. These are the details:

1. Allow the program to choose two random integers, each between 0 and 10.

2. Build and pose an addition question for the user, using the following form:

   What is <num1> + <num2>?

3. Compare the user's answer to the correct answer.

4. Give feedback: correct or incorrect (if incorrect, show the correct answer).

Here is the output of two sample runs of the program:

```
>>>
What is:  10 + 3?  13
Yes, you got it!
>>>

>>>
What is:  10 + 5?  14
No, sorry, the correct answer was:    15
>>>
```

Your code should look something like this:

```
# Adding game version 1

import random

firstNumber = random.randrange(0, 11)
secondNumber = random.randrange(0, 11)
correctAnswer = firstNumber + secondNumber

question = 'What is:  ' + str(firstNumber) + ' + ' + str(secondNumber) + '? '
userAnswer = input(question)
userAnswer = int(userAnswer)

if userAnswer == correctAnswer:
    print('Yes, you got it!')
else:
    print('No, sorry, the correct answer was:  ', correctAnswer)
```

The key to this program is generating two random numbers within the appropriate range and adding them together so that you know what the correct answer should be. Then you ask the user for their answer. Finally, you compare the correct answer to the user's answer and give appropriate feedback.

# Programming Challenge 2

Once you have the first challenge code running correctly, the next steps are to modify it to allow the program to run in a loop and keep score. The details are as follows:

1. Add a score counter (start at zero).

2. Add a loop (to ask multiple questions).

3. If the user presses Return/Enter, exit loop.

4. If the user answers correctly, add 2 points to score.

5. Otherwise, for an incorrect answer, subtract 1 point from score.

6. Print the score.

7. When the user chooses to leave the program, say goodbye.

Here is the output of a sample run of this version of the program:

```
What is:  7 + 6?  13
Yes, you got it!
Your current score is:  2

What is:  1 + 4?  5
Yes, you got it!
Your current score is:  4

What is:  4 + 1?  5
Yes, you got it!
Your current score is:  6

What is:  10 + 1?  11
Yes, you got it!
Your current score is:  8

What is:  3 + 8?  9
No, sorry, the correct answer was:  11
Your current score is:  7

What is:  5 + 0?
Thanks for playing
>>>
```

This is the solution to the challenge:

```python
# Adding game version 2

import random

score = 0

# Main loop
while True:
    firstNumber = random.randrange(0, 11)
    secondNumber = random.randrange(0, 11)
    correctAnswer = firstNumber + secondNumber

    question = 'What is:  ' + str(firstNumber) + ' + ' + str(secondNumber)
    + '? '
```

```
    userAnswer = input(question)
    if userAnswer == ":
        break  # user wants to quit

    userAnswer = int(userAnswer)

    if userAnswer == correctAnswer:
        print('Yes, you got it!'(
        score = score + 2

    else:
        print('No, sorry, the correct answer was:  ', correctAnswer)
        score = score - 1

    print(Your current score is: ', score)
    print()

print('Thanks for playing')
```

In this version, the changes are relatively small. We kept score (using a variable called score) by adding two points for each correct answer and subtracting one if an answer was incorrect. The important change was to put the main portion of the code in a while loop so that the user had as many addition questions as they wanted. We also checked for no answer (the empty string), which is the indication that the user wanted to quit the game.

# Writing/Reading One Piece of Data to and from a File

In the next version of the game, let's add the ability to have persistent data by modifying the program so that when the user quits the program, the code writes out the score to a file. When the user chooses to start the program again, the score is read in from the file, and the program starts up using the previous score.

I'll present the code of this version, as follows, and then I'll explain the changes:

```
# Adding game version 3
# Save only the score

import random
from FileReadWrite import *    # means import everything as though it were
typed here
```

```
DATA_FILE_PATH = 'GameData.txt'

# Start up code
if not fileExists(DATA_FILE_PATH):
    score = 0
    print('Hi, and welcome to the adding game.')
else:
    score = readFile(DATA_FILE_PATH)
    score = int(score)
    print('Welcome back. Your saved score is:', score)

# Main loop

while True:
    firstNumber = random.randrange(0, 11)
    secondNumber = random.randrange(0, 11)
    correctAnswer = firstNumber + secondNumber

    question = 'What is:  ' + str(firstNumber) + ' + ' + str(secondNumber)
    + '? '
    userAnswer = input(question)
    if userAnswer == ":
        break

    userAnswer = int(userAnswer)

    if userAnswer == correctAnswer:
        print('Yes, you got it!')
        score = score + 2
    else:
        print('No, sorry, the correct answer was:  ', correctAnswer)
        score = score - 1

    print('Your current score is: ', score)
    print()

writeFile(DATA_FILE_PATH, str(score))
print('Thanks for playing')
```

In this version, the key changes are at the beginning and end of the program. The first thing we do in this program is bring in the code we developed earlier, which allows us to do file I/O. We import the code using this line:

```
from FileReadWrite import *
```

That gives us access to the previously written `fileExists`, `readFile`, and `writeFile` functions. In order for this `import` to work correctly, the source file we are developing and the `FileReadWrite.py` file must be in the same folder.

Next, we define a constant for our file path. Any file name will work, so let's choose the very clear name of `GameData.txt`. Because the content is string data, we choose to use a `.txt` extension, meaning that it is filled with only text.

When the program starts, similar to our earlier `IncrementTest` program, we check for the existence (actually, the nonexistence) of our data file. If the data file does not exist, then we know this is the first time we are running the program. In that case, we welcome the user to our game and set our `score` variable to 0. If we find that the file does exist, we read the contents of the file into our `score` variable. Data read from a text file comes in as text in the same way that `input` produces text. Therefore, we have to convert the score to an integer. Then we welcome the user back to the game and tell them their previous score.

The central part of the code is identical. The user plays as many rounds as they like. When the user is ready to quit the program, we take the current score and write it out to the data file. Finally, we thank the user for playing.

The data file is created (or updated) in the same folder as the source file and the `FileReadWrite.py` file. You can easily open it and view the contents with any text editor. When we look at the contents of the file after playing any number of rounds, all we see is a text version of the most recent score. If you write to a file that already exists (any run after the first run), the previous contents of the file are overwritten.

# Writing/Reading Multiple Pieces of Data to and from a File

In the final version of the game, we'll want to keep track of, write out, and read back four pieces of information:

- User name
- Score
- Number of problems tried
- Number of problems answered correctly

To write out and read back multiple pieces of information, we need two more built-in functions: `split` and `join`.

# The join Function

Let's start with the `join` function. The data we want to write to a file must be one long text string. If we want to write out multiple pieces of data, we need to build a string that incorporates of all of them. We'll do this in two steps:

1. Take all data that we want to save (converting any numbers to string versions) and then create a list containing the data.

2. Combine the list into a string.

The purpose of the `join` function is to take a list (of strings) and concatenate all elements to create a single long string. In the resulting string, each piece of original data is separated by a character of your choice. The comma is the most typical character used to separate this type of data. `join` is a string operation, but it has an odd syntax. It is most often used in an assignment statement, like this:

```
<string> = <separatorCharacter>.join(<list>)
```

`join` takes the list (of strings) and creates a new string by concatenating all the elements of the list, separated by the given separator character. Here is an example:

```
>>> myList = ['abc', 'de', '123', 'fghi', '-3.21']
>>>
>>> # Use a comma as a separator character
```

```
>>> myString = ','.join(myList)
>>>
>>> print(myString)
abc,de,123,fghi,-3.21
>>>
```

Here you can see that the `join` function has taken a list of string data and created a single comma-separated string.

## The split Function

The other built-in function is the `split` function, which takes a string and splits it at every point where it finds a given separator character, into multiple pieces of data in a list. `split` is typically used in an assignment statement, like this:

```
<list> = <string>.split(<separatorChar>)
```

Here is an example:

```
>>>
>>> myString = 'abc,de,123,fghi,-3.21'
>>>
>>> myList = myString.split(',')
>>>
>>> print(myList)
['abc', 'de', '123', 'fghi', '-3.21']
>>>
```

Because `split` is an operation on a string, we can use it after we read in data from a file and separate out the individual pieces of data that were used to make up the string when the file was written.

Because of the syntax, `split` and `join` are both considered string operations. `join` operates on a separator character, whereas `split` operates on a string to be broken apart. But these operations perform complimentary or opposite actions. Think of it like this: `join` is passed a list and produces a string, but `split` takes a string and produces a list. `join` is often used for writing out to a file, whereas `split` is often used for reading data in from a file.

# Final Version of the Adding Game

Now, in addition to remembering the score, let's modify the game further by keeping track of three more pieces of data. The first time we play the game, we'll ask for and remember the user's name. We'll also remember the number of problems the user has seen and the number of problems the user has answered correctly.

To keep track of this additional information, we'll add three more variables: userName, nProblems, and nCorrect. When the user chooses to quit the program (by pressing Return or Enter), we'll add some code to write the information we want to remember out to a file. As a format for the content of the file, we'll use the following:

```
<name>,<score>,<nProblems>,<nCorrect>
```

For example, after playing the game once and answering 14 out of 15 questions correctly, the file for our user Joe Schmoe looks like this:

```
Joe Schmoe,27,15,14
```

Here is the code of the final version that implements these changes. The modifications are significant, but everything should be understandable:

```
# Adding Game version 4
# Saving lots of data

import random
from FileReadWrite import *     # means import everything as though it were
typed here

DATA_FILE_PATH = 'AddingGameData.txt'

#  Main program starts here

if not fileExists(DATA_FILE_PATH):
    userName = input('You must be new here, please enter your name:  ')
    score = 0
    nProblems = 0
    nCorrect = 0

    print('To quit the game, press RETURN/ENTER and your info will be saved')
    print('OK', userName, "let's get started ...")
    print()
```

```python
else:
    savedDataString = readFile(DATA_FILE_PATH)  #read the whole file into a
    variable
    savedDataList = savedDataString.split(',')  # turn that into a list
    userName = savedDataList[0]
    score = savedDataList[1]
    score = int(score)
    nProblems = savedDataList[2]
    nProblems = int(nProblems)
    nCorrect = int(savedDataList[3])  # can do both in a  combined step

    print('Welcome back', userName, 'nice to see you again! ')
    print('Your current score is: ', score)
    print()

# Main loop

while True:
    firstNumber = random.randrange(0, 11)
    secondNumber = random.randrange(0, 11)
    correctAnswer = firstNumber + secondNumber

    question = 'What is: ' + str(firstNumber) + ' + ' + str(secondNumber)
    + '? '
    userAnswer = input(question)
    if userAnswer == '':
        break

    userAnswer = int(userAnswer)
    nProblems = nProblems + 1

    if userAnswer == correctAnswer:
        print('Yes, you got it!')
        score = score + 2
        nCorrect = nCorrect + 1
```

```
    else:
        print('No, sorry, the correct answer was:  ', correctAnswer)
        score = score - 1

    print('Your current score is: ', score)
    print()

print('Thanks for playing')
print()
print('You have tried', nProblems, 'problems and you have correctly
answered', nCorrect)

# Make a list of the useruserName,  userScore, nProblems, nCorrect then
# create a string from that using join
dataList = [userName, str(score), str(nProblems), str(nCorrect)]
outputText = ','.join(dataList)

writeFile(DATA_FILE_PATH, outputText)
```

We chose to use a different file path from the previous version because this version writes out different data.

As with the previous version, we start by checking to see if our data file exists. If it does not, we conclude that this is the first time the user is playing the game. If the file does exist, we assume the user has played the game before and we need to read in the data from the file.

If this is the first time playing the game, we give a greeting to the user, ask their name, and initialize the variables score, nProblems, and nCorrect all to zero.

If the user has played the game before, we read the contents of the file using the readFile function we developed earlier and use the split function on the data that we read in. That generates a list. In the list that is created, we know that element 0 contains the user's name, element 1 contains the score, element 2 contains the number of problems, and element 3 contains the number of problems answered correctly. We extract these pieces of information from the list and store them into the same three variables. Finally, we print out some messages to welcome the user back and tell them their current score.

The central part of the game is nearly identical, except we have added code to increment the number of problems asked and to increment the number of problems answered correctly.

When the user chooses to quit the program, we tell them the number of problems they have seen and the number they answered correctly. Then we take the data we want to save, build a list out of it (while ensuring that each piece of information is converted to a string), and then use the `join` function to turn that list into one comma-separated string. Finally, we write that string out to the data file using the `writeFile` function we developed earlier.

Though this program was set up to write out and read in four pieces of data, you can use these same techniques to write out, and later read back in, any number of pieces of data.

# Writing and Reading a Line at a Time with a File

In the code we have developed so far, you have seen how to write a text file from a single variable or read a text file into a single variable. But there are times where we want to write data to a file a line at a time or read data from a file a line at a time. Here are five more small functions that should be added to the bottom of the earlier file, `FileReadWrite.py`. These additional functions allow us to write and read files this way:

```
#   (Earlier code for fileExists, writeFile, readFile)
#
#  Functions for opening a file, writing & reading a line at a time, and
closing the file

def openFileForWriting(filePath):
    fileHandle = open(filePath, 'w')
    return fileHandle

def writeALine(fileHandle, lineToWrite):
    # Add a newline character '\n' at the end and write the line
    lineToWrite = lineToWrite + '\n'
    fileHandle.write(lineToWrite)

def openFileForReading(filePath):
    if not fileExists(filePath):
        print('The file, ' + filePath + ' does not exist - cannot read it.')
        return "
```

```
    fileHandle = open(filePath, 'r')
    return fileHandle

def readALine(fileHandle):
    theLine = fileHandle.readline()

    # This is a special check for attempting to read past the end of the
      file (EOF).
    # If this occurs, let's return something unusual: False (which is not a
      string)
    # If the caller wishes to check, their code can easily detect the end
      of the file this way
    if not theLine:
        return False

    # If the line ends with a newline character '\n', then strip that off
      the end
    if theLine.endswith('\n'):
        theLine = theLine.rstrip('\n')

    return theLine

def closeFile(fileHandle):
    fileHandle.close()
```

Here is the basic idea of how to use these functions. If you have a case where you want to write data one line at a time, you have to follow the same three steps outlined earlier: open the file, write to the file, and close the file. Rather than doing the three steps in a single call (as we did with writeFile), here we use three separate functions to implement the three steps:

- openFileForWriting: Opens the file for writing.

- writeALine: Call this as many times as you want; each call writes a line of text.

- closeFile: Closes the file.

Feel free to read the code of these three functions, but once you know that they work correctly, you do not need to remember the details of the implementation. By adding these functions to the earlier FileReadWrite.py file, these functions become part of your reusable library. As discussed earlier in the chapter, to make these functions available in your Python source file, you import the FileReadWrite package using this line:

```
from FileReadWrite import *
```

Let's look at an example of how you might use these new functions. In the following code, we will write three lines of text to a file named MultiLineData.txt. The FileReadWrite.py file must be in the same folder as our source file because it is imported into the source file:

```
# Write multiple lines of text to a file

from FileReadWrite import *

DATA_FILE_PATH = 'MultiLineData.txt'

myFileHandle = openFileForWriting(DATA_FILE_PATH)

data1 = 'Here is some data as a string'
writeALine(myFileHandle, data1)
data2 = 'Here is a second line of string data'
writeALine(myFileHandle, data2)

# Could have some code join several pieces of data into a single string
data3 = '123,Joe Schmoe,123.45,0'
writeALine(myFileHandle, data3)

closeFile(myFileHandle)
```

The code should be very clear. We open the file for writing, write three lines of text, and then close the file. The key to using these functions is that the call to open the file returns a file handle. You then use this file handle in every call to writeALine. When you are done writing, you close the file with a call to closeFile passing in the file handle. Running this program creates a text file (in the same folder as the program) called MultiLineData.txt, with the following contents:

```
Here is some data as a string
Here is a second line of string data
123,Joe Schmoe,123.45,0
```

If we have a file such as this `MultiLineData.txt` and we want to read it into our program, we perform very similar steps: open the file for reading, read the data, close the file. We use calls to the following functions to read in the data:

- `openFileForReading`: Opens the file for reading.

- `readALine`: Call this as many times as you need to; each call reads in a line of text.

- `closeFile`: Closes the file.

To read in the data that was previously written out to our `MultiLineData.txt` file, we could have a program like this:

```
# Read in multiple lines of text

DATA_FILE_PATH = 'MultiLineData.txt'

myFileHandle = openFile(DATA_FILE_PATH)

data1 = readALine(myFileHandle)
print(data1)
data2 = readALine(myFileHandle)
print(data2)
data3 = readALine(myFileHandle)
print(data3)
# Could add code to split data3 into several different pieces of data

closeFile(myFileHandle)
```

Again, the key concept is the file handle that is generated by a call to `openFileForReading`. We use this file handle in every call to `readALine`. When we are finished reading, we call `closeFile`, passing in the file handle.

Having all these functions bundled into a separate file (`FileReadWrite.py`) makes for a nice reusable package. We only need to know the names of the functions and what data each one needs to be passed.

# Example: Multiple Choice Test

Let's put many of these concepts together and build a useful example program. We'll create a program that allows the user to take a multiple-choice test. The interesting thing about the program is that we'll write it in a way that it can be used to pose any number of questions on any topic.

---

**Definition**    *Content independence* is a program's ability to use data that is not built into the program.

---

We will build our multiple-choice test program in a content-independent way by having the questions and answers in an external text file. If we define and use a clear layout for this text file, the program can be used as a generic "engine" that runs through any number of questions on any topic.

We'll first make the decision that each multiple-choice question has four possible answers. We'll define a layout for our questions file, like this:

```
<Test title line>
<Number of questions>
<Question 1>
<Correct answer for question 1>
<Incorrect answer 1 for question 1>
<incorrect answer 2 for question 1>
<Incorrect answer 3 for question 1>
<Question 2>
<Correct answer for question 2>
<Incorrect answer 1 for question 2>
<incorrect answer 2 for question 2>
<Incorrect answer 3 for question 2>
...
<Question n>
<Correct answer for question n>
<Incorrect answer 1 for question n>
<incorrect answer 2 for question n>
<Incorrect answer 3 for question n>
```

In this layout, the first line of the file is a title line that will be presented to the user. The second line contains a text version of an integer that will tell us how many questions there are in the test.

After that, each question is made up of a grouping of five lines. The first line of each group is the question itself. After that is the correct answer to the question. Then there are three incorrect or "distracter" answers.

Here is a sample test file with four questions:

```
Stupid answers quiz
4
What color was Washington's white horse?
White
Blue
Red
Beige
How many green Chinese pots are there in a dozen?
12
1
10
-6
What is the state song of Alabama?
Alabama
New Jersey is the place for me
My home is in Australia
I like monkeys
What is the first verb in the Pledge of Allegiance?
pledge
I
allegiance
snorkel
```

For each question, the program reads in five lines, poses the question, randomizes the answers, and presents the randomized answers. It waits for a user response, checks to see whether the user got the question correct or not, and gives appropriate correct or incorrect feedback.

During the test, the program keeps and presents a running score. At the end of the test, the program calculates the percentage correct.

Here is the code for the multiple-choice test program:

```
# Multiple choice test

import random
from FileReadWrite import *

FILE_PATH = 'MultipleChoiceQuestions.txt'
LETTERS_LIST = ['a', 'b', 'c', 'd']

# Open the file for reading, read in the title line
fileHandle = openFileForReading(FILE_PATH)
titleText = readALine(fileHandle)

# Find out how many questions there will be
nQuestions = readALine(fileHandle)
nQuestions = int(nQuestions)

print('Welcome!  This test is:')
print()
print(titleText)  # print whatever title we got from the file
print()
print('There will be', nQuestions, 'questions.')
print()
print("Let's go ...")
print()

score = 0
# Each time through the loop, handle a single question
for questionNumber in range(0, nQuestions):
    questionText = readALine(fileHandle)  # read a line of a question

    answers =[]
    for i in range(0, 4):
        thisAnswer = readALine(fileHandle)  # read each answer
        answers.append(thisAnswer)
```

```
    correctAnswer = answers[0]  # save away the correct answer
    random.shuffle(answers)  # randomize the 4 answers
    indexOfCorrectAnswer = answers.index(correctAnswer) # see where the
    correct answer is

    # present the question and the four randomized answers
    print
    print(str(questionNumber + 1) +'. ' + questionText) #ask question
    for index in range(0, 4):
        thisLetter = LETTERS_LIST [index]
        thisAnswer = answers[index]
        thisAnswerLine = " + thisLetter  + ')  ' + thisAnswer
        print(thisAnswerLine)

    print

    # Ensure that the user enters a valid letter answer
    while True:
        userAnswer = input('Your answer (a, b, c, or d): ')
        userAnswer = userAnswer.lower()  # convert usersAnswer to lowercase
        if userAnswer in LETTERS_LIST:  # valid answer
            break
        else:  # invalid answer
            print('Please enter a, b, c, or d')

    # Find the index associated with the user's answer
    # The following maps a to 0, b to 1, c to 2, d to 3
    indexOfUsersAnswer = LETTERS_LIST.index(userAnswer)

    # Give feedback
    if indexOfCorrectAnswer == indexOfUsersAnswer:
        score = score + 1
        print('Correct!'          )
    else:
        print("Sorry, that's not it.")
        correctLetter = LETTERS_LIST[indexOfCorrectAnswer]
        print('The correct answer was: ', correctLetter + ')  ' +
        correctAnswer)
```

```
    print()
    print('Your score is:', score)
```

```
# Done, show the percent correct and close the file
pctCorrect = (score * 100.)/ nQuestions
print()
print('All done!    You got:', str(pctCorrect) + '% correct')
```

```
closeFile(fileHandle)
```

I won't go into all the details of this program because it is well commented. The only tricky part is finding the index of the correct answer and matching it up to the index of the answer the user chose. We use the built-in list index operation to find the index of where the correct answer wound up in our randomized list. We also use the index operation to map the user's letter answer (*a*, *b*, *c*, or *d*) into an index (0, 1, 2, 3). We compare the user's choice index to the correct index to see if the user answered the question correctly. When we run the program, the output looks like this:

```
>>>
Welcome! This test is:

Stupid answers quiz

There will be 4 questions.

Let's go ...

1. What color was Washington's white horse?
a)   Red
b)   White
c)   Blue
d)   Beige

Your answer (a, b, c, or d): b
Correct!

Your score is: 1
```

2. How many green Chinese pots are there in a dozen?
a)   10
b)   -6
c)   1
d)   12

Your answer (a, b, c, or d): d
Correct!

Your score is: 2

3. What is the state song of Alabama?
a)   New Jersey is the place for me
b)   I like monkeys
c)   Alabama
d)   My home is in Australia

Your answer (a, b, c, or d): c
Correct!

Your score is: 3

4. What is the first verb in the Pledge of Allegiance?
a)   snorkel
b)   allegiance
c)   pledge
d)   I

Your answer (a, b, c, or d): a
Sorry, that's not it.
The correct answer was: c)  pledge

Your score is: 3

All done! You got: 75.0% correct
>>>

The ability to put data (such as the question data for this program) in an external file is a very powerful technique. Content-independent programs like this can have very wide applicability.

# A Compiled Version of a Module

If you have run a program that imports the `FileReadWrite` module that we built in this chapter, you might notice that in the same folder, there is now a folder named `__pycache__`. In that folder is a file named `FileReadWrite.cpython-3x.pyc`. I'll explain what this is.

Earlier I said that when you run a Python program, the Python compiler reads your code and "compiles" it into a simpler form called *bytecode*. The bytecode version is what actually runs on the computer. Whenever a program imports another Python file, the imported file must also be compiled. To simplify, let's say that we have a program called `A.py` that imports B (from the Python source file `B.py`). In this case, both `A.py` and `B.py` must be compiled. Python does this in a very smart way. Because you are typically editing `A.py` before your run, it makes sense to recompile that file every time you run. But most of the time, `B.py` does not change. Therefore, when Python sees a statement to import B, it checks to see if `B.pyc` exists in the folder named `__pycache__`. If that file does not exist, it compiles `B.py` and produces a compiled bytecode version named `B.pyc`. The .pyc extension stands for *Python compiled*. The next time you go to run your `A.py` program, Python sees the `B.pyc` file and uses that version of B since it has already been compiled. This results in faster compile times (the time between when you say, "Run," and when the program actually starts to run).

If you make a change to `B.py`, Python must recompile that file and produce a new `B.pyc`. The way it knows when to do this is simple and clever. Whenever Python finds an `import` statement asking to import a module, it checks to see if there is a related `.pyc` file. If there is, it compares the last edited date/time of the `.py` file against the last edited date/time of the `.pyc` file. If the date/time of the `.py` file is after the date/time of the related `.pyc` file, it knows that the source file has been changed and it must recompile the `.py` file to produce a new `.pyc` file.

When you write a program that imports `FileReadWrite.py`, Python looks for `FileReadWrite.pyc`. in the `__pycache__` folder. If that file does not exist in that folder, Python reads your `FileReadWrite.py`, compiles it, and produces the bytecode version of the file: `FileReadWrite.pyc`. It now uses the bytecode version of the file.

Now it should be clearer that when you write an `import` statement, you only specify a module name (such as `FileReadWrite`) and leave off the file extension.

# Summary

In this chapter, you learned how to write to and read from a file. To use a file, you must first identify the file that you want to use by specifying its path as a string. Reading from or writing to a file involves three steps: open the file, read from or write to it, and close the file. Whenever you programmatically open a file, the operating system gives you back a file handle that you use in subsequent calls to write or read data. When you are finished, you must close the file, again using the file handle. You saw that Python's built-in os package contains many useful operating systems functions.

We then built a set of three reusable functions: fileExists, writeFile, and readFile. Given these functions, we built a small example that used those functions to write a string of text to a file and read it back in. To make the functions truly reusable, we learned how to keep the functions in a separate Python source file and use the import statement to bring an external file into our code.

We then built four versions of a simple children's adding program. The final version was able to save its state by writing out and reading back multiple pieces of data used by the program. This allowed the program to pick up right where the user left off. Internally, we used two new functions: join (to combine the data into a single string before writing to a file) and split (to read back the data from the file and break it up into the original data).

Our final topic on file I/O was the ability to read and write a line of data at a time with a file. Although we still must use the same three steps of opening a file, reading or writing it, and closing the file, we built a set of functions for these three steps. You saw how to use the file handle provided when you open the file in subsequent calls to read a single line of data or write a single line of data and then to close the file. This technique allows us to read and write large quantities of data using text files. I provided an example of building a generic multiple-choice testing program that is completely content independent by moving the data into a text file.

Lastly, we discussed how Python creates a compiled version of a Python module that is imported into other Python source files.

# CHAPTER 10

# Internet Data

In the previous two chapters, we discussed different ways to get and manipulate strings. That makes this our third chapter on strings. Earlier, I talked about how a program can get text input from the user by using a call to `input`. In the previous chapter, I showed how a program could get data from and save data to a file. But there is another place where programs can get text data from: the Internet!

This chapter discusses the following topics:

- Request/response model

- Getting a stock price

- Pretending to be a browser

- API

- Requests with values

- API Key

- Example program to get stock price information using an API

- Example program to get weather information

- URL encoding

## Request/Response Model

When you use a browser to go to a web site, you enter a URL (which stands for *Universal Resource Locator*), you press Enter or Return, and soon you see a nicely formatted web page. I'll explain what happens behind the scenes when you use a browser this way (see Figure 10-1).

283

© Irv Kalb 2018
I. Kalb, *Learn to Program with Python 3*, https://doi.org/10.1007/978-1-4842-3879-0_10

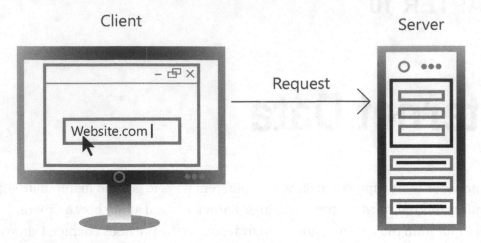

**Figure 10-1.** *Client computer making a request to a server*

When you use any browser on any device (computer, tablet, phone, and so on) to go to a web site, the system you are using is called the *client* and the computer that hosts the web site is called the *server*. After typing a URL, when you press Enter or Return the browser on the client makes a query called a *request* that is sent across the Internet. Assuming that the URL is well formatted, the request is sent to the appropriate server of the site given in the URL. The browser running on the client then waits for an answer to the query from the server.

Having received the request, the server does whatever it needs to do to answer the request. In the case of a typical request to display a web page, it prepares and formats its answer. The answer is known as a *response* (see Figure 10-2).

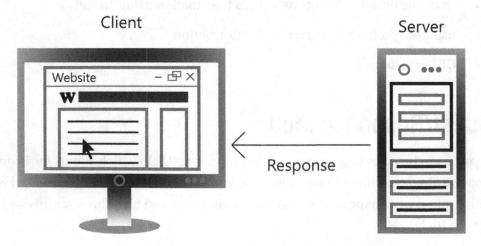

**Figure 10-2.** *Server sending back a response to a client computer*

284

The response is made up of text, formatted in a language called HTML (for *HyperText Markup Language*). Additionally, the response can contain other data, such as pictures, sounds, videos, and so forth. For this discussion, we'll concentrate only on the HTML portion of the response. When the response is ready, it is sent back from the server to the client's browser.

The browser reads through the returned HTML, formats the resulting page, and shows the page in the browser window.

This sequence is commonly known as the *request/response model*. The key thing to realize here is that the browser sends a string (the request URL) to the server and then receives a string (the response HTML) from the server.

If you think about what the browser is doing, the steps are very similar to the way we make a function call. The main difference is that instead of calling a function in its own program, or a built-in function in its own language, the action of the browser making a request is like making a function call, but across the Internet. Similar to what happens when you make a call to a function in Python where the caller waits until the function is finished, the browser waits until the server returns a response.

---

**Note**   In this chapter we will discuss a number of Internet web sites. As of this writing (summer 2018), all the examples and related sample code work perfectly. But some of these examples may fail later if the companies that provide them change the way things are done on their sites. The important thing to learn is the generalized underlying concepts.

---

# Getting a Stock Price

Suppose you want to find out the current stock price of a company. First, you have to know the stock symbol. (If you don't know a company's stock symbol, you can find it by using a search engine and entering "stock symbol for xxx," where xxx is the name of the company.) Let's say you wanted to find the price of Apple stock, whose symbol is AAPL. There are a number of sites that you can go to in order to get the price of a stock. One very useful one is the site of the NASDAQ stock exchange. You can use any browser and enter the following URL to get the current price of Apple stock:

```
https://www.nasdaq.com/symbol/aapl
```

When you press Enter or Return, the browser sends the request. The NASDAQ server receives the request and looks up current information about Apple stock. It then builds the appropriate HTML code to send back to the browser. The browser receives all of the returned HTML as a single string, formats the information, and displays the page on the screen. You see the current stock price for Apple near the top of the page. You also see the change and percent change of the stock price, some key stock data (such as the best bid/ask price, 1-year target, today's high value, and many more), along with an interactive chart of previous prices, and even some recent news about Apple.

The underlying HTML code that makes up any web page is available to view in the browser. In Google Chrome, you can see it by right-clicking any web page and, from the context menu, choosing View Source. In Safari, you can see it by clicking Develop ➤ Show Page Source.

In the source of the page, you can see that a huge amount of text has been returned from this request—more than a thousand lines of text. Somewhere in there is the price of Apple stock.

Let's remember what we just did and relate it back to the world of Python.

# Pretending to Be a Browser

In Python, we can write a program that effectively pretends to be a browser. That is, instead of the browser making the request to get information from the NASDAQ site (or other similar site), we can write a Python program that can make the same request. The response—all the HTML text—will come back to our program, and we can save all that text into a variable. But instead of painting the entire page like the browser does, we'll just look for the specific information we want to find: the price of a stock.

Python has a module called `urllib` and a submodule called `request` that provide the code needed to allow programs to make requests over the Internet. As with other packages we have discussed, you bring this package into your code with this line:

```
import urllib.request
```

Once you have done that, the following two lines can be used to make the request across the Internet:

```
connection = urllib.request.urlopen(<URL>)
responseString = connection.read().decode()
```

First, we call `urllib.request.urlopen`, specifying the URL you want to connect to. This call returns a value similar to the file handle we used when dealing with file I/O in Chapter 9. Across the Internet, this call returns what you can think of as a connection. Assuming that works, the returned connection value is then used in a call to the `read` function to get the data from the given URL. However, we need to do one more step. The data that is read from a site is often *encoded* (I'll explain more about this later in this chapter). We have to *decode* the data to turn it into a string that we can use in a Python program. The resulting string is stored into a variable.

For example, to get stock-quote information for Apple, we can use this code:

```
nasdaqAppleURL = 'https://www.nasdaq.com/symbol/aapl'
connection = urllib.request.urlopen(nasdaqAppleURL)
responseString = connection.read().decode()
```

When these lines run, the variable `responseString` is set to the exact same underlying HTML information that the browser gets for that page when it makes the request. We know that the stock price is included somewhere in the returned text because when the browser makes the request and gets the response, we see the stock price on the screen. If we were to spend a lot of time analyzing the HTML we got back as a response, we could find an identifying tag that precedes the actual price string. In this case, there is an HTML tag `<div id="qwidget_lastsale" class="qwidget-dollar">` right before the price of the stock. Knowing that this exists in the HTML, we can write some code that reaches into the long HTML string an using a slice, grabs just the characters that make up the price.

This technique is called *screen scraping*. That is, we are taking data that is intended for drawing on the screen of the computer and reading through it to find the particular piece or pieces of information we want.

This approach does work, but it can fail. The problem is that the code to find our specific piece of information is based on knowledge of how the page looks on the screen today. The company that owns the base URL (NASDAQ, in this example) could decide at any time to change the way the page is laid out. Further, we were able to find the piece of information because we noticed that the specific tag was built into the HTML of the page. At any point, the company responding to a request could also change the internal tag—for example, to `<div id="qwidget_lastprice" class="qwidget-dollar">`. In either of these cases, the program would break because the page is no longer formatted the way the program expects.

The bottom line is that although this technique works (temporarily), it is *not* a good way to get information from the Internet into your program. Let's look at a much better way.

# API

Companies that want to share their data make it available to computer programmers by publishing a set of guidelines for retrieving this type of data in a much more efficient way. These guidelines are called an API.

---

**Definition**    An API (short for *Application Programming Interface*) is a set of URLs and parameters that is designed to be called by programs across the Internet.

---

The idea is that instead of receiving a full page of HTML designed for display, using an API programmers can ask for and get just the information they want and use it in their programs. For example, there is a company named Alpha Vantage that has a set of APIs for retrieving data about stocks, physical and crypto currencies, stock indicators, and sector performances. It is fully documented at `www.alphavantage.co/documentation/`.

To get a stock quote, there is a single URL with a number of different parameters you can specify. The base URL is `www.alphavantage.com/query`. But in order to make a useful request, you must also specify a number of additional values.

# Requests with Values

If we think of the request/response model being like a function call, it would make the model more complete if we could pass data with a request, just as we pass values when we make a call to a Python function. It turns out that you can do exactly that. However, passing data with a URL has a different syntax than the way we do it in Python. The reason for this difference is that requests over the Internet are independent of the programming language. When passing data with a URL, there has to be a very general syntax. That syntax looks like this:

```
http://<URL>?<parameterName1>=<value1>&<parameterName2>=<value2> etc.
```

At the end of the base URL, you add a question mark to indicate that more information is coming. Following the question mark, you build any number of sequences of the form `parameterName=value` (with no spaces). Each grouping is commonly known as a *name/value pair*. After the first name/value pair, additional `parameterName=value` pairs must be separated by an ampersand character (&). This syntax is different from how we make a call in Python, where we pass an argument simply as a variable or a value. With a URL request, you must supply the exact name of each parameter that the site expects. The names of these parameters are typically given in the documentation of the API. Each value to be passed must be a string, but without quotes, because the entire URL is specified as one long string. Some example name/value pairs in a URL could look like this:

```
?firstname=Joe&lastname=Schmoe&age=36
```

These name/value pairs say that for the `firstname` parameter, use a value of `Joe`; for the `lastname` parameter, use a value of `Schmoe`; and for the `age` parameter, use a value of 36.

Now we are almost ready to build the full URL to get a stock quote using the Alpha Vantage API. According to its documentation, to get a stock quote we need to specify three pieces of information. The first two are very straightforward.

The first piece of information tells the site what "function" to perform. In this case, we want a stock quote (there are many other options). To indicate that, we need to add this to the URL:

```
?function=BATCH_STOCK_QUOTES
```

Next, we need to specify which stock symbol to get a quote for. To do that, we add the stock symbol for Apple like this:

```
&symbols=AAPL
```

The last piece of information is an identifier called an API key.

# API Key

Companies (and government agencies) that provide data via APIs often provide the data free to programmers who use their extensive APIs. But in order to prevent overuse and/or potential malicious intent, organizations often require that you obtain an identifying key from them. An *API key* is a unique string that identifies you as the person whose code is making a request. API keys are typically given out for free by filling out an online form. Once you get an API key, you need use it in all your API queries to that company. If you expect to build a commercial program, or you expect to make extensive uses of their APIs, you may have to pay a fee to the company for the use of the API key.

The process of obtaining an API key from a company is typically very easy. An API key can be obtained from Alpha Vantage at this site: `www.alphavantage.co/support/#api-key`. There are only a few questions to answer in the form, as shown in Figure 10-3.

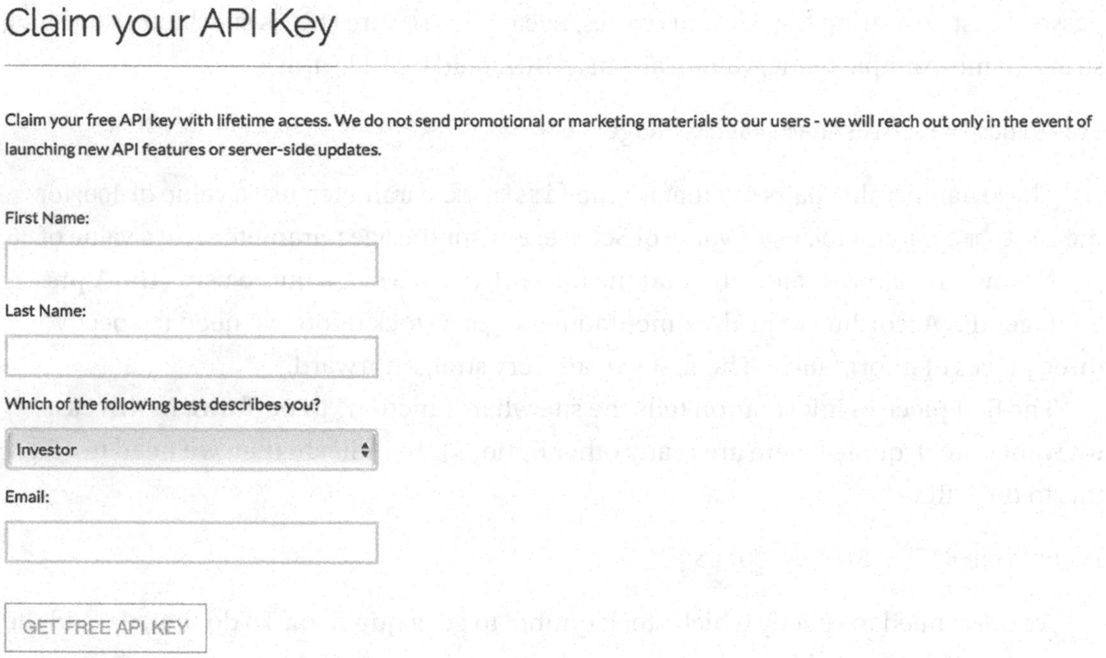

## Claim your API Key

Claim your free API key with lifetime access. We do not send promotional or marketing materials to our users - we will reach out only in the event of launching new API features or server-side updates.

First Name:

Last Name:

Which of the following best describes you?

Investor

Email:

GET FREE API KEY

**Figure 10-3.** *Requesting an API key from Alpha Vantage*

If you fill out the form and press the GET FREE API KEY button, you should soon get an e-mail back that includes a string of about 16 characters. This is your API key. You can use that key to make API requests to Alpha Vantage.

As the final piece of information, you need to add the following:

```
&apikey=<yourAPIKeyHere>
```

Let's put it all together. In order to get the stock proce of Apple, you would build up this URL:

`https://www.alphavantage.co/query?function=BATCH_STOCK_QUOTES&symbols=AAPL&apikey=xxxxxxx`

The xxxxxx is the API key you received from AlphaVantage.

# Example Program to Get Stock Price Information Using an API

Now that we have all the pieces, we can build a program to get the price of a stock using an API. If we make a call using the API just discussed, with a valid API key, the answer comes back as a single string that looks like this:

```
{
    "Meta Data": {
        "1. Information": "Batch Stock Market Quotes",
        "2. Notes": "IEX Real-Time Price provided for free by IEX
        (https://iextrading.com/developer/).",
        "3. Time Zone": "US/Eastern"
    },
    "Stock Quotes": [
        {
            "1. symbol": "AAPL",
            "2. price": "177.8500",
            "3. volume": "20536464",
            "4. timestamp": "2018-04-18 16:30:20"
        }
    ]
}
```

In the next chapter, I show you how this information is laid out in a special text format (called JSON). For now, let's just view this information as one long string. We can see that the stock price for today is 177.8500. But in order to find the price of a stock in this string generically, we will have to write code to build a slice to extract it. In the preceding string, we see that the price is preceded by the string `"2. price":` and is ended by a double quotation mark. We'll write some code to calculate the indeces needed to identify that slice.

Here is our full program to make the request, get the response, and extract the price information, based on any stock symbol entered by the user:

```python
# Getting a stock quote

import urllib.request

API_KEY = 'xxxxx'  ##  <- Replace xxxxx with your API key

#  Data provided for free by Alpha Vantage.  Website: alphavantage.co
#
#  typical URL:
#        https://www.alphavantage.co/query?function=BATCH_STOCK_QUOTES&
#        symbols=AAPL&apikey=<key>

def getStockData(symbol):
    baseURL = 'https://www.alphavantage.co/query?function=BATCH_STOCK_
    QUOTES&symbols='
    ending = '&apikey=' + API_KEY

    fullURL = baseURL + symbol + ending
    print()
    print('Sending URL:', fullURL)

    # open the URL
    connection = urllib.request.urlopen(fullURL)

    # read and convert bytes to a string
    responseString = connection.read().decode()

    print('Response is: ', responseString)

    # Look for a prefix in the response
    prefixString = '"2. price": "'

    # do a little math to figure out the start and end index of the real price:
    prefixStringPosition = responseString.index(prefixString)
    prefixStringLength = len(prefixString)

    start = prefixStringPosition + prefixStringLength
    end = responseString.index('"', start)
```

```
    # extract the price using a slice, and return it
    price = responseString[start:end]
    return price

while True:
    print()
    userSymbol = input('Enter a stock symbol (or press ENTER to quit): ')
    if userSymbol == '':
        break
    thisStockPrice = getStockData(userSymbol)

    print()
    print('The current price of', userSymbol, 'is:', thisStockPrice)
    print()

print('OK bye')
```

This program's code is very straightforward. At the bottom, the main code has an infinite loop where we ask the user for a stock symbol. That symbol is passed to the getStockData function. That function builds a full URL including the operation we want to perform, the stock symbol, and our API key. The function makes a request over the Internet using that URL. The server hands back a long string as documented earlier. (I've left in the print statements that show the URL that is sent and the response string that is returned—you can comment these lines out or remove them if you want.) The function then extracts the price of the stock by calculating the start and end indices for the appropriate slice. Finally, it returns that price to the caller.

An important point here is that companies build APIs like this so that programs running on computers and devices can quickly get the data they are asking for. Some APIs are intended only for the use of the company's employees. Others, like the Alpha Vantage's stock API, are available to the general public. Unlike using the screen-scraping technique, where the screen layout may change at any time, APIs are designed not to change, although as a company learns how its users (programmers) are using its data, it may choose to amend some API details and/or add new API calls.

> **Caution**   APIs have the potential for abuse. If you wind up making too many calls to an API per hour, or if you make calls too quickly, you may be locked out from making such calls. Owners of sites that have APIs often *throttle* the number of calls allowable within a certain time period. Please do not abuse APIs with your code.

# Example Program to Get Weather Information

There is a wonderful site at OpenWeatherMap.org that allows programmers to retrieve a wide variety of weather data from around the world. Its APIs are well documented at `http://openweathermap.org/API`. In order to use any of the APIs, you must first obtain a free API key using a similar form to the one you saw earlier.

There are many choices for the types and quantities of weather information you can retrieve. As a demonstration, I'll show you how to get the current weather information for any city. Our more specific goal is to retrieve the current temperature in that city.

The API works as follows. You make a call to the base API and, as data, supply the city you want information about, the return format for your data, and your API key. For example:

```
api.openweathermap.org/data/2.5/weather?q=Phoenix&mode=xml&APPID=xxxxx
```

Using that URL, here is an example of the current weather information returned for the city of Phoenix:

```
<?xml version="1.0" encoding="UTF-8"?>
<current><city id="5308655" name="Phoenix"><coord lon="-112.08"
lat="33.45"></coord><country>US</country><sun rise="2018-04-20T12:50:59"
set="2018-04-21T02:03:33"></sun></city><temperature value="292.37"
min="291.15" max="293.15" unit="kelvin"></temperature><humidity
value="22" unit="%"></humidity><pressure value="1016" unit="hPa">
</pressure><wind><speed value="4.6" name="Gentle Breeze"></speed><gusts
value="9.3"></gusts><direction value="270" code="W" name="West">
</direction></wind><clouds value="20" name="few clouds">
</clouds><visibility value="16093"></visibility><precipitation mode="no">
</precipitation><weather number="801" value="few clouds" icon="02d">
</weather><lastupdate value="2018-04-20T17:58:00"></lastupdate></current>
```

There is a lot of information there, and it may seem intimidating. In the next chapter, I show you how this information is laid out in another text format called XML. For now, let's just view this as one long string. If you look through the string, you will see a tag that says `<temperature value="`. Immediately following that is the actual temperature. We can use the same approach we used for getting stock data. That is, we can calculate the indices of the start and end points of the temperature and use a slice to extract the information we want.

However, the data this program generated for the temperature in Phoenix shows a value of 292.37, which seems quite hot, even for Phoenix. In the United States, we use the Fahrenheit scale, and most of the rest of the world uses the Centigrade scale, so when reporting temperatures, OpenWeatherMap.org decided to represent temperatures in yet a third scale: Kelvin. The Kelvin scale is based on the concept of absolute zero. To make the answers clearer for readers in the United States, I wrote and used a small function to convert a temperature from degrees Kelvin into degrees Fahrenheit. The resulting Fahrenheit temperature is a much more enjoyable 66.866 degrees.

The following full program allows the user to enter the name of any major city. The program makes an API call to get all the weather information for that city. After the server responds, the program then extracts the temperature information and converts it to a Fahrenheit value that it reports to the user:

```
import urllib.request

# API documentation from:  http://openweathermap.org/API

# Sample, try:  api.openweathermap.org/data/2.5/weather?q=Phoenix&mode=xml&
APPID=xxxxx

API_KEY = 'xxxxx'  ##  <- Replace xxxxx with your API key

def getInfo(city):
    URL = 'http://api.openweathermap.org/data/2.5/weather?q=' + city +
    '&mode=xml'+ '&APPID=' + API_KEY
    print("URL request is: " + URL)
    print()

    # Make the request and save the response as a string.
    connection = urllib.request.urlopen(URL)
    responseString = connection.read().decode()
```

```
    print(responseString)
    print()

    prefixString = '<temperature value="'
    # do some small math to figure out the start and end index of the
    temperature:
    prefixStringLength = len(prefixString)
    prefixStringPos = responseString.index(prefixString)
    start = prefixStringPos + prefixStringLength
    end = responseString.index('"', start)

    # extract the temperature and return it
    degreesK = responseString[start : end]  # this is in degrees Kelvin
    degreesK = float(degreesK)
    return degreesK

# Convert from Kelvin degrees to Fahrenheit
def convertKToF(degreesK):
    degreesF = (1.8 * (degreesK - 273.)) + 32
    return degreesF

while True:
    city = input('What city would you like the temperature of? ')
    if city == ":
        break
    tempK = getInfo(city)
    # Convert from Kelvin degrees to Fahrenheit
    tempF = convertKToF(tempK)
    print(tempF)
    print()

print('Bye')
```

This program includes `print` statements to show the URL that was created and the response string that was returned. If you comment those lines out, a typical run would look like this:

```
What city would you like the temperature of? Phoenix
```

```
68.99000000000002
```

```
What city would you like the temperature of? Boston
```

```
38.714000000000034
```

# URL Encoding

When we use parameter values in conjunction with API calls, the values that are passed in are always strings. For most strings made up of standard characters, everything works fine, but certain characters are considered "unsafe" when used in parameter values. Most importantly, the *space* character is considered not to be safe. The original reason has to do with people reading values from one place and typing them into fields or forms that wind up in URLs. Because the space character is essentially an invisible character, the number of spaces that were in the original text may not be clear.

In order to include a space in a parameter value, the space character must be translated to either the plus character (+) or the numeric value of the space character. Every character is assigned a unique number. All characters can be represented by a special string that gives the number associated with that character as a hexadecimal (base 16) number. For example, the space character as a hexadecimal number is written as %20. The process of replacing a character with another character or sequence of characters is called *encoding*.

If we wanted to only encode the space character, we could take any string that we might use as a parameter value in a URL and apply a string `replace` operation to it. For example:

```
>>> originalString = 'New Jersey'
>>> encodedString = originalString.replace(' ', '+')
>>> print(encodedString)
New+Jersey
>>>
```

Or this:

```
>>> originalString = 'New Jersey'
>>> encodedString = originalString.replace(' ', '%20')
>>> print(encodedString)
New%20Jersey
>>>
```

Either of these versions of the encoded string could then be used within a URL in an API call. When a parameter value is received by a server, any plus character or %20 sequence is decoded back to the space character.

There are a number of other characters that are also considered unsafe for use in a URL, including the following:

- " (Quote mark)
- < and > (Less-than and greater-than symbols)
- # (Pound sign)
- % (Percent sign)
- And the following: {, }, |, \, ^, ~, [, ], `

That is a lot of characters to remember and find replacement hexadecimal representations for. Fortunately, there is a built-in Python function that can do this work for us. If we ever believe that a value of a parameter to be passed in a URL might contain any of these characters, then before building the value into a URL, we can use the following function from the urllib package:

```
import urllib.parse
encodedString = urllib.parse.quote_plus(<original string>)
```

To use it, you pass in the original string, and it returns an encoded version of the string that works within a URL. For example, if we want to make an API call where we want to specify a value of the string 'New Jersey', we would encode it this way:

```
>>> import url.libparse
>>> originalString = 'New Jersey'
>>> encodedString = urllib.parse.quote_plus(originalString)
>>> print(encodedString)
New+Jersey
>>>
```

This call encodes the space as a plus in the same way you saw earlier with the string `replace` operation. However, the call to `urllib.parse.quote_plus` takes care of encoding *all* potentially unsafe characters for us. Here is an example:

```
>>> import url.libparse
>>> originalString = 'The sales tax of "New Jersey" is > 1%'
>>> encodedString = urllib.parse.quote_plus(originalString)
>>> print(encodedString)
The+sales+tax+of+%22New+Jersey%22+is+%3E+1%25
>>>
```

As a result of this call, in addition to encoding the spaces into plus signs, the double-quote characters have been converted to their hexadecimal form (%22), the greater-than character has been changed to a %3E, and the percent sign has been replaced with %25. After doing this type of encoding using `urllib.parse.quote_plus`, you can be assured that your parameter values are safe for transmission to a server within a full URL.

## Summary

This chapter was all about getting text data over the Internet. I explained the request/response model, which is used to exchange information between a computer and a server. I then showed you how to take a request and add parameter values by adding them in as name/value pairs to the end of a URL string. After reading the response and decoding it, the response string is typically saved in a Python variable. I demonstrated this technique by showing you how to get a stock price from a financial site. We built a Python program that made the same request that we made in a browser, and got back the same HTML the browser got back. Then we extracted the stock price we were looking for. Although this was an interesting demonstration, it is not the proper way to get information because the HTML is designed for display on the screen.

The proper way to get data over the Internet is to use an API. Using an API allows us to get the data we are looking for in a much more concise way. Many companies attempt to ensure that their APIs are not overused or used maliciously by issuing and requiring the use of an API key. I explained how to build a URL (for an API) that includes a base URL and add parameters onto the end. Using an API, I showed you how to a get the price of a given stock. I also showed a program that uses an API to get weather information for any given city.

The chapter wrapped up by discussing a technique used to ensure that potentially unsafe characters can be encoded so that they are correctly transmitted in requests.

# CHAPTER 11

# Data Structures

Let's start this chapter with a definition.

---

**Definition**    A *data structure* is a collection of multiple pieces of data, arranged in a way that the data can be accessed efficiently.

---

The only data structure we have discussed so far is a list. A list allows us to refer to any one of multiple pieces of data using an index. Python has a few more built-in data structures.

This chapter covers the following topics:

- Tuples

- Lists of lists

- Representing a grid or a spreadsheet

- Representing the world of an adventure game

- Reading a comma-separated value (`.csv`) file

- Dictionary

- Using the `in` operator on a dictionary

- Programming challenge

- A Python dictionary to represent a programming dictionary

- Iterating through a dictionary

- Combining lists and dictionaries

- JSON: JavaScript Object Notation

- Example program to get weather data

© Irv Kalb 2018
I. Kalb, *Learn to Program with Python 3*, https://doi.org/10.1007/978-1-4842-3879-0_11

- XML data

- Accessing repeating groupings in JSON and XML

# Tuples

Python has a built-in data structure called a tuple. (There is ongoing debate about whether this should be pronounced "toople" or "tuhpple." The latter, pronounced as in "quintuple," seems more popular, but both are acceptable.) A *tuple* is essentially a list that cannot be changed. We'll review some basic operations of a list and then look at how a tuple differs from it. Let's start by creating a list:

```
>>> friendsList = ['Joe', 'Martha', 'John', 'Susan']
>>> print(friendsList)
['Joe', 'Martha', 'John', 'Susan']
>>>
```

We can find the length of the list using the len function and access any element in this list using an index:

```
>>> print(len(friendsList))
4
>>> print(friendsList[0])
Joe
>>> print(friendsList[3])
Susan
>>>
```

We can also change the value of a given element in the list and add (append) an element to the list:

```
>>> friendsList[2] = 'Greg'
>>> print(friendsList)
['Joe', 'Martha', 'Greg', 'Susan']
>>> friendsList.append('Diane')
>>> print(friendsList)
['Joe', 'Martha', 'Greg', 'Susan', 'Diane']
>>>
```

We can set a new value and perform the append operation because lists are mutable (changeable). By contrast, a tuple is immutable (not changeable).

A tuple is defined using a similar, but slightly different syntax from a list. Instead of the left and right square brackets used to define a list, a tuple is defined using left and right parentheses:

```
(<element1>, <element2>, ... <elementN>)
```

Like a list, a tuple is typically created in an assignment statement:

```
<tupleVariable> = (<element1>, <element2>, ... <elementN>)
```

Let's say we want to create a list of friends. If we know that the list of friends will not change during a run of the program, we would create a tuple of friends and initialize it at the start of the program, as follows:

```
>>> friendsTuple = ('Joe', 'Martha', 'John', 'Susan')
>>> print(friendsTuple)
('Joe', 'Martha', 'John', 'Susan')
>>>
```

So far, it looks the same as our earlier friendsList, except for the use of parentheses instead of square brackets. We can use the len function to see how many elements are in a tuple and the bracket syntax to get at an individual element of a tuple:

```
>>> print(len(friendsTuple))
4
>>> print(friendsTuple[0])
Joe
>>> print(friendsTuple[3])
Susan
>>>
```

But if we try to modify an individual element of the friendsTuple, we get an error message:

```
>>> friendsTuple[2] = 'George'

Traceback (most recent call last):
  File "<pyshell#19>", line 1, in <module>
```

```
    friendsTuple[2] = 'George'
TypeError: 'tuple' object does not support item assignment
>>>
```

If we try to append a new name onto the tuple, we also get an error message:

```
>>> friendsTuple.append('Diane')
```

```
Traceback (most recent call last):
  File "<pyshell#21>", line 1, in <module>
    friendsTuple.append('Diane')
AttributeError: 'tuple' object has no attribute 'append'
>>>
```

Both of these error messages show that the contents of a tuple cannot be changed.

You might be asking, "What good is this? Why would I ever want to use a tuple over a list?" The answer is speed. When a list is represented as a tuple, Python internally organizes the data in a way that it can access each individual element faster than in a list. Therefore, if you want to write code that runs as fast as possible, then look for any case where you have a list that never changes in your program. You can redefine it from a list to a tuple by changing the square brackets to parentheses. Eventually, this concept becomes second nature. You start thinking of unchanging lists as tuples and define them that way right from the start.

There is one additional small benefit to using a tuple. If you have a list of data and you want to ensure that there is no code that makes any changes to it, use a tuple. Any code that attempts to append to, delete from, or modify an element of a tuple will generate an error message. The offending code can quickly be identified and corrected.

---

**Note**    If you ever write any code using PyGame (an extension to Python that allows you to put graphics on the screen), you will notice that screen coordinates are almost always written as x, y tuples, and in (<xValue>, <yValue>). Further, rectangles in PyGame are typically written as four-element tuples: (<xValue>, <yValue>, <width>, <height>).

---

# Lists of Lists

In our earlier discussion of lists, I said that one interesting thing about a list is that the content—the data inside a list—can be of any data type. It turns out that not only can the data be of type integer, float, string, or Boolean, but any element of a list can also be a list. For example, consider the following list:

```
>>> myList = [5, -1, [23, 45, 14], 62]
>>> print(myList)
[5, -1, [23, 45, 14], 62]
```

To find out how many elements are in this list, we'll use the len function:

```
>>> print(len(myList))
4
```

The list has four elements, but element 2 is also a list:

```
>>> print(myList[2])
[23, 45, 14]
>>>
```

If we wanted to get to a value in this list within a list, there are two approaches. First, we could assign the inner list to a new list variable, and then reference the particular element we want from that list:

```
>>>
>>> innerList = myList[2]
>>> print(innerList)
[23, 45, 14]
>>> print(innerList[1])
45
>>>
```

Or we could use a different syntax. To get to an element of a list within a list, we can do this:

```
<outerList>[<outerListIndex>][<innerListIndex>]
```

For example:

```
>>> myList = [5, -1, [23, 45, 14], 62]
>>> print(myList[2][1])
45
>>>
```

This syntax reaches into myList and gets element 2 (which is the inner list of [23, 45, 14]). Because that is a list, we then get element 1 of that list (which is the value 45) and print it. (As you will soon see, this concept can extend to lists of lists of lists, and so on.)

# Representing a Grid or a Spreadsheet

Lists within lists are a great way to represent data in a grid or a spreadsheet, or any application where you have a need for rows and columns. Grids can be used to represent the playing boards of many games. For example, we could represent a tic-tac-toe board as a grid of three rows and three columns, like this:

```
EMPTY = "
X = 'x'
O = 'o'

# Build a 3 by 3 grid
grid = [\
        [EMPTY, EMPTY, EMPTY],\
        [EMPTY, EMPTY, EMPTY],\
        [EMPTY, EMPTY, EMPTY]\
        ]
```

As each player makes a move in the game, we would write code to put an X or an O into the appropriate spot in the grid. For example, if a player decided to place an X in the upper right-hand square, we would use this code to modify that cell:

```
# Typically set the row and col based on user input, this is just for
demonstration:
row = 0
col = 2
grid[row][col] = X
```

Any game board that is made up of any number of rows and columns can be represented this way. For example, you could build an eight-by-eight grid to represent the board for a game of checkers or chess.

# Representing the World of an Adventure Game

Adventure games are a very popular form of text-based games. In an adventure game, the user is placed in a world that can also be represented as a grid. Here is an example of a start to a program that builds a six-by-six grid:

```
#  Adventure game demo
import random

EMPTY = 'e'
TREASURE = 't'
MONSTER = 'm'

# Build 6 by 6 grid
NROWS_IN_GRID = 6
NCOLS_IN_GRID = 6
grid = [\
        [EMPTY, TREASURE, EMPTY, EMPTY, EMPTY, MONSTER],\
        [EMPTY, EMPTY, EMPTY, EMPTY, EMPTY, EMPTY],\
        [EMPTY, EMPTY, EMPTY, EMPTY, MONSTER, EMPTY],\
        [EMPTY, MONSTER, EMPTY, EMPTY, EMPTY, EMPTY],\
        [EMPTY, EMPTY, EMPTY, EMPTY, TREASURE, EMPTY],\
        [EMPTY, TREASURE, EMPTY, EMPTY, EMPTY, EMPTY],\
        ]

# Find a random starting cell that is empty
while True:
    locRow = random.randrange(NROWS_IN_GRID)
    locCol = random.randrange(NCOLS_IN_GRID)
    if grid[locRow][locCol] == EMPTY:
        break   # found an empty cell, we will place the player here

print('Starting at  row:', locRow, '  col:', locCol)
print()
```

```
while True:  # move around the grid
    direction = input('Press L, U, R, or D to move: ')
    direction = direction.lower()
    print()

    if direction == 'l':
        locCol = locCol - 1

    elif direction == 'u':
        locRow = locRow - 1

    elif direction == 'r':
        locCol = locCol + 1

    elif direction == 'd':
        locRow = locRow + 1

    else:
        print('Oops - staying where we are ... ')

    foundInCell = grid[locRow][locCol]
    print('Now at row:', locRow, '   col:', locCol, '    cell contains:',
    foundInCell)

    # Add code here to do whatever you want with the contents of the
        current cell
    # (e.g., fight, run, pick up, etc.)
```

This code is a good start for creating and populating the world represented by the grid, and for handling the navigation within it. To make it fun, you would want to add code to handle the interactions between the player and whatever they find as they navigate around in the world. Additionally, it would be important to add code to check and handle the cases of potentially moving off all edges. For example, the user might be in the first column (column 0) and press the l key to say that they want to go left. In a case like this, you could either have some code that gives the user a message saying that they cannot go there, or allow an action like this to wrap around the grid. That is, if the user tries to go off the left edge of the world, they reappear on the right edge in the same row. A similar thing could be done for an attempt to move off any edge.

The preceding code works fine, but every time the game is played, the grid is laid out the same way. The following is some code that generates a random grid every time the game is played:

```
# Adventure game demo dynamic
import random

# Define some constants for items that will be found in the grid
EMPTY = 'e'
TREASURE = 't'
MONSTER = 'm'
SWORD = 's'
POTION = 'p'
addInToGrid = (TREASURE, TREASURE, TREASURE, MONSTER, MONSTER, MONSTER,\
               SWORD, SWORD, POTION, POTION)

NROWS_IN_GRID = 6
NCOLS_IN_GRID = 8

# Find a random cell that is empty
def findEmptyCell(aGrid, nRows, nCols):
    while True:
        aRow = random.randrange(nRows)
        aCol = random.randrange(nCols)
        if aGrid[aRow][aCol] == EMPTY:
            return aRow, aCol

# Build grid, start it off all empty
grid = []
for r in range(0, NROWS_IN_GRID):
    aRow = []
    for c in range(0, NCOLS_IN_GRID):
        aRow.append(EMPTY)
    grid.append(aRow)

# Add in items randomly
for item in addInToGrid:
    locRow, locCol = findEmptyCell(grid, NROWS_IN_GRID, NCOLS_IN_GRID)
    grid[locRow][locCol] = item
```

```
# For testing, print the grid, row by row
for thisRow in grid:
    print(thisRow)

print()
locRow, locCol = findEmptyCell(grid, NROWS_IN_GRID, NCOLS_IN_GRID)
# For testing, print out the starting location so we know where we are in
the grid
print('Starting at  row:', locRow, '  col:', locCol)

< ... same navigation code as before>
```

The important difference in this code is that the grid is built dynamically. To do that, we start our grid variable as an empty list. Then we use a for loop to iterate through all the potential rows in the grid. Notice that we are using constants to define the number of rows and columns in the grid, and that we use these constants in our for loops. Each time through our outer loop, we initialize an aRow variable to the empty list. Then we have a nested for loop that appends a value of EMPTY to aRow. At the end of the inner loop, we have built a single row of our grid, represented as a list of all EMPTYs. Each time through the outer loop (for each row), we then append this list to our grid. This ends up building the grid as a list of lists.

Next, we iterate over a tuple of items to be added to the grid that were stored in a variable named addInToGrid. For each item in that tuple, we call findEmptyCell. This function returns both a row and a column of an empty cell in the grid. We use the syntax of two indices in brackets to identify the outer index (the row) and an inner index (the column) of the cell into which we will store a value. The code calls the same function to find a random starting point for the user in the grid.

Just for demonstration purposes, let's print the resulting grid, a row at a time, so that you can see what was built. Here is the output from a typical run:

```
['e', 'p', 'e', 'e', 't', 'm', 'e', 'e']
['e', 'e', 'e', 'e', 'e', 'p', 'e', 'e']
['e', 'e', 'e', 'e', 'e', 't', 'e', 'e']
['e', 'e', 'e', 'e', 'm', 'm', 's', 'e']
['e', 'e', 'e', 'e', 'e', 'e', 'e', 'e']
['t', 's', 'e', 'e', 'e', 'e', 'e', 'e']

Starting at  row: 5   col: 5
Press L, U, R, or D to move:
```

# Reading a Comma-Separated Value (.csv) File

Another example of data that can be represented as a list of lists is data that comes from a spreadsheet program. We'll work through an example of how we can take data from a spreadsheet created in Microsoft Excel (and probably other spreadsheet programs) and bring it into a Python program.

Figure 11-1 shows a spreadsheet that a teacher might construct for keeping track of grades on homework assignments, a midterm exam, and a final exam.

| ◇ | A | B | C | D | E | F | G | H |
|---|---|---|---|---|---|---|---|---|
| 1 | Name | Homework 1 | Homework 2 | Homework 3 | Homework 4 | Homework 5 | Midterm | Final |
| 2 | Joe | 20 | 20 | 19 | 20 | 20 | 34 | 45 |
| 3 | Mariah | 20 | 17 | 20 | 20 | 20 | 34 | 52 |
| 4 | John | 20 | 18 | | 18 | 16 | 40 | 55 |
| 5 | Mary | 20 | 20 | 20 | 16 | 20 | 27 | 48 |
| 6 | Fred | | 20 | 20 | | 20 | 33 | 45 |
| 7 | Martha | 20 | 20 | 20 | 20 | 20 | 38 | 58 |
| 8 | Craig | 19 | 20 | 20 | 18 | 19 | 40 | 60 |
| 9 | Kathy | 15 | | 20 | | 20 | 40 | 56 |
| 10 | Miles | 20 | 20 | 20 | 20 | 20 | 26 | 58 |
| 11 | Stacey | 17 | 18 | 15 | 16 | 18 | 38 | 44 |
| 12 | George | 20 | | 20 | | 20 | 25 | 34 |
| 13 | Sue | 20 | 20 | | 20 | 19 | 27 | 54 |
| 14 | Tom | 20 | 20 | 20 | 20 | 20 | 35 | 58 |

*Figure 11-1.* *Grades spreadsheet*

In this course, the homework assignments have a maximum of 20 points each, the midterm has a maximum of 40 points, and the final has a maximum of 60 points. Therefore, the maximum total possible points for the class is 200 points. If a student does not turn in an assignment, the cell representing that assignment is left blank.

Spreadsheet files like this are typically saved with the default format and the .xls or .xlsx extension. These are standard file formats for Microsoft Excel. However, as an option, you can click Save As and choose to save the file as a .csv file, which stands for *comma-separated value*. If you choose to save a spreadsheet as a .csv file, the data is written out line by line in plain text, where the data of each cell is separated from the adjacent one by inserting a comma character. I have saved the spreadsheet shown in Figure 11-1 in .csv format; the resulting file looks like what's shown in Figure 11-2.

```
Name,Homework 1,Homework 2,Homework 3,Homework 4,Homework 5,Midterm,Final
Joe,20,20,19,20,20,34,45
Mariah,20,17,20,20,20,34,52
John,20,18,,18,16,40,55
Mary,20,20,20,16,20,27,48
Fred,,20,20,,20,33,45
Martha,20,20,20,20,20,38,58
Craig,19,20,20,18,19,40,60
Kathy,15,,20,,20,40,56
Miles,20,20,20,20,20,26,58
Stacey,17,18,15,16,18,38,44
George,20,,20,20,,25,34
Sue,20,20,,20,19,27,54
Tom,20,20,20,20,20,35,58
```

***Figure 11-2.*** *Grades spreadsheet data saved as a comma-separated value file*

The first line contains the titles of the columns. Following that is one line for each student. As you can see, the data values in each of these lines are separated by commas. Notice also that any cell that was empty is represented as zero characters in the text line—that is, a missing entry is represented by two commas. Now we need a way to read data formatted this way into a Python program.

---

**Definition**    *Parse* means to take information and separate it into more easily processed components. For example, the Python compiler parses the code you write and breaks it down into the individual words and symbols in each line, so that it can turn your code into the bytecode form that can run on the computer.

---

To help read in and parse the data, let's use another of Python's many built-in packages. There is a package (not surprisingly, called the csv package) that is designed to read in CSV-formatted files.

In the following code, we read in the data from this .csv file, calculate a score for each student, and then translate that score into a letter grade (the translation to a letter grade comes from code that we developed earlier with the if/elif/else statements):

```
# Read grades from csv file, compute grade letter for course

import csv   # Comma separated value package

DATA_FILE_NAME = 'GradesExample.csv'

#Convert a number score to a letter grade:
def letterGrade(score):
    if score >= 90:
        letter = 'A'
    elif score >= 80:
        letter = 'B'
    elif score >= 70:
        letter = 'C'
    elif score >= 60:
        letter = 'D'
    else:
        letter = 'F'   #fall through or default case
    return letter

# Open the file in 'read Universal' (return char) mode)
# This allows for dealing with files created by spreadsheet programs like Excel
fileHandle = open(DATA_FILE_NAME, 'rU')

# Let the csv reader parse the file into rows
csvParsed = csv.reader(fileHandle)

# Treat each row (which represents data for a single student) as a list
readingHeaderLine = True
for row in csvParsed:   # iterate through each line

    if readingHeaderLine:  # first line?
        readingHeaderLine = False
        continue   #  skip the header line
```

```
    # This is what the data looks like coming in to the program
    #print('Original: ', row)

    name = row[0]  # save the student's name
    total = 0  # prepare to add 'em up
    for index in range(1, 8):   # elements 1 through 7 are the scores
        thisGrade = row[index]
        if thisGrade == ":
            thisGrade = 0.0  # change a nothing to a zero
        else:
            thisGrade = float(thisGrade)  # convert score from string to
            float
        total = total + thisGrade

    percent = (total  * 100.)/ 200.  # out of a possible 200 points

    gradeToReport = letterGrade(percent)

    print(name, '    Percent:', percent, '   Letter Grade:',  gradeToReport)
fileHandle.close()  #close the file
```

This code starts by importing the `csv` package. In the main code, we open the file in a new way, specifying the open mode as `'rU'`, which stands for *read universal*. This mode allows programs to read text files that were created on any operating system, because these files may have a variety of different end-of-line and/or newline characters. Once the file is opened, we call `csv.reader`. This is an operation in the `csv` package that reads through the entire file and modifies the data so that each line of the file is represented as a Python list. (Internally, it most likely calls the Python `split` function to separate the individual pieces of data.) When that completes, our code goes through a loop, iterating for each row in the original file.

We set a `readingHeaderLine` Boolean variable to `True` before the loop started. Inside the loop, we treat each row as a list. The first row is a list containing the header information (`Name`, `Homework1`, `Homework2`, and so on). We don't want to do anything with this line, so all we do is set the `readingHeaderLine` Boolean to `False` to indicate that we are no longer looking at the header line. Then we use a `continue` statement to send control back to the top of the loop.

For each subsequent row, we now can deal with the data representing a single student. That data is made up of a list of eight elements: element 0 is the student's name, and elements 1 through 7 are the score values, where each is a string. We build another loop to add up the scores of all homework values and the two test scores. If we find that a value is missing (which would come into the program as an empty string), then we give the student a zero for that score. When we are finished with that loop, we have the total score for that student. We then call our letterGrade function to convert the score into a letter grade. As the last thing in our loop, we write out this student's name, percentage, and letter grade. When we are done, we close the file.

Running the program generates the following output:

```
Joe        Percent: 89.0    Letter Grade: B
Mariah     Percent: 91.5    Letter Grade: A
John       Percent: 83.5    Letter Grade: B
Mary       Percent: 85.5    Letter Grade: B
Fred       Percent: 69.0    Letter Grade: D
Martha     Percent: 98.0    Letter Grade: A
Craig      Percent: 98.0    Letter Grade: A
Kathy      Percent: 75.5    Letter Grade: C
Miles      Percent: 92.0    Letter Grade: A
Stacey     Percent: 83.0    Letter Grade: B
George     Percent: 59.5    Letter Grade: F
Sue        Percent: 80.0    Letter Grade: B
Tom        Percent: 96.5    Letter Grade: A
```

If we want to, we could easily modify the code to write a new .csv file where each student line could contain the existing information and the additional percent and/or letter grade information (separated by commas). The resulting .csv file could then be opened in a spreadsheet program, such as Microsoft Excel.

Also, if we had wanted to do more analysis of the scores data—for example, ranking students or scores per assignment or test—we could have saved all the information in a larger list of lists data structure. In other words, we could have created an empty list, like this:

```
allScores = [ ]
```

Then every time we iterated through the loop, we could have appended the current row of data into that list, like this:

```
allScores.append(row)
```

With this approach, we can have all the data from the original .csv file in a single Python list of lists, and we can do any analysis we want.

# Dictionary

Another extremely important data structure available in Python is called a dictionary. A *dictionary* is similar to a list in that it allows you to refer to a collection of data by a single variable name. However, it differs from a list in one fundamental way. In a list, order is important, and the order of the elements in a list never changes (unless you explicitly do so). Because the order of elements in a list is important, you refer to each element in a list using its index (its position within the list).

In a dictionary, the data is represented in what are called *key/value* pairs. The syntax of a dictionary looks like this:

```
{<key>:<value>, <key>:<value>, ..., <key>:<value>}
```

Note that this is the only place in Python where the curly braces { and } are used.

I'll show you an example of how this works. Imagine that we wanted to represent several attributes or properties of a physical object using Python. We could create a single variable for each item. For example, let's try to describe a house using several variables:

```
color = 'blue'
style = 'colonial'
numberOfBedrooms = 4
garage = True
burglarAlarm = False
streetNumber = 123
streetName = 'Any Street'
city = 'Anytown'
state = 'CA'
price = 625000
```

Variables like these work fine. But the data in these variables is all related—each variable is a property of a single house. We could build a dictionary to represent the related data about the house. The same information built as a dictionary would look like this:

```
houseDict = {'color' : 'blue', 'style' : 'colonial', 'numberOfBedrooms' : 4,\
'garage' : True, 'burglarAlarm' : False, 'streetNumber' : 123,\
'streetName' : 'Any Street', 'city' : 'Anytown', 'state' : 'CA',\
'price' : 625000}
```

We are naming this dictionary houseDict to make it clear that this is a dictionary. Again, this is not a requirement; we are using a name like this as an extension to our naming convention. In this example, all the keys of this dictionary are strings, which is a very common practice. However, the keys in a dictionary can be of any type of immutable data—integers, floats, Booleans, and tuples can also be used as keys. Whatever data type you use for keys, each key in a dictionary must be unique. The values in a dictionary can be of any type.

Let's print out houseDict to show that Python understands the dictionary data structure:

```
print(houseDict)
{'color': 'blue', 'style': 'colonial', 'numberOfBedrooms': 4, 'garage': True,
'burglarAlarm': False, 'streetNumber': 123, 'streetName': 'Any Street',
'city': 'Anytown', 'state': 'CA', 'price': 625000}
```

Dictionaries rely on the key/value pair relationships rather than on positioning. Therefore, when we want to access any piece of data in a dictionary, we do it by using a key as an index (rather than the position index that we use with a list). Here are some examples:

```
>>> print(houseDict['color'])
blue
>>> print(houseDict['state'])
CA
>>> print(houseDict['numberOfBedrooms'])
4
>>>
```

To assign a new value for an existing key in a dictionary, we use an assignment statement, like this:

```
>>> houseDict['price'] = 575000   #change value of an existing key
>>> print(houseDict)
{'color': 'blue', 'style': 'colonial', 'numberOfBedrooms': 4, 'garage': True,
'burglarAlarm': False, 'streetNumber': 123, 'streetName': 'Any Street',
'city': 'Anytown', 'state': 'CA', 'price': 575000}
>>>
```

To add a new key/value pair into a dictionary, we use an assignment statement the same way. If the key we are specifying does not exist in the dictionary, then the key/value pair is added to the dictionary:

```
>>> houseDict['numberOfBathrooms'] = 2.5  # numberOfBathrooms is not in the
dictionary yet
>>> print(houseDict)
{'color': 'blue', 'style': 'colonial', 'numberOfBedrooms': 4, 'garage': True,
'burglarAlarm': False, 'streetNumber': 123, 'streetName': 'Any Street',
'city': 'Anytown', 'state': 'CA', 'price': 575000, 'numberOfBathrooms': 2.5}
>>>
```

Notice that the numberOfBathrooms key has been added to the dictionary.

There are two additional operations (functions) you can use on a dictionary. If you want, you can find all the keys defined in a dictionary with a call to <dictionary>. keys(). You can find all the values with a call to <dictionary>.values(). Both calls return an iterable list—perfect for use in a for statement. Here is an example using our previously defined dictionary:

```
>>> print(houseDict.keys())
dict_keys(['color', 'style', 'numberOfBedrooms', 'garage',
'burglarAlarm', 'streetNumber', 'streetName', 'city', 'state', 'price',
'numberOfBathrooms'])
>>> print(houseDict.values())
dict_values(['blue', 'colonial', 4, True, False, 123, 'Any Street',
'Anytown', 'CA', 575000, 2.5])
>>>
```

# Using the in Operator on a Dictionary

When we try to access an element in a list, we need to ensure that any index we use is a valid number. That is, the index has to have a value between 0 and the length of the list minus 1. (Remember that if a list has *N* elements, then the valid indices are 0 to *N* − 1.)

When accessing items in a dictionary, we have to ensure that we are using a valid key; that is, we have to use a key that exists in the dictionary. If the key we use is in the dictionary, we get the value associated with that key. But if we try to use a key that is not in the dictionary, we get an error:

```
>>> print(houseDict)
{'color': 'blue', 'style': 'colonial', 'numberOfBedrooms': 4, 'garage':
True, 'burglarAlarm': False, 'streetNumber': 123, 'streetName':
'Any Street', 'city': 'Anytown', 'state': 'CA', 'price': 575000,
'numberOfBathrooms': 2.5}
>>>
>>> print(houseDict['streetName'])
Any Street
>>>
>>> print(houseDict['roofType'])

Traceback (most recent call last):
  File "<pyshell#65>", line 1, in <module>
    print(houseDict['roofType'])
KeyError: 'roofType'
>>>
```

This is similar to what happens if we try to use an index that is too large or too small for a list. In that case, we get an "index out of range" error. With a dictionary, we get a KeyError, meaning the key does not exist in the dictionary.

To ensure that we are using a valid key, we can use the in operator before attempting to use a key in a dictionary. The in operator is used like this:

```
<key> in <dictionary>
```

It returns True if the key is found in the dictionary, or False if the key is not found:

```
>>> print('city' in houseDict)
True
>>> print('roofType' in houseDict)
False
>>>
```

In any code where we think a key might not be found, it's a good idea to add some defensive coding to check and ensure that the key is in the dictionary before we attempt to use it on the dictionary. Typically, we build this type of check using an if statement:

```
if myKey in myDict:
    # OK, we can now successfully use myDict[myKey]
else:
    #  The key was not found, print some error message or take some other
action
```

Sometimes, it may make more logical sense to code the reverse test. We can use not in to test for the key not being in the dictionary:

```
if myKey not in myDict:
    # The key was not found, do whatever you need to do
```

# Programming Challenge

This challenge asks you to build a dictionary and use keys into that dictionary to extract information. The information is given as a table of state names (keys) and the population of each state (values). The program should allow the user to enter the name of a state. If the state is found in the dictionary, then the program should report the population of that state. If the state is not found, then the program should output a message like "Sorry, but we do not have information for that state." The program should run in a loop, allow the user to enter any number of states, and then exit when the user presses Return (Mac) or Enter (Windows). As of 2018, the data for the 12 states with the highest populations is shown in Table 11-1.

***Table 11-1.*** *U.S. States with Highest Population*

| State | Population |
| --- | --- |
| California | 39776830 |
| Texas | 28704330 |
| Florida | 21312211 |
| New York | 19862512 |
| Pennsylvania | 12823989 |
| Illinois | 12768320 |
| Ohio | 11694664 |
| Georgia | 10545138 |
| North Carolina | 10390149 |
| Michigan | 9991177 |
| New Jersey | 9032872 |
| Virginia | 8525660 |

This is the solution using a dictionary:

```
# Get the population of a given state

statesDict = {
    'California':39776830, 'Texas':28704330, 'Florida':21312211,
    'New York':19862512,\
    'Pennsylvania': 12823989, 'Illinois': 12768320, 'Ohio':11694664,
    'Georgia': 10097000,\
    'North Carolina': 10390149, 'Michigan':9991177, 'New Jersey': 9032872,
    'Virginia': 8525660}

while True:
    usersState = input('Enter a state: ')
    if usersState == '':
        break
    if usersState in statesDict:
        population = statesDict[usersState]
        print('The population of', usersState, 'is', population)
```

```
    else:
        print('Sorry, but we do not have any information about',
        usersState)
    print()
```

The code for this program is based on a dictionary of state/population key/value pairs. The main loop allows the user to enter a state name. The program tests to see if the given state is in the dictionary by using the in operator. If the state is found, then the program finds the population of that state and reports it. Otherwise, the program says that it does not have any information about that state.

# A Python Dictionary to Represent a Programming Dictionary

Another example of using a dictionary is a program that works as a real dictionary. In this example, it will be a dictionary of a few of the programming terms introduced in this book. In the following program, programming terms are used as keys, and their matching definitions are specified as values:

```
# Using a dictionary to represent a dictionary of programming terms

programmingDict = {
    'variable': 'A named memory location that holds a value',
    'loop' : 'A block of code that is repeated until a certain condition is met.',
    'function' : 'A series of related steps that form a larger task, often
     called from multiple places in a program',
    'constant' : 'A variable whose value does not change',
    'Boolean' : 'A data type that can only have values of True or False'}

while True:
    print()
    usersWord = input('Enter a word to look up (or Return to quit): ')
    if usersWord == ":
        break

    if usersWord in programmingDict:
```

```
        definition = programmingDict[usersWord]
        print('The definition of', usersWord, 'is:')
        print(definition)

    else:
        print()
        print('The word', usersWord, 'is not in our dictionary.')
        yesOrNo = input('Would you like to add a definition for ' +
        usersWord + ' (y/n) ')
        if yesOrNo.lower() == 'y':
            usersDefinition = input('Please give a definition for ' +
            usersWord + ': ')
            programmingDict[usersWord] = usersDefinition
            print('Thanks, got it!')

print('Done.')
```

This example is very similar to the previous challenge. It starts with a dictionary of programming terms, where the words are the keys and the values are the definitions. However, this program has an additional twist. If the user enters a word that is not in the dictionary, it asks the user if they want to add a definition for the word they entered. If the user chooses to add a definition, the program allows the user to enter the definition, and the key/value pair is added to the dictionary.

# Iterating Through a Dictionary

If you need to iterate through all the elements in a dictionary, similar to a list, you can use a for loop. In the case of a dictionary, however, the variable you specify in the for statement is given the value of a key in the dictionary every time through the loop. Here is an example using the earlier dictionary of state populations:

```
>>> statesDict = {
    'California':39776830, 'Texas':28704330, 'Florida':21312211,
    'New York':19862512,\
    'Pennsylvania': 12823989, 'Illinois': 12768320, 'Ohio':11694664,
    'Georgia': 10097000,\
    'North Carolina': 10390149, 'Michigan':9991177, 'New Jersey': 9032872,
    'Virginia': 8525660}
```

```
>>> for state in statesDict:
        print(state)

California
Texas
Florida
New York
Pennsylvania
Illinois
Ohio
Georgia
North Carolina
Michigan
New Jersey
Virginia
>>>
```

You can be assured that using a for loop this way will iterate through every key in the dictionary. If you need each matching value while iterating through a dictionary, you can reach into the dictionary using the current key in the body of the loop. For example:

```
>>> statesDict = {
    'California':39776830, 'Texas':28704330, 'Florida':21312211,
    'New York':19862512,\
    'Pennsylvania': 12823989, 'Illinois': 12768320, 'Ohio':11694664,
    'Georgia': 10097000,\
    'North Carolina': 10390149, 'Michigan':9991177, 'New Jersey': 9032872,
    'Virginia': 8525660}
```

```
>>> for state in statesDict:
        population = statesDict[state]
        print(state, population)

California 39776830
Texas 28704330
Florida 21312211
New York 19862512
Pennsylvania 12823989
```

```
Illinois 12768320
Ohio 11694664
Georgia 10097000
North Carolina 10390149
Michigan 9991177
New Jersey 9032872
Virginia 8525660
>>>
```

# Combining Lists and Dictionaries

Now you have seen examples of lists of lists and you can build dictionaries of dictionaries. But highly complex data structures can be built by mixing and matching lists and dictionaries. You can have a list of dictionaries or a dictionary where all values are lists. Beyond that, every sublist or subdictionary can also be a dictionary or a list. Although that may seem very complicated, data structures like this can be extremely useful in representing hierarchical data.

In this first example, we want to represent a number of cars. This data could refer to cars we own, cars we are interested in purchasing, or even cars that are at a used car dealership waiting to be sold:

```
carsList = [\
    {
'make':'Toyota', 'model':'Prius', 'year': 2006, 'color':'gold', 'doors':4,
'leather':False, 'license': 'ABC123', 'mileage': 777777},\
    {
'make':'Honda', 'model':'Civic', 'year': 2010, 'color':'red', 'doors':2,
'leather':False, 'license': 'DEF444', 'mileage': 54321},\
    {
'make':'Ford', 'model':'Fusion', 'year': 2012, 'color':'blue', 'doors':4,
'leather':True, 'license': 'GHI999', 'mileage': 24680},\
    {
'make':'Chevy', 'model':'Volt', 'year': 2015, 'color':'black', 'doors':4,
'leather':False, 'license': 'JKL444', 'mileage': 7890}\
    ]
```

In this example, each element in the list is a dictionary. Each dictionary has an identical set of keys. Given this structure, it would be easy to iterate through all the cars, searching for all cars that match a given set of criteria. For example, if we wanted to search through our list of cars and find all cars that have four doors and mileage less than 50,000 miles, we could use the following code:

```
for carDict in carsList:
    if (carDict['doors'] == 4) and (carDict['mileage'] < 50000):
        print(carDict['make'], carDict['model'], carDict['license'])
```

That would produce the following results:

```
Ford Fusion GHI999
Chevy Volt JKL444
```

The following example is slightly more complicated:

```
personalDataDict = {
    'Joe': {'height':73, 'weight': 200, 'sex':'M', 'age':35,
    'allergies':['tree pollen', 'carrots', 'onions']},\
    'Sally':{'height':58, 'weight': 100, 'sex':'F', 'age':32,
    'allergies':['bee stings']},\
    'John': {'height':36, 'weight': 75, 'sex':'M', 'age':8,
    'allergies':['peanuts']},\
    'Mary': {'height':35, 'weight': 60, 'sex':'F', 'age':7,
    'allergies':[]}\
    }
```

In this example, we have a dictionary of people. We use their names as keys. Each person is represented as a dictionary of key/value pairs. But if you look at the allergies key, you can see the value for each person is a list of all things that person is allergic to. The list can have any number of elements, including zero. We can find the list of allergies for a specific person in this way:

```
joesData = personalDataDict['Joe']
joesAllergies = joesData['allergies']
print(joesAllergies)
```

```
marysData = personalDataDict['Mary']
marysAllergies = marysData['allergies']
print(marysAllergies)
```

The code produces this output:

```
['tree pollen', 'carrots', 'onions']
[]
```

Using a person's name as a key provides a dictionary of information about them. Within that dictionary, if you use a key of allergies, you get back the list of things that person is allergic to. In the case of Joe, we see that he is allergic to tree pollen, carrots, and onions. Mary's list of things she is allergic to is empty, meaning she is not allergic to anything.

If we wanted to generate a printout of all people and their allergies, we could use the following:

```
for personName in personalDataDict:
    onePersonDict = personalDataDict[personName]
    allergyList = onePersonDict['allergies']
    if allergyList == []:
        print(personName, 'is not allergic to anything')
    else:
        print(personName, 'is allergic to the following:')
        for allergy in allergyList:
            print('    ', allergy)
```

That would produce this output:

```
John is allergic to the following:
    peanuts
Sally is allergic to the following:
    bee stings
Joe is allergic to the following:
    tree pollen
    carrots
    onions
Mary is not allergic to anything
```

Using lists and dictionaries together allows us to build up highly complex data structures. As long as you understand the layers that make up the data structure, Python code can be written in a very straightforward way to get the specific information you want. As shown, extracting the data that is important to you is done using an appropriate sequence of indices and/or keys.

# JSON: JavaScript Object Notation

In Chapter 10, there is an example of a program that displays stock quote information. The program asks the user to enter a stock symbol, uses an API call to get current information about the stock, and extracts the stock price from the returned string. As an example, when we created a request for the price of Apple (stock symbol AAPL), the returned string looked like this:

```
{
    "Meta Data": {
        "1. Information": "Batch Stock Market Quotes",
        "2. Notes": "IEX Real-Time Price provided for free by IEX
        (https://iextrading.com/developer/).",
        "3. Time Zone": "US/Eastern"
    },
    "Stock Quotes": [
        {
            "1. symbol": "AAPL",
            "2. price": "165.7500",
            "3. volume": "65336628",
            "4. timestamp": "2018-04-20 16:59:43"
        }
    ]
}
```

Now that we have discussed Python's dictionaries, the layout of this string should look more familiar. The information is returned in a special format called JSON (short for *JavaScript Object Notation*). JSON format is a generalized text-based format for structuring data. JSON-formatted data is often used as a mechanism for transmitting hierarchical data in response to requests sent to servers.

The JSON format is almost identical to Python's data structures. In fact, it is so close that there is a Python `json` package that allows us to translate a string formatted in JSON into Python lists and dictionaries. If we make the same API call that we did earlier, we can translate the returned string into a Python dictionary using a single call in the `json` package. Then, rather than using a slice, we can pick out the specific information we are looking for more easily, in a clearer way, and with much less code.

If you look at the preceding response, you will see that the returned string is the equivalent of a Python dictionary. At the top level, there are two key/value pairs. The keys are `Meta Data` and `Stock Quotes`. Interestingly, the value associated with the `Stock Quotes` key is a list. That's because the API allows for more than one stock symbol in the query. However, our program is only supplying one stock symbol in each request. In the list of `Stock Quotes`, each element is a dictionary of information about one stock symbol. We can now easily get the stock price for our stock by asking for the data associated with the key `"2. price"`.

Here is our full program that makes the same request but handles the returned data as JSON-formatted data:

```
# Getting a stock quote

import urllib.request
import json

API_KEY = 'xxxxx'    # <- replace this with your API key

# Data provided for free by Alpha Vantage.  Website: alphavantage.co
#
# typical URL:
#       https://www.alphavantage.co/query?function=BATCH_STOCK_QUOTES&
        symbols=AAPL&apikey=<key>

def getStockData(symbol):
    baseURL = 'https://www.alphavantage.co/query?function=BATCH_STOCK_
    QUOTES&symbols='
    ending = '&apikey=' + API_KEY

    fullURL = baseURL + symbol + ending
    print()
    print('Sending URL:', fullURL)
```

```
    # open the URL
    connection = urllib.request.urlopen(fullURL)

    # read and convert to a string
    responseString = connection.read().decode()

    print('Response is: ', responseString)
    responseDict = json.loads(responseString) # convert from JSON to a
    Python dictionary
    print('Response as a dict is:', responseDict)

    # The dictionary has an entry with a key of Stock Quotes
    stockList = responseDict['Stock Quotes']

    # We get back one dictionary for every stock symbol
    # Since we only gave 1 stock symbol, we look at element 0
    stockDict = stockList[0]

    # Reach into the stock dict and pull out the price
    price = stockDict['2. price']

    return price

while True:
    print()
    userSymbol = input('Enter a stock symbol (or press ENTER to quit): ')
    if userSymbol == ":
        break
    thisStockPrice = getStockData(userSymbol)

    print()
    print('The current price of', userSymbol, 'is:', thisStockPrice)
    print()

print('OK bye')
```

The main code of this program is identical to the one introduced in Chapter 10. All the changes have been made in the getStockData function. In that function, the call to json.loads (the s means that the input comes from a string) converts the returned JSON data into its Python form, which in this case is a dictionary. Then, understanding the structure of the dictionary, we get the value associated with the Stock Quotes key. That gives us another list. But because we know that it will only have one element, we can extract element zero, which is a dictionary. Finally, we get the price by using the key 2. price as a key.

The responses to many different APIs are returned in JSON format. Often the response string is made up of combinations of lists and dictionaries. Applying the techniques demonstrated here allows us to reach into these complex data structures to get the desired information.

# Example Program to Get Weather Data

In the previous chapter, we showed a program that retrieved weather information using an API from OpenWeatherMap.org. The OpenWeatherMap API can return data in a number of different text formats. Here is an example of the result of requesting current weather information for the city of Boston as a JSON string:

```
{"coord":{"lon":-71.06,"lat":42.36},"weather":[{"id":800,"main":"Clear",
"description":"clear sky","icon":"01d"}],"base":"stations","main":{"temp":
288.53,"pressure":1026,"humidity":13,"temp_min":286.15,"temp_max":290.15},
"visibility":16093,"wind":{"speed":4.1,"deg":310,"gust":7.7},"clouds":
{"all":1},"dt":1524423120,"sys":{"type":1,"id":1296,"message":0.004,
"country":"US","sunrise":1524390672,"sunset":1524440080},"id":4930956,
"name":"Boston","cod":200}
```

In this form, this data may seem rather intimidating. With just a quick glance, you can tell there are a number of nested dictionaries and lists. Let's make this more human readable by adding some newline characters. That should make it easier to understand the overall structure of the data as a dictionary:

```
{"coord":{"lon":-71.06,"lat":42.36},
"weather":[{"id":800,
    "main":"Clear",
    "description":"clear sky",
    "icon":"01d"}],
"base":"stations",
        "main":{"temp":288.53,
        "pressure":1026,
```

```
        "humidity":13,
        "temp_min":286.15,
        "temp_max":290.15},
"visibility":16093,
"wind":{"speed":4.1,
        "deg":310,
        "gust":7.7},
"clouds":{"all":1},
"dt":1524423120,
"sys":{"type":1,"id":1296,
        "message":0.004,
        "country":"US",
        "sunrise":1524390672,
        "sunset":1524440080},
        "id":4930956,
        "name":"Boston",
        "cod":200}
```

You can see that there is a great deal of weather information available here. To get to the temperature value, we first have to use the main key. The value found there is another dictionary. In that dictionary, you can see the temp key (you also see information about the minimum and maximum temperatures, humidity, pressure, and so on).

The following code is used to get the temperature for any city the user specifies. To run this code, you need to obtain your own API key and assign it to the API_KEY constant. Note that in the URL that is built up, we are specifying json (as the mode parameter) to indicate that we want the data to be returned in JSON format:

```
# Get temperature for a given city

import urllib
import json

# API documentation from:  http://openweathermap.org/API

# Go to openweathermap.org, get an API Key, and paste it between the quotes
below'
API_KEY = 'xxxxxx'    # <- replace with your API Key
```

```
def getTemperature(city):

    urlAndParams = 'http://api.openweathermap.org/data/2.5/weather?q=' +
    city + '&mode=json'+ '&APPID=' + API_KEY

    # Make the request and save the response as a string.
    response = urllib.urlopen(urlAndParams).read()

    responseDict = json.loads(response)  # convert from JSON to a Python
    dictionary

    mainDict = responseDict['main']  # get the information associated with
    the main key

    degrees = mainDict['temp']    # get the temperature from that dictionary

    return float(degrees)

# Convert from Kelvin degrees to Fahrenheit
def convertKToF(degreesK):
    degreesF = (1.8 * (degreesK - 273.)) + 32
    return degreesF

while True:
    city = input('What city would you like the temperature of? ')
    if city == "":
        break
    tempK = getTemperature(city)
    tempF = convertKToF(tempK)
    print(tempF)
    print()
```

The main code is a loop that continually asks the user to choose a city. It then calls a function called getTemperature, passing in the city. getTemperature builds the URL and makes the request. Once we get the returned data back, we convert the response from a JSON-formatted string into a Python dictionary. From there, it is a matter of using the appropriate dictionary keys. First, we use the main key to get the main dictionary. Within that dictionary, we get the temperature using the temp key. (You can see how we could now extract any of the other weather information just as easily.) We convert the temperature string to a float and return it to the main code. Finally, we convert the temperature from Kelvin to Fahrenheit and report the result to the user.

# XML Data

In the OpenWeatherMap API we just used, we set the `mode` parameter to return the data in `json` format. One of the other options is `xml` (short for *eXtensible Markup Language*). In many ways, XML is similar to HTML, the HyperText Markup Language used to define web pages. XML is designed as a self-documenting format that allows computers to exchange data. Similar to HTML, the information to be exchanged is formatted using tags (opening and closing tags). Whereas HTML has a well-defined set of tags that can be used, XML allows you to create your own tags to describe your data.

There are entire books written to explain the intricacies of XML, and I will certainly not try to cover the details here. Instead, I'll show an example of XML-formatted data and explain how to access that data in Python.

If we make the same request to get the temperature of Boston, but we specify the mode as `xml`, the XML formatted response looks like this:

```
<current><city id="4930956" name="Boston"><coord lon="-71.06"
lat="42.36"></coord><country>US</country><sun rise="2018-04-22T09:51:13"
set="2018-04-22T23:34:40"></sun></city><temperature value="288.53"
min="286.15" max="290.15" unit="kelvin"></temperature><humidity
value="13" unit="%"></humidity><pressure value="1026" unit="hPa">
</pressure><wind><speed value="4.1" name="Gentle Breeze">
</speed><gusts value="7.7"></gusts><direction value="310" code="NW"
name="Northwest"></direction></wind><clouds value="1" name="clear sky">
</clouds><visibility value="16093"></visibility><precipitation mode="no">
</precipitation><weather number="800" value="clear sky" icon="01d">
</weather><lastupdate value="2018-04-22T18:52:00"></lastupdate></current>
```

Let's take that XML data and reformat it a little to make it more human readable by adding newline characters and some indenting:

```
<current>
    <city id="4930956" name="Boston">
        <coord lon="-71.06" lat="42.36"></coord>
        <country>US</country>
        <sun rise="2018-04-22T09:51:13" set="2018-04-22T23:34:40"></sun>
    </city>
```

```
<temperature value="288.53" min="286.15" max="290.15" unit="kelvin">
</temperature>
<humidity value="13" unit="%"></humidity>
<pressure value="1026" unit="hPa"></pressure>
<wind>
    <speed value="4.1" name="Gentle Breeze"></speed>
    <gusts value="7.7"></gusts>
    <direction value="310" code="NW" name="Northwest"></direction>
</wind>
<clouds value="1" name="clear sky"></clouds>
<visibility value="16093"></visibility>
<precipitation mode="no"></precipitation>
<weather number="800" value="clear sky" icon="01d"></weather>
    <lastupdate value="2018-04-22T18:52:00"></lastupdate>
</current>
```

The formatting of the XML data looks very similar to HTML data. Every grouping has start and end tags (for example, <current> and </current>, <city> and </city>, and so forth). Each grouping like this is called an *element* or *node*. We'll use the term *node* here so as not to confuse you with elements in a list. Then there are nodes within nodes, each with its own start and end tags. When a node only has text inside it, it is called the *text of the node*. For example, within the city node, there is a country node that looks like this:

```
<country>US</country>
```

Additionally, nodes can have individual name/value pairs. For example, the coord node has values for lon (longitude) and lat (latitude):

```
<coord lon="-122.08" lat="37.39"></coord>
```

In XML, items like these are called *attributes*.

Fortunately, Python provides a package (not surprisingly, called xml) that allows programmers to extract the information from XML-formatted data. To use the package, we first have to bring the xml package into our programs with an import statement. Rather than import the entire xml package (which includes the ability to write and modify XML documents), we only need the part that allows us to turn XML strings into XML documents and retrieve information. That portion is called xml.etree.

ElementTree. That is a rather long name—Python provides a way to import a package and give it a shorthand name. You do that using the following variation of the import statement:

```
import <full imported package name> as <shorthand version of package name>
```

In the following code, we use this variation of the import statement and use a shortened name of etree. This is not required, but is often done as a convenience by programmers so that they won't have to type long names when specifying a function in a package.

XML data is often thought of as a tree. Using our example data, try to think of the data in the form of a tree lying on its side. The root of the tree is the node named current. From that node, we see the following nodes: city, temperature, humidity, pressure, wind, clouds, visibility, precipitation, weather, and lastupdate. Coming off of the city node are the coord, country, and sunrise nodes. The coord and sunrise nodes each have two attributes. What we need is a way of taking the data that we have as a string and turning it into a tree-structured document. That is done with a call to a function in the xml package, like this:

```
tree = etree.fromstring(XMLAsAString)
```

After that call, we have the data in a form that allows us to get any information we want to from the XML in its tree form. The xml package has a number of functions that can be used to easily find any individual piece of information we want.

Here is the code for the XML-based version of the program:

```
# Get weather data from openweathermap.org - as XML

import urllib.request
import xml.etree.ElementTree as etree

# API documentation from:  http://openweathermap.org/API

API_KEY = 'xxxxxx'  # <- replace with your API Key

def getInfo(city):

    urlWithParams = 'http://api.openweathermap.org/data/2.5/weather?q=' \
                + city + '&mode=xml' + '&APPID=' + API_KEY
```

```
# Make the request and save the response as an XML-formatted string.
connection = urllib.request.urlopen(urlWithParams)

# Read the data and convert to a string:
responseString = connection.read().decode()

print(responseString)

# Turn the string into an XML document
tree = etree.fromstring(responseString)

# Find the temperature node, then get the value attribute inside it
temperatureInfo =  tree.find('temperature')
degrees = temperatureInfo.attrib['value']

    return float(degrees)

# Convert from Kelvin degrees to Fahrenheit
def convertKToF(degreesK):
    degreesF - (1.8 * (degreesK - 273.)) + 32
    return degreesF

while True:
    city = input('What city would you like the temperature of? ')
    if city == ":
        break
    tempK = getInfo(city)

    tempF = convertKToF(tempK)
    print(tempF)
    print()
```

The main code and the function to convert from Kelvin are identical to those of the previous example. The changes are in the getInfo function. As mentioned earlier, the URL in this version specifies that the mode of the response should be XML. Once we receive the response, we use the following lines to get the specific information we want:

```
# Turn the string into an XML tree
tree = etree.fromstring(responseString)
```

```
# Find the temperature tag, then the value attribute inside that
temperatureInfo = tree.find('temperature')
degrees = temperatureInfo.attrib['value']
```

The first line converts the response string from the server into an XML tree. The next line reaches into the resulting XML tree structure and finds the `temperature` group. Within that group, the last line finds the `value` attribute. If we wanted to, we could now get to any other piece of data in the XML tree.

There are many more functions available within the `etree` package. More information on all the functions available to parse XML documents is in the official Python documentation at `https://docs.python.org/3/library/xml.etree.elementtree.html`.

JSON and XML are two solutions to the same problem of representing arbitrary hierarchical data. Most often, these two formats are used to transmit data between two computers. JSON is much more succinct and Python-like, or *Pythonic*. JSON is easily accessible in pure Python because JSON-formatted data can be parsed using Python lists and dictionaries. XML is more descriptive because it has tags that identify the data built into the data structure itself. Because of that, equivalent XML-formatted data tends to be considerably longer. Further, when attempting to read XML-formatted data, code must be written using a set of calls defined in the `xml` package.

# Accessing Repeating Groupings in JSON and XML

Sometimes, the data returned by an API has repeating groupings. For example, imagine you made a request to a site to get information about all the members of a band. In response, you get back a set of blocks where each block contains information about one member of the band—for example, the member's name, age, and instrument played. I'll show what this data structure might look like in JSON format and then in XML format. I'll also show how we can use Python to access the data about each band member:

```
# Demonstration of repeating blocks in JSON and XML

import json
import xml.etree.ElementTree as etree

# Build a JSON structure as a triple quoted string
myJSON = '''{
```

```
  "bandMembers": [
    {
      "name": "Keith Emerson",
      "age": 32,
      "instrument": "keyboards"
    },
    {
      "name": "Greg Lake",
      "age": 42,
      "instrument": "guitar"
    },
    {
      "name": "Carl Palmer",
      "age": 35,
      "instrument": "drums"
    }
  ]
}"'

bandMembersDict = json.loads(myJSON)
memberList = bandMembersDict['bandMembers']
for member in memberList:
    print(member['name'], member['age'], member['instrument'])
```

As you might expect, the repeating blocks are handled as a list.

In the JSON code, the entire structure is converted into a dictionary with only one name/value pair. Using a bandMembers key, we get a list of band members. We then iterate through the list, and each member is represented as a dictionary. For each member, we print out their name, age, and instrument using an appropriate key:

```
# Build an XML structure as a triple quoted string
myXML = "'
<bandMembers>
    <member>
        <name>Keith Emerson</name>
        <age>32</age>
        <instrument>keyboards</instrument>
```

```
        </member>
        <member>
            <name>Greg Lake</name>
            <age>42</age>
            <instrument>guitar</instrument>
        </member>
        <member>
            <name>Carl Palmer</name>
            <age>35</age>
            <instrument>drums</instrument>
        </member>
</bandMembers>"'

tree = etree.fromstring(myXML)
bandMembersList = tree.findall('member')
for member in bandMembersList:
    (print member.find('name').text, member.find('age').text,
    member.find('instrument').text)
```

The XML code is similar. We first convert the structure into an XML tree. We then use a call in the xml package to find all the band members (each is a node). That returns a list of all band members. Like the JSON code, we iterate through all band members. Within each band member, we use the find operation in the xml package to find each member's name, age, and instrument and print out the text associated with each of these nodes.

The output of both of these sections of code is exactly the same:

```
>>>
Keith Emerson 32 keyboards
Greg Lake 42 guitar
Carl Palmer 35 drums
Keith Emerson 32 keyboards
Greg Lake 42 guitar
Carl Palmer 35 drums
>>>
```

# Summary

This chapter introduced a number of data structures that can be used in Python. It started by showing a tuple—a list that cannot change. Then I gave examples of the uses of a list of lists, a construct that can be used to represent grids, spreadsheets, the world of an adventure game, and anything that you can think of that is arranged as a number of rows and columns. We went through the process of taking data that was exported as a comma-separated value file (`.csv`) and bringing that data into a Python program as a list of lists.

I introduced the Python dictionary. In a dictionary, the data is structured as key/value pairs. You only access the data using keys. Using the `in` operator is an easy way to determine whether a key is in a dictionary. I then gave you a challenge to build a dictionary and write some code to access data found in it.

As another example, we built a dictionary of programming terms, where the keys were programming terms and each related value was the definition of the term. This demonstrated the ability to add keys and values to a dictionary. I then showed you how to iterate through a dictionary using a `for` loop. Next, I explained how lists and dictionaries could be combined to build highly complex data structures.

Finally, we went through examples of how APIs often return data using either JavaScript Object Notation (JSON) or eXtensible Markup Language (XML). There were examples of how to convert API responses into these two data structures and how to retrieve data from each.

# CHAPTER 12

# Where to Go from Here

As I said in Chapter 1, this book is not intended to be comprehensive. Instead, the goal is to provide you with a general understanding of programming using the Python language. The good news is that if you have made it this far, you should have a solid understanding of most of the syntax and constructs of Python. However, the more exciting news (if you want to look at it that way) is that there is much more to explore.

This chapter discusses the following topics:

- Python language documentation
- Python Standard Library
- Python external packages
- Python development environments
- Places to find answers to questions
- Projects and practice, practice, practice

## Python Language Documentation

The Python Software Foundation is the owner/developer of the Python language. In addition to the language itself, it provides a number of pages of documentation about the language, libraries, and other information useful to Python developers. The official top-level documentation for the Python language can be found at https://docs.python.org/3.6/ (the current version at the time of writing).

343

© Irv Kalb 2018
I. Kalb, *Learn to Program with Python 3*, https://doi.org/10.1007/978-1-4842-3879-0_12

# Python Standard Library

The Python Standard Library (which is installed when you download and install Python) contains a large number of built-in packages, each with many built-in functions just waiting for you to find and take advantage of them. We have only had space to scratch the surface of a few of these packages. We only talked about one or two functions of a handful of packages. Each of these packages provides functionality that is much more extensive.

There are many other built-in packages that we didn't even get to. In Table 12-1, I present the ones mentioned, along with a few more of the more well-known packages available in the Python Standard Library that you may be interested in learning more about.

***Table 12-1.***  *Built-in Python Packages*

| Package Name | General Functionality |
| --- | --- |
| csv | Reading and writing comma-separated values |
| datetime | Basic date and time types |
| itertools | Functions for creating iterators for efficient looping |
| time | Time access and conversions |
| json | Creating and processing JSON-formatted data |
| logging | Logging facility |
| os | Many operating systems functions |
| math | Trig functions (sin, cos, tan, etc.) and constants (such as pi) |
| random | Generating random numbers |
| re | Regular expression operations |
| TKInter | Graphical user interface package |
| turtle | Turtle graphics |
| urllib | Opening arbitrary resources by URL |
| xml | Creating and processing XML-formatted data |

A description of the entire Python Standard Library is at `https://docs.python.org/3.6/library/`.

An alphabetical module index is at `https://docs.python.org/3.6/py-modindex.html`.

# Python External Packages

The Python "ecosystem" is extremely large and healthy and continues to grow. A huge number of external packages is available to Python programmers. Table 12-2 contains some of the most well-known external packages.

***Table 12-2.*** *External Python Packages*

| Package Name | General Functionality |
|---|---|
| beautifulsoup | Library for parsing HTML and XML files |
| django | High-level framework for building Python-based web applications |
| flask | Microframework for building Python-based web applications |
| Matplotlib | 2D plotting library, produces publication quality figures |
| MySQL-Python | Python connector to a MySQL database |
| NumPy | Adds support for large, multidimensional array and high-level math functions |
| SciPy | Library used by scientists, analysts, and engineers doing scientific computing |
| Pandas | Data structures and data analysis tools |
| PyGame | Designed for writing games, adds support for windows, mice, and more |
| Requests | Makes HTTP requests in a syntax easier for humans |
| Scikit-learn | Software machine learning library |

The official Python wiki (https://wiki.python.org/moin/UsefulModules) has a listing of what it thinks are the most useful external modules.

There is a site called PyPI (the Python Package Index) that calls itself "a repository of software for the Python programming language." It may be a little difficult and intimidating to find what you are looking for there because there are over 80,000 packages cataloged. Before considering writing a package of your own, it may be worth your time checking to see whether someone has already built and published a similar module. PyPI is at https://pypi.python.org/pypi.

# Python Development Environments

This book has demonstrated the use of the IDLE development environment that comes free with Python. It is a very good place to start. However, if you want to do "real" software development, you soon find that IDLE has a number of deficiencies. As mentioned earlier, the lack of line numbers is truly annoying. Perhaps most importantly, IDLE does not have a usable debugger. A *debugger* is a tool that allows a programmer to set places in a program (called *breakpoints*) where the program will stop and allow the programmer to see the value of variables, and allows the program to be executed a line at a time. IDLE claims to have a debugger, but its debugger is impossible for the average human to use. If you decide to get into serious Python development, you will probably want to graduate from using IDLE. There are a number of alternatives. I'll tell you about some of the most popular.

Surprisingly (to me), many people develop Python code by using any basic text editor (for example, Notepad++, TextEdit, and so on). Many programmers use a text editor like Sublime Text that (using a settings file) can be configured to have some Python-specific settings. Files are edited in the text editor and then run from the command line.

There is a well-known language-independent software development environment called Eclipse that has a plug-in called PyDev that enables Eclipse to be used as a Python development environment. If you have experience setting up an Eclipse environment, this might be a good choice for you.

The IPython Notebook is now known as the Jupyter Notebook. It is an interactive computational environment in which you can combine code execution, rich text, mathematics, plots, and rich media. A key thing about Jupyter Notebook files is that they can contain any number of small to medium-sized pieces of Python code in a single file, and you can run any of them separately. It is an excellent environment for demonstrations and classroom use and for sharing code. It allows a wide variety of documentation types, including text with special fonts, images, YouTube videos, and so on.

PyCharm (by JetBrains) is a serious, full-featured Python IDE (short for *integrated development environment*). It comes in two flavors: Community Edition (free) and Professional Edition (paid). Beginning programmers should find the free Community Edition to have everything you need. The Professional Edition has additional features that make it worthwhile to someone who is developing Python code for a living.

Yet another option is Visual Studio from Microsoft. Visual Studio is a generic development environment that markets itself as "any language, any OS." It has full support for Python with a downloadable source plug-in.

# Places to Find Answers to Questions

The official Python documentation is a great place to go for detailed information on any Python syntax or documentation on any Python Standard library call.

Programmers often go to the web site `www.stackoverflow.com` to ask and answer programming questions. If you are stuck trying to figure out how to code something in Python, try going there and searching through the questions and answers. Often, you find that someone else has had the same question before you and other programmers have chimed in with answers. (When you start to feel comfortable with the language, try to answer some questions posed there.)

Many major cities have a local "user group" where programmers get together for talks and/or socialization. Python user groups are sometimes called PIGgies, for Python Interest Groups. A listing of many of these groups is at `https://wiki.python.org/moin/LocalUserGroups`.

Although there are many local conferences about Python, PyCon (Python Conference) calls itself "the largest annual gathering for the community using and developing the open-source Python programming language." Go to `www.pycon.org` for details.

# Projects and Practice, Practice, Practice

The only way to truly learn programming is through practice. As with a foreign language, it takes time to feel comfortable using a computer programming language. With experience, you start to recognize useful patterns in programming problems and in your solutions. To that end, I suggest that you take the time to work on developing projects on your own to gain experience. The following are some suggestions for projects that you should be able to build, using just the information presented in this book. These are all text-based projects:

- *Rock, paper, scissors*: The user chooses rock, paper, or scissors by entering the first letter, and the computer randomly chooses one. Rock crushes scissors, paper covers rock, scissors cuts paper.

- *Hangman*: Challenge the user to discover a randomly chosen word within a given number of guesses of individual letters.

- *Blackjack*: Build a game of 21, where the player plays against the dealer. Add in a betting system and keep track of how much the player wins or loses.

- *Craps*: The rules are a little complicated, but this is a good programming challenge. A betting system for wins and losses makes this fun.

- *Flash cards*: Build a generic flash card testing program. Build a program that reads a file of questions and answers. Read in the file, randomize the questions, pose them to the user, and compare their answers to correct answers. For an extra challenge, allow the program to handle multiple forms of correct answers.

- *Adventure game*: Take the program we built that demonstrated the concept of a list of lists to represent a grid and turn it into a real game. Add battles against monsters, treasure hunts, and anything else you like.

- *Use an API*: Like our stock price information and weather information examples, find a publicly available API that gives you data about some topic that you care about. Build a user interface that allows the user to get the information they are interested in.

# Summary

This chapter was more of a reference chapter, suggesting places to go to get more information about Python. I provided links to the official documentation, where to find more information about the Standard Python Library, and external packages. I gave a listing of what I consider some of the important packages within the Standard Python Library and some of the most important external packages.

I discussed a number of alternative development environments that you can use when you outgrow IDLE. Then I listed a number of sites, groups, and conferences that you can contact for more information about what's going on with the language. I wrapped up with suggestions for projects that you might consider building to give you experience.

Most importantly, becoming a good Python programmer requires practice, practice, practice!

# Index

© Irv Kalb 2018
I. Kalb, *Learn to Program with Python 3*, https://doi.org/10.1007/978-1-4842-3879-0

Printed in the United States
By Bookmasters